FINANCE, GROWTH AND STABILITY

Finance, Growth and Stability

Financing Economic Development in Thailand, 1960–86

KAREL JANSEN
Institute of Social Studies
The Hague

Avebury

Aldershot · Brookfield USA · Hong Kong · Singapore · Sydney

Published by

Avebury

Gower Publishing Company Limited
Gower House
Croft Road
Aldershot
Hants GU11 3HR
England

Gower Publishing Company
Old Post Road
Brookfield
Vermont 05036
USA

Printed and Bound in Great Britain by
Athenaeum Press Ltd., Newcastle upon Tyne.

ISBN 0 566 07125 8

Contents

Acknowledgements

This study is the result of research conducted within the framework of the Research Programme on Money, Finance and Development of the Institute of Social Studies (ISS), my employer. Financial support from the ISS for a number of study trips to Thailand is gratefully acknowledged.

In Thailand I benefited from support and advice from the staff of the Faculty of Economics of the Chulalongkorn University and from several staff members of the Research Department of the Bank of Thailand. I thank them all and I hope that the result of my work is not a disappointment to them.

This book is a substantially revised and updated version of the doctoral dissertation that I defended in 1987. I am very grateful to my promotor, Professor Hans Linnemann and the referent, Professor H. Visser, who made many valuable comments that helped to improve the dissertation.

At the ISS, I thank my colleagues in the Money and Finance group for their support. In particular, I want to thank Valpy FitzGerald and Rob Vos for their detailed and helpful comments on an earlier draft of this study.

Many colleagues at the ISS have helped in the technical production of this book; I am grateful to the staff of the Publications Office, the typing pool and the computer department. Although I cannot list the names of all people who have helped in putting the book together, I should make an exception for Koos van Wieringen who drew the charts.

List of Tables

List of Charts

Introduction

A structuralist approach to finance

This study aims to present a structuralist analysis of the role of finance in the process of economic development taking the experience of Thailand as a basis. Economic development is a process consisting of two parts: growth of output and productivity in the various sectors of the economy and structural change in which the balance between the sectors shifts. In this study the link between financial development and structural change will be the central concern. It will be argued that the process of financial development can only be properly understood if it is analysed in the context of shifting balances between sectors and of transfers of resources between sectors.

The central hypothesis of this study is that the causes and effects of financial development cannot be meaningfully analysed at the level of macroeconomic aggregates, such as aggregate savings or the rate of growth. The crucial causes and effects of financial development lie at the microeconomic level, where an individual economic unit that saves more than it can or wishes to invest decides to deposit its savings with a bank; and where another unit that wishes to invest more than it can save obtains credit from that bank. It is to be expected that the surplus units, as well as the deficit units, will be concentrated in particular sectors of the economy, so that financial flows will be, to a considerable extent, intersectoral flows. The analysis of the nature, size, causes and effects of these flows form the subject of this study.

Most of the recent literature on finance and development has concentrated on the link between financial development and economic growth. It is argued that financial development will increase aggregate savings and will increase the efficiency of the allocation of investment resources and will so help to improve the rate of economic growth. There is generally less attention for the link between financial development and structural change.

The approach followed places this book in the classical tradition of development economics. Early authors, like Kalecki (1976), Lewis (1954) and Nurkse (1953) were concerned with two main problems: firstly, how to raise the share of resources devoted to capital formation and, secondly, how to change the structure of the economy (industrialize) without running into unsustainable imbalances. In their analysis there was no explicit attention for the role of financial institutions. This study will argue that the role of these institutions with respect to their concerns is very important.

The basic premise on which this study is built is that financial factors are important and influence the speed, direction and stability of economic growth. The experience of most countries has been that in the early stages of economic development, the role of financial institutions rapidly expands. This reflects a change in the way capital formation is financed. Usually, three ways of financing investment are distinguished (for example, Drake 1980). In the case of 'self-finance' the saver and the investor are the same economic unit and investments are financed out of accumulated own savings. The second form, 'direct finance', creates a separation between saver and investor; the saver lends directly to the investor. With 'indirect finance' a financial intermediary comes between saver and investor: the saver deposits his savings in a financial institution which channels these funds to investors.

Financial development may be defined as the process by which the role of indirect finance in financing capital formation is increased. It implies an increased separation of the acts of saving and investing, or an increased division of labour in the economy between saving and investing units. In practice, net saving and net investing units will be concentrated in particular groups, regions or sectors, so that an increase in financial intermediation will generate intersectoral flows of funds and will affect sectoral balances in the economy.

The framework in which to analyse these intersectoral flows is partly dictated by available statistics and partly by theoretical considerations. In the classic models of Lewis and Kalecki attention was focused on the two main productive sectors: agriculture and industry. To a considerable extent, such a breakdown overlaps with other dichotomies suggested in the development literature, such as the formal versus the informal sector, modern versus traditional sector or urban versus rural sector.

Besides the breakdown of economic activities by productive sectors (agriculture, industry, etc.), National Accounts and Flow-of-Funds statistics present a breakdown by institution: households and unincorporated enterprises, corporations and government. According to this breakdown it can be observed that the household sector generally has a savings surplus and the corporate and government sector generally a deficit. It is important to note that the household sector in a developing country is quite different from that in a rich country. In Western countries the household sector consists mainly of wage- and salary-earning households. In developing countries in general, and certainly in Thailand, the proportion of the labour force in wage employment is much smaller; most households are self-employed units engaged in farming, retail trade, services, etc. Under these conditions, an alternative name for the household sector might be the sector of unincorporated enterprises. This breakdown of the productive sector of the economy into the unincorporated and corporate sectors will be applied in the subsequent chapters.

In this study the terms 'household sector' and 'unincorporated sector' are used to refer to that part of the productive sector that is organized in small-scale units, generally based on family labour and operating on competitive markets. The term 'corporate sector' refers to large-scale firms, using extensively hired labour and operating on more oligopolistic markets. The breakdown of production units according to the organization of production and to the market conditions they face is of crucial importance to the analysis of saving and investment behaviour and of the role of financial intermediation.

The analysis of the consequences of financial development may be summarized in three questions:

(a) Does financial development speed up the rate of economic growth?
(b) Does financial development affect the structure of economic development? and
(c) Does financial development affect the short-term macroeconomic stability?

Financial development and economic growth

Financial development could speed up economic growth if it enabled the mobilization of more investable resources or lead to a more efficient allocation of such resources.

Whether financial development increases investable resources has been a subject of some debate. This study asserts that most savings are made out of profit incomes of corporate and unincorporated enterprises. The level of these profits is determined by the overall conditions of production in which financial development plays only a small role. Chapter 3 provides a detailed analysis of the saving behaviour of the corporate and the unincorporated sectors. Usually, household savings are analysed from a consumption theory perspective. However, it is widely established and recognized that most household savings in developing countries come from self-employed households. This study emphasizes that household savings are in fact retained profits of household firms and that the analysis of household saving behaviour should be approached from the production conditions facing the household firm rather than from consumption considerations. As household firms and large corporations face quite different production conditions, their saving behaviour is separately analysed in Chapter 3 and is explained by quite different factors.

It will be shown that financial development, by itself, does little to increase the amount of investable resources. Does it then accelerate economic growth by improving the allocation of such resources? Obviously, the answer to that question depends on the behaviour of financial institutions, such as commercial banks. This behaviour is analysed in some detail in Chapter 4, where it is argued that these financial institutions in fact ration credit; they prefer to deal with the corporate sector where they can deal with established firms, run by people they know. These firms operate often on regulated or protected markets so that risks are small. Because of these market imperfections, the term 'efficiency' is ambiguous anyway. The smaller firms in the unincorporated sector have far less access to bank credit, not necessarily because their investment plans are inferior but because the loan amounts are small, the projects more risky and because they lack the personal contacts with the bank managers. It can, in addition, be noted that financial institutions allocate part of their resources to uses that are clearly 'inefficient' (for example consumption credit or luxury buildings). It is, therefore, not obvious a priori that an increased role of financial institutions will increase the overall efficiency for allocation.

Financial development and structural change

It is far more likely, turning to our second question, that financial intermediation will influence the sectoral allocation of resources in the economy. Surplus (saving) units and deficit (investing) units are not randomly distributed over the economy; they tend to be concentrated in particular groups of society and in particular economic sectors and regions. Financial intermediation therefore shifts the resources of some groups, sectors or regions to others and in this way contributes to the changing structure of the economy. These intersectoral financial transfers are the crux of the cause and the impact of financial development.

In Chapter 4 the Flow-of-Funds Accounts of Thailand will be used to trace the directions of financial flows. It will be shown that the household sector is the main net supplier of funds to the financial institutions and that the corporate sector is the main net receiver of funds from them. It is surprising that the household savings, which in Chapter 3 are argued to be the operating surplus of household firms, are not used to a greater extent for own investments in the household firms themselves. Chapter 4 concludes that this may be explained by the high concentration of incomes in the household sector and by the limited incentives for investment in the sector. The mobilization of resources from the household sector through the financial institutions comes in addition to resources appropriated through other mechanisms, such as taxation and agricultural price intervention, and together amount to a substantial transfer of resources from the unincorporated to the corporate sector of the economy. This transfer has helped to finance the rapid growth of the corporate sector. And, as Chapter 4 concludes, it cannot be shown to have had excessively negative effects on growth and income levels in the unincorporated sector.

Financial development and stability

The third and final question raised above deals with the relationship between financial development and macroeconomic stability. A consequence of financial development is the separation of the acts of saving and investing and this may result in short-term macroeconomic instability when planned savings do not tally with planned investments. Financial institutions can, through credit expansion, contribute to such imbalances. On the other hand, financial development will create scope for the use of instruments of monetary policy that may help to manage short-term imbalances.

Chapter 5 will show that the problem of short-term stability in Thailand cannot be satisfactorily analysed at an aggregated macroeconomic level. A more disaggregated analysis reveals that imbalances between planned savings and investment can have two sources. Firstly, the main component of domestic savings, household savings, fluctuates considerably in the short run, while the other components, corporate and government savings, are more stable over time. Secondly, the main component of domestic investment, corporate investment, also fluctuates strongly, while household and government investments tend to be more stable. The outcome of this is that aggregated domestic savings tend to follow the fluctuations in household savings and aggregated investment those in corporate investment. The overall macroeconomic balance is thus the outcome of quite separate events in these two sectors. The nature of the instability, and of the adjustment process it brings, cannot be adequately understood and traced using conventional stabilization models, as these have either an aggregated saving function or a simplistic analysis of saving behaviour, and generally both.

The analysis in Chapter 5 will show that the short-term discrepancies between private savings and investments are accommodated by domestic and international financial markets rather than being corrected by active stabilization policies.

Financial and monetary policies

In most countries the growth of the financial system has invited active intervention by governments in financial markets. This has led to considerable debate about the most appropriate monetary and financial policies in developing countries. In a neo-classical world with perfect capital (and other) markets, there would be no need for such policies. The level of aggregate savings would be determined by interest rates and time preferences, and the level and sectoral distribution of investments would be dependent on rates of return and risk perceptions and preferences. Short-term imbalances would be readily adjusted through price fluctuations in the capital, labour, commodity and foreign exchange markets (see Beenstock 1980).

The reality of the developing world, though, is that markets are far from perfect and that, for economic or political reasons, governments have ideas about how they intend to control and improve the speed and direction of economic development. So, from an early stage in development theory, there has been a concern with the question of how to accelerate economic growth, how to channel resources to modern sectors of the economy and how to maintain macroeconomic stability under conditions of rapid growth and change. In this study there will be special attention for such policies as they relate to the activities of the financial system. In Chapter 4 it will be argued that, in general, such policies in Thailand have tried to stem the net outflow of financial resources from the agricultural or rural sector.

Thailand

Thailand is a very appropriate case for the analysis of the interaction between financial and economic development. As Chapter 2 will describe in more detail, the country has gone through a period of rapid growth over the last twenty-five years and the structure of the economy has changed significantly. For most years, growth has been accompanied by a macroeconomic stability that is remarkable for a developing country. Financial intermediation has grown even faster than the economy. The financial system is relatively free, although, of course, the government intervenes in its activities in various ways, but these controls are not so pervasive as to make financial intermediation unimportant or the financial system a mere extension of the government apparatus. There are elements of what could be called financial repression, for example, selective credit controls, but their impact is limited. The rate of inflation has generally been low and the loan and deposit rates of interest in almost all years were positive in real terms. The financial system is unrestricted in its contacts with international markets. It seems reasonable to assume that Thailand presents a pattern of financial behaviour that is close to what a fully liberalized financial system would produce. Therefore an analysis of the role played by the financial system in the mobilization of investment resources and the sectoral allocation of these resources, as well as of its role in creating and/or managing short-term instabilities would be interesting.

Outline of the study

Chapter 1 presents an overview of the main issues raised in the literature on finance and development. In early contributions the problem of 'financing' development was seen as the mobilization of real resources, mainly from the agricultural sector, to finance industrialization. In later contributions monetary and financial variables, and financial institutions, came to play a more explicit and central role, but the perspective on the sectoral balances and transfers was lost. Also the literature on stabilization in developing countries lacks a proper sectoral analysis of macroeconomic behaviour. Chapter 1 concludes by proposing a structuralist approach to the study of finance and development that would integrate the concerns with growth, resource mobilization, intersectoral transfers and short-term stabilization.

Chapter 2 provides a brief outline of the main trends in economic and financial development in Thailand. Over the last 25 years the country has gone through a period of very rapid growth and significant structural change. Growth of the financial system has also been very rapid. The investment resources required for this growth and change have come mainly from domestic sources, and a significant part of these resources has been channelled through the financial institutions. The rapid growth of export earnings has helped on average to keep the current account deficits relatively small. This implies that domestic saving and investment behaviour has not been constrained by foreign exchange availability.

Chapter 3 concentrates on the analysis of saving behaviour. After a brief review of existing theories of saving it is concluded that these look at households exclusively as consumption units. Most households in developing countries like Thailand, however, are self-employed production units whose incomes and savings fluctuate with the prices obtained for their products. A model for household saving that places these production conditions at the centre of the analysis is developed and tested. Similarly, the saving of the corporate sector is analysed in Chapter 3 as the outcome of the pricing decisions made by firms. To complete the analysis of domestic savings a simple model of government saving is tested.

Having established the determinants of saving behaviour, Chapter 4 uses Flow-of-Funds Accounts to study the allocation of these resources in the household sector and the corporate sector, and to trace the role of financial institutions in the flows between sectors. It is concluded that the household sector in Thailand has a substantial savings surplus which is channelled, largely through the financial system, to the corporate and government sector. An attempt is made to explain these flows, but for lack of detailed and reliable data such explanation often has to remain at a rather intuitive level. Chapter 4 also discusses whether the outflow of funds from the household sector of unincorporated enterprises has unacceptable negative effects on output, productivity, employment and income levels in this sector. So far there is little evidence of this in Thailand.

Chapter 5 proceeds from the observation that the saving patterns of the unincorporated and corporate sectors of Thailand are quite different. The household sector has a highly fluctuating savings ratio, a result of the variations in its output prices; the corporate sector, which largely determines its own prices, has a much more stable saving pattern. But the investments undertaken by the corporations vary quite strongly. The financial system, and foreign capital flows, have to cope with the resulting fluctuations in the financing deficit of the corporate sector. It is shown in Chapter 5 that, if one analyses savings at a disaggregated level, separating household from corporate savings, the analysis of stabilization patterns will lead to conclusions different from those reached in available models using an aggregated saving function.

Chapter 6 summarizes the findings of the earlier chapters, and assesses whether the method applied and the findings reached in this study on the financial development of Thailand have a wider relevance for other developing countries.

1 Finance and development: a survey of issues

1.1 Introduction

This first chapter aims to provide a survey of the parts of the general development literature that have dealt with the role of finance in economic development.

Such a review must start with the 'classics' who, at an early stage, were concerned with the problem of 'financing development' (Kalecki 1976; Lewis 1954; Nurkse 1953). Their central concern was with sectoral balance and macroeconomic stability during the process of industrialization. Typically, in their contributions the role of financial institutions is neglected, probably because at the time of writing the financial system in most developing countries was still underdeveloped. As Chapter 4 will show, however, financial flows and institutions can be easily integrated into their analysis. A discussion of the 'classical' approach will follow in section 1.2. The question of how to increase investments and accelerate growth was also the central inspiration for the two-gap models (Chenery and Strout 1966). The answer was that if, in poor countries, domestic savings are low, international capital transfers can help to increase the resources available for investment. Such capital flows have the advantage that they not only add to available savings but also relieve the foreign exchange constraint. This approach is interesting because it has led to a debate about the relationship between domestic savings and capital inflows. It has less to say about the sectoral allocation of resources or about the role of financial institutions. A review of the foreign capital approach will follow in section 1.3. The role of financial institutions and of financial intermediation is central to the theme of financial development, on which subject there is substantial literature. Initially, there was a concentration on historical and institutional analysis, describing patterns of financial development and their relationship to economic growth (for example, Cameron et al. 1967; Goldsmith 1969). Subsequent work has emphasized the policy aspects of financial development, arguing strongly for financial policies that would stimulate financial intermediation to accelerate growth (for instance, Patrick 1966; McKinnon 1973; Shaw 1973). In this approach, which will be discussed in section 1.4, less explicit attention is given specifically to the processes of structural change. In the literature on short-term macroeconomic management in developing countries, the role of monetary policy has been a focal point from the outset (see Polak 1957). With the advance of financial development the instruments available for demand management have changed and the complexities of monetary policies have increased, as will be discussed in section 1.5. The review of the relevant literature in sections 1.2 - 1.5 will serve as a background for section 1.6 where the approach to be followed in this study is set out. That approach may be labelled 'structuralist', as it is basically concerned with the problem of sectoral balance and structural change. Questions of financial development, financial policies and short-term stability are analysed from that standpoint.

1.2   Financing economic growth and structural change

The early and seminal writings on the question of how to finance development dealt with two basic problems (Nurkse 1953; Lewis 1954; Kalecki 1976): the first was how to increase the resources available for investment and the second was how to diversify the structure of the economy (industrialization) without running into unsustainable sectoral imbalances.

The first question can be rephrased using the often-quoted words of Arthur Lewis:

> The central problem in the theory of economic development is to understand the process by which a community which was previously saving and investing 4 or 5 per cent of national income converts itself into an economy where voluntary saving is running at about 12 to 15 per cent of national income or more. (Lewis 1954, p. 416)

In answering that question Lewis himself followed the classical tradition, rooted in Smith and Ricardo, arguing that practically all saving is done by the capitalist class; workers and middle classes save very little and the *rentier* class engages in excessive consumption. Thus the share of savings in income can increase when the profit share increases. These classical saving assumptions also underlie the neo-Keynesian growth models (see, for example, Kaldor 1955). A brief look at these models may help to understand the mechanisms involved.[1] The saving function is defined as:

(1) $S = a\, YL + b\, YP$
       S = gross domestic savings
       YL = labour income (wages)
       YP = profit income

This function goes back to the classical saving theory in which the income of wage-earners is assumed to be at subsistence level and therefore fully consumed, so that the value of the coefficient a in equation (1) is equal or close to zero. The profit income of capitalists is assumed to be fully or almost fully saved, so that 'b' is close to 1. The landlord class could save from their rent income, but they were generally assumed to engage in wasteful consumption (see Lewis 1954).

Since total income is defined as (ignoring rent income):

(2) $Y = YL + YP$

Equation (1) may be rewritten as:

(3) $S/Y = (b - a)\, YP/Y + a$

Equation (3) makes savings dependent on the distribution of income. The crucial question now becomes: how can the profit share YP/Y be increased? Through such an increase, savings and investment could be increased and growth enhanced. Since *ex post,* $S = I$, equation (3) may be rewritten as follows:

(4) $$\frac{YP}{Y} = \frac{1}{b-a}\,\frac{I}{Y} - \frac{a}{b-a}$$

in which I = investment.

In the Keynesian analysis, investment is an exogenous variable determined by the desire to invest and the availability of finance. Equation (4) shows that if I/Y can be increased, YP/Y increases too, so that savings rise and growth accelerates.

Pasinetti (1961) refined Kaldor's model by pointing out that if workers save they will also receive profit income and, therefore, the income distribution between the income categories, profits and wages is different from the distribution between the social classes, workers and capitalists. But he also showed that this does not affect the basic conclusion of the model, because as capitalists continue exclusively to determine the level of investment they also determine the level and proportion of profits in income. Workers' incomes have to adjust passively.

Arthur Lewis's model is an application of the classical saving theory to less developed countries (LDCs). Through increased investment in the modern sector the share of profits in national income can increase, because labour is available in unlimited supply and can be drawn from the backward agricultural sector without any rise in aggregate consumption. Kalecki (1976, Chapter 5) also presented a model in which credit-financed investment raises output and the profit share, and thus savings.

These post-Keynesian models seem almost too good to be true; it would appear that any desired savings ratio and growth rate can be achieved, but that interpretation is too optimistic as a closer look at the mechanisms behind this model will show.

Although capitalists make the investments and receive the profits, which they then save, this is not a model of self-financed investments. The initial investment has to be financed out of credit as investment precedes profit. Implicitly, therefore, this theory assumes a certain level of financial development. Credit-financed investment is restricted to the modern, capitalist sector of the economy.

In the Lewis model, credit financing, and thus an increase in the money supply, leads to excess demand for (agricultural) consumer goods whose prices will then rise. At a later stage, when investments in the industrial sector mature, the supply of industrial goods increases and aggregate supply of agricultural and industrial commodities rises and prices may fall again. This is not a model of forced saving through inflation because total consumption does not fall. What is 'forced' is the saving potential present in the disguised unemployment in the agricultural sector. The mechanism through which these savings are forced is the price rise; Nurkse (1953) points out that taxation may be necessary. One could consider the price rise or the taxation as the mechanism to transfer the food that the workers first shared in the rural areas to the urban areas, where they now work on investment projects and in factories. When the investment projects have matured, this transfer can take place through the exchange of commodities between the agricultural and industrial sectors.[2]

In this way, with constant output in the agricultural sector, investment in the industrial sector can increase the profit share and the savings ratio because the share of the capitalist sector in the economy is increasing.

In a more dynamic setting, the growth of the economy results in an increase in the demand for agricultural output, both for food and for inputs into industry. In Kalecki's terms inflation can only be avoided if the output of what he calls department II (that is consumer goods) grows fast enough to satisfy this growing demand. If the supply of the agricultural sector is inelastic, the increased demand can easily result in rising food prices and falling real wages. This fall in the real wage will help to protect the level of the profit share and of savings, but it may at the same time reduce the size of the market for the output of the modern sector (Kalecki 1976). FitzGerald (1986) analysed these processes in more detail and showed that the outcome is less simple than suggested here. The increased food prices may increase the income of the farmers, who can then provide the market for the output of the modern sector, but it may also increase the income of landlords, traders or money-lenders who mainly engage in luxury consumption and hence do not constitute a market for most of the domestic industrial sector. Matters become still more complex when not only food prices but also prices of manufactured commodities, the products of the modern sector, are allowed to increase. The real wage will then fall as prices of both agricultural and industrial goods increase, and the terms of trade between agriculture and industry may or may not turn against agriculture.

There may be limits to the income redistribution towards profits. If there is a real wage level below which the real wage cannot fall (a subsistence wage), then the profit share will not increase any further and the savings ratio will stagnate (Kaldor 1955). The same would apply if workers were able to organize themselves and resist a fall in real wages through collective bargaining. Farmers will have less chance of defending themselves against falling terms of trade if alternative crops or alternative employment opportunities are not available.

It would appear, then, that a redistribution of income, along the lines of the post-Keynesian models, would realistically occur under the impact of inflation. If workers are unable to defend their real wages, and if the terms of trade can be turned against the farmers, inflation can shift the income distribution towards profits. Assuming that the propensity to save out of profits is greater than that out of wages or farm income, this could lead to a rise in the savings ratio.

The role of inflation in this context needs to be well understood. Price rises will shift the income distribution towards profits only if some prices rise faster than others so that relative prices change. In particular, the real wage and the relative prices of agricultural goods have to fall for the profit share to increase. These price shifts would increase profits and thus shift funds to entrepreneurs who will use these to finance investment (Gurley and Shaw 1967). Generalized inflation, in which all prices rise at the same rate, would not have an effect on the income distribution. But it could shift resources to the government as the money-creating authority (Thirlwall 1974b).[3]

The acceleration of economic growth and the development of an industrial sector requires an investable surplus. In the early stages of the process of industrialization, the industrial sector is too small and immature to generate such a surplus all by itself. Agriculture is then virtually the only sector where such a surplus can be generated. It is thus inevitable that part of this surplus is mobilized for investment elsewhere in the economy. As discussed above, this mobilization can take various forms. Surplus rural labour can be transferred to the industrial sector at low wages. The terms at which commodity transfers between agriculture and industry take place can be biased against agriculture through relative price changes or taxation.

The transfer of resources and the bias in the incentive structure make modern sector investments possible and profitable. And as investments rise, profits and savings can increase. But this picture is too simplistic. In a country like Thailand, and the same is likely to be true in many other developing

5

countries, the agricultural sector and the related trading and processing activities are an important source of profits and savings in themselves. Such profits can be invested in agriculture itself, but, if the incentive structure is biased against agriculture, such investment may be unattractive. Agricultural profits may be directly transferred to the industrial sector when, for example, traders or landlords participate in industrial projects. They might also be *indirectly* transferred to the industrial sector, through the intermediation of the financial system. As Chapter 4 will show, this indirect transfer has been the major channel of intersectoral transfers in Thailand, with the agricultural sector, broadly defined to include related rural trade and services, depositing their savings with financial institutions which, in turn, used these funds for financing investments in the modern corporate sector.

The analysis of growth and of intersectoral balances and transfers can only be complete, therefore, if the role of financial intermediation is explicitly included. Also, the relationship between financial development and economic growth can only be understood in the context of a sectoral analysis.

The repercussions of the surplus extraction on the agricultural sector need to be analysed carefully. In this context the role of this sector may be analysed from the supply side and from the demand side.

On the supply side, Kalecki (1976) considered the main task of agriculture to be the supply of necessities (food) for a growing industrial labour force and for a growing population, and the supply of raw material inputs for industry. As agricultural supply may be relatively inelastic, the agricultural sector could easily act as a constraint on overall growth leading to inflation and stagnation.

In an open economy these problems could be avoided through the importation of necessities and raw materials. But if the supply of export goods required to pay for these imports is again relatively inelastic, the same problem will recur. In most LDCs exports are typically produced in the agricultural sector, often under conditions of short-term and medium-term inelasticity of supply.

The role of agriculture has been analysed from the demand side by Mundle (1985) who argued that growth of the industrial sector crucially depends on the demand arising from growing agricultural incomes. With a growing rural population the demand for own food (that is, subsistence) increases and thus the surplus of goods that could be supplied to the industrial sector declines. Stagnation in industrial growth can only be avoided if the productivity of agriculture rises, so that the supply of inputs to industry can increase and, in turn, the growing agricultural income will provide a strong demand for the output of the industrial sector.[4]

It is important, then, to consider whether the organization of production in the agricultural sector is such that investments and innovations that will generate productivity growth are stimulated. The best guarantees for this are given by a rural social organization in which the producers themselves appropriate the surplus generated by their output. For example, if land tenancy

6

is predominant, such incentives may not be available (Mundle 1985). But it is also important to emphasize that such investments will only be undertaken if agricultural producers can finance them out of profits or from credits.

One could argue that the short supply of necessities would turn the internal terms of trade in favour of agriculture and increase agricultural profits. This would, if supply is not totally inelastic, stimulate agricultural output and so relieve the constraint on growth (FitzGerald 1986). In the case of agricultural exports, it is often argued that a devaluation of the currency could have a similar effect. But Mitra, after observing an improvement in the agricultural terms of trade in India, concluded that this had no effect on the growth of output and productivity because the rich farmers who appropriated the gains of the price increases preferred to use these funds elsewhere. They may have feared that investing these funds in agriculture would increase output and would turn the terms of trade against them (Mitra 1977).

If agricultural growth is crucial to economic development, one has to raise the question whether the outflow of funds from agriculture leaves enough incentives and resources for the investments required to ensure the growth of output and productivity. Over the longer term agriculture can only continue to generate an outflow of surplus while maintaining growth of its output, if agricultural productivity increases (Mellor 1973). Does the outflow leave enough resources to finance the investment that will guarantee this growth of productivity? Mundle and Okhawa (1979), in discussing Japan's experience, observed that in the period 1888–1937 the surplus outflow from agriculture was generally higher than the investments made in the sector. Yet an increase in agricultural productivity was achieved by applying techniques that were not very capital intensive.

It will be argued later (see Chapters 2 and 4) that in Thailand something similar occurred. Agricultural output grew rapidly as more land was taken under cultivation and labour was used more intensively. Measured as yield per acre, productivity stagnated. The availability of excess land and labour led to a pattern of agricultural growth which was not dependent on heavy financial investments. On the one hand, it was rapid enough to create the demand and supply necessary for rapid industrial growth and, on the other, it allowed an extraction of a surplus without undermining agricultural growth.

Of course, the balance between the sectors and the growth of productivity in agriculture is also dependent on government policies. Governments can directly intervene in agricultural markets through price-setting; they can also indirectly influence relative prices through manipulation of the exchange rate: a low exchange rate (in terms of domestic currency) will keep the cost of imported (industrial) inputs and the earnings on (agricultural) exports low. Governments can impose differential tax burdens on various sectors or income groups and, through public investment projects, can help to increase the productivity of chosen sectors. In the use of these instruments, they are directed by economic and political objectives. Lipton accused governments of developing countries of an 'urban bias' in their policies, turning the balance excessively against the agricultural sector where most of the poor have to live and work (Lipton 1977). Such a bias was certainly present in Thailand in recent decades.

This section may be summarized by three comments pertinent to the analysis in this study.

(a) It is rooted in the classical tradition, because it recognizes that a central feature of the process of economic development is the changing balance between the productive sectors in the economy. In this process the 'new' sectors depend, for their investment resources, partly on the surplus generated by the 'old' sectors. In the literature reviewed above, 'old' and 'new' is simplified to an agriculture–industry dichotomy, but a more general interpretation is worthwhile. The financing of industrialization through the surplus appropriated from agriculture is often called 'primitive accumulation'. It is useful to point out that in the strict Marxist interpretation of that term, it refers to the transfer of resources from the pre-capitalist mode of production to the capitalist one (Saith 1985). Thus the term is not confined to the agriculture–industry flows, but could be used more broadly to cover flows between the sector of small household firms and the modern corporate sector of the economy. Chenery also observed that 'it is useful to conceive of development as a transition from traditional to modern forms of organization' (Chenery 1979, p. 1). This more institutional sectoral breakdown is a central feature of the analysis in this study. Of course, it overlaps considerably with the agriculture-industry dichotomy, but it makes it easier to deal with the fact that within the agricultural and the industrial sector, as well as within other sectors of the economy, both forms of organization may exist side by side and that there may be transitions from one form of organization of production to another.

(b) The analysis of intersectoral flows in the contributions reviewed in this section has been in terms of real resource flows rather than of financial ones. The former can be forced through relative price changes, government interventions, taxation and other means. These forced real resource flows are important, but do not form the main focus of this study, which instead concentrates on the analysis of the voluntary flows through financial institutions. It will be shown that the latter institutions provide an important channel through which the savings of the household sector flow voluntarily to the modern sector.

(c) The contributions reviewed here all point to the crucial importance of increasing domestic savings. Yet the analysis of actual saving behaviour is rather simplistic. For Lewis and Kalecki savings come out of capitalists' profits. Nurkse argued that in developing countries, most people are too poor to save, and those with more income try to emulate foreign consumption levels and patterns. He emphasized the need for taxation to increase aggregate savings.

These approaches ignore the fact that the agricultural sector, or more generally the sector of household firms, can be an important source of voluntary savings, part of which will be used for investment in the family enterprise, but part of which may also be made available, through financial institutions, for investment elsewhere in the economy. In this study a more complete analysis of the saving behaviour in the various sectors of the economy will be attempted.

1.3   Financing development: the role of international capital flows

The role that capital inflows or foreign savings play in the process of accumulation is quite complex. Foreign savings are an addition to domestic savings in that they increase the resources available for investment. The special role of foreign savings, though, derives from the fact that they also provide foreign exchange. This dual role is fully recognized in the two-gap models. Chenery and Strout (1966) is the classic work in this tradition. They identified three constraints on growth: (i) the absorption capacity of the economy; (ii) the supply of domestic savings, which sets the maximum rate of investment that can be financed; and (iii) the supply of foreign exchange, which sets a limit to the amount of investment goods that can be imported. Capital inflows may help to soften all these constraints. The absorption capacity can be increased through technical assistance and financial aid can supplement domestic savings and foreign exchange earnings.

In a closed economy any desired rate of growth in excess of available domestic savings cannot be financed. But in an open economy, capital inflows can supplement domestic savings and raise the rate of growth as long as the absorptive capacity is large enough. In fact, with the inflow of foreign savings any desired growth rate within the absorptive capacity is possible. Of course, such a higher rate of growth can be sustained only if foreign finance will flow forever, an unlikely assumption. To maintain the high growth rate, but gradually reduce foreign dependence, requires that either the average propensity to save (APS) increases, or that the incremental capital/output ratio (ICOR) falls. This latter possibility will not be discussed here. The APS will gradually rise if the marginal propensity to save (MPS) exceeds the APS.

If capital inflows were eventually to decline, there would also be a foreign-exchange problem. The higher growth rate requires a higher level of imports and these can only be continuously financed if export earnings rise. The fact that capital inflows create a debt which has to be serviced and repaid makes these conditions even more severe. If capital inflows fall and countries have to provide the resources to service the debt, domestic savings and export earnings

9

then have to increase to finance a continuously high rate of growth. Studies to be reviewed in Chapter 3 suggest that the MPS in most LDCs is not much higher than the APS, which means that continuous dependence on capital inflows to maintain a high level of growth is likely. Grinols and Bhagwati (1976) showed that, given reasonable assumptions about the capital–output ratio, saving behaviour and initial import-export balances, it is easily possible, though not necessary, that an increased capital inflow will lead to permanent dependence on such inflows rather than to self-sustained growth. Wasow (1979) extended their analysis by explicitly introducing debt servicing, which, of course, increases the chance of permanent dependence.

The importance and relevance of such considerations need little arguing at the present time, for the concern about the large external debt of some developing countries is great. They raise two questions of great importance: firstly, does the inflow of foreign capital contribute to a pattern of investment that will generate the required foreign exchange earnings (either through import savings or export earnings)? And, secondly, what is the impact of the capital inflow on domestic saving behaviour? The first question will not be analysed here, but some interesting work done on the second question should be reviewed.

It has been suggested that the inflow of foreign capital may lower domestic savings. The macroeconomic balance equation states:

(5) $I - S = F$

in which F = current account deficit or foreign capital inflow.

This *ex post* identity shows that an increase in F that is not fully reflected in an increase in investment will show up as a fall in domestic savings. There are various ways in which this may in fact happen. If capital inflows are partly used to finance increased consumption, the effect of an increased capital inflow will be that the estimate of domestic savings falls. Capital inflows and the resulting expenditures have also multiplier effects which may lead to an increase in consumption. On the basis of utility maximization, one could argue that an inflow of funds shifts the budget constraint and that one would normally expect that this extra income would be allocated partly to investment and partly to consumption (Griffin 1970). In fact, however, many capital inflows from abroad may be directly related to specific investment projects. Less clear, however, is whether and how an inflow of capital would affect saving behaviour out of domestic income. There may be a number of ways in which it could do so.

Griffin (1970) argued strongly that a capital inflow could have a negative effect on domestic saving efforts. He suggested the following ways in which this could happen:

(i)   The inflow of capital might have a negative effect on government savings. Tax revenue can be used to pay for more consumption expenditure now that aid finances investment. Alternatively, tax efforts might be softened.

(ii) Corporate savings might fall if access to international capital reduces the need to retain profits for self-financing. The activities of multinational corporations might also pre-empt investment opportunities of local firms, thus reducing their incentive to save.

(iii) Household savings might fall if increased availability of foreign exchange that follows a capital inflow leads to a lowering of import controls and increased consumption of imported consumer goods.

But capital inflows could also stimulate domestic saving efforts. Papanek (1972) suggested that there might be a number of ways in which capital inflows would increase domestic saving.

(iv) In countries with a tight foreign-exchange constraint, the inflow of capital makes investments possible that previously could not be undertaken for lack of foreign exchange. It might be that the increased opportunity to invest would generate a greater willingness to save.

(v) Capital inflows might increase particularly the incomes of groups with high saving propensities (for example industrialists).

(vi) Most capital inflows initially flow to investment projects which increase income, and therefore consumption and savings. The ultimate effect on saving could be manipulated by government policy.

The six points listed above, for and against, provide a number of hypotheses on how capital inflows from abroad could influence domestic saving behaviour. Empirical testing of these hypotheses, as it has taken place, leaves much to be desired.[5] Most studies have relied on cross-country comparisons.

Griffin (1970) ran a regression in the form

(6) $S/Y = a + b\ F/Y$

on a sample of countries and found for b values between -0.6 and -0.8. Weisskopf (1972) criticized these estimates because Griffin failed to exclude countries with a capital outflow from the sample and because it is only possible to estimate the saving function if the saving constraint is binding. In some countries with a very tight foreign exchange situation, the level of investment that can be undertaken is determined by available foreign exchange, and the level of actual savings adjusts to the amount of investment that can be financed. Correcting for these shortcomings, Weisskopf arrived at an estimate for b of -0.23. He, in turn was attacked by Newlyn who argued that these results were strongly influenced by a few exceptional cases and that a better estimate would be -0.5 (see Newlyn 1977). Papanek (1973) also ran a similar regression and arrived at a result of -0.64. The various estimates of the coefficient are within the range expected: part of the capital inflows are consumed, part contribute to increasing investment. The implication of all these findings is that international capital flows add less to investment resources than one might have expected. Of course, on balance, they do add to the total investment resources.

This aggregated analysis on a comparative basis is not very useful in shedding light on the more complex question of how capital inflows could affect saving behaviour. Some progress towards such understanding can be made if one breaks down the aggregate 'capital inflow' into its component parts. Newlyn (1977) ran a regression on pooled data for 18 developing countries covering a 10-year period. The dependent variable is gross investment and the explanatory variables include the various types of capital inflows:

- private current transfers (accounting for 6 per cent of total inflows in the sample),
- government current transfers (19 per cent),
- direct investment (18 per cent),
- contractual borrowing by public and private sector (61 per cent),
- accommodating finance (2 per cent).

Newlyn used a number of specifications for the regression equation, each of which gave somewhat different results, but the tendencies that emerged are that the coefficients related to private transfers and short-term finance are generally not significant. The coefficient of public current transfers is negative and close to -1. Of course, if all such inflows were used for consumption one would expect the coefficient to be equal to zero. Thus the significantly negative estimate indicates that such inflows have complementary consumption effects. The estimate for the coefficient of direct investment varies between 0.7 and 1.0, and that of contractual borrowing is around 0.75. The combined effect of all inflows (taking into account the outflow of debt servicing) is positive: investments are increased by about 50 per cent of total capital inflows, a figure that tallies with the results of the regression at the aggregated level reported above. But the more disaggregated analysis shows that this overall outcome is the result of quite different reactions to different types of capital flows (see also Papanek, 1973).

These findings suggest that this outcome is the result of different reactions on the side of the various sectors in the economy (e.g. public and private sector) to the different types of capital inflows. In Chapter 3 this suggestion is further worked out by including the relevant part of the total capital inflows in the analysis of the saving behaviour of the separate sectors.

This brief review of literature on international capital flows leads to two comments relevant for this study:

Firstly, the literature reviewed deals with the same problem as that discussed in section 1.2, that is how can the resources available for investment be increased? It was found that capital inflows are partly used to increase consumption and may reduce the domestic willingness to save, but on balance the inflows increase investment and growth. It should be noted though that most of the studies reported above are somewhat dated and generally precede the debt crisis. One could say that most of the studies assume capital inflows to consist of aid that does not create a debt burden. In the light of the current debt servicing burden faced by many developing countries, few countries are enthusiastic to increase further external indebtedness. That still leaves the question on the relationship between the capital inflows that took place and domestic saving behaviour. The effects on domestic saving behaviour should not be investigated only at the aggregated level. Different types of inflows are likely to influence the saving behaviour of different groups or sectors; Chapter 3 will attempt to analyse the impact of capital inflows on the saving behaviour at a more disaggregated level. Aid flows, for example, may reduce the need for and the willingness of the government to save, but they may have little effect on household savings.

Secondly, studies of the impact of capital inflows on domestic investment, growth and saving generally assume that the level of the inflows is exogenously determined. A particular amount of international capital is available to the country and the level of investment and savings will adjust to this. Recent changes on international financial markets have increased the access of many developing countries to these markets and have made capital inflows more endogenous, that is they adjust to a given *ex ante* imbalance between domestic savings and investment. This raises important new questions of macroeconomic management, in particular on acceptable external debt burdens. These questions will form the substance of Chapter 5.

1.4 Financial development

The two areas of development literature reviewed in the last two sections dealt with the problems of financing development mainly in terms of real resource flows; the role of financial institutions was hardly mentioned. Of course, in the study of long-term economic development it is the allocation of the real resources that matters. But financial flows through financial institutions do influence the real resource flows as well, and financial development, defined as an increasing role of financial intermediation, does have implications for the direction and stability of economic development.

It is a well-established fact that, with economic development, the financial system of a country also grows (Cameron et al. 1967; Goldsmith 1969; Goldsmith 1983). Several quantitative indicators have been designed to measure the extent of financial development in relation to economic development. The most detailed attempt at measurement is still Goldsmith (1969). Most of his indicators, however, are very demanding in terms of data availability and quality. Goldsmith (1969, 1983) used concepts like the 'Financial Interrelations Ratio' (the value of all financial assets as a proportion of the value of all tangible assets), and 'Financial Intermediation Ratio' (the value of assets of financial institutions as a proportion of the value of all financial assets). Given the data problems encountered in many countries, there has been a tendency to use rather simpler indicators, such as the number of bank offices per head of population or total bank assets as a percentage of National Income (see Cameron et al. 1967) – or even simpler the M2/GDP and M3/GDP ratios – as indicators of financial development.[6] The findings of the studies on these indicators can be summarized with Goldsmith's main conclusions:

(a) In the early stages of economic development, the financial superstructure grows faster than the economy.
(b) The level of the indicators of financial development and their change-over time can differ between countries, depending on for instance differences between the rates of growth and in the economic structure (for example, concentration of production in larger corporations which are dependent on external finance, or in household firms relying on self-finance).
(c) Financial development tends to start with the banking system and gradually to diversify into non-bank financial institutions (Goldsmith 1969).

The observation that economic growth and financial development go together has led to a debate about the causality between these two phenomena. Does the growth of the financial system contribute to economic growth or is it economic growth that creates the demand for more financial services? In other words, is the direction of causality supply-leading or demand-following? Goldsmith (1969) addressed this question but observed that the interactions are quite complex and that no clear direction of causation can be established.

Some authors have narrowed down this question to a simplistic econometric test using Granger/Sims causality tests. Gupta (1984) performed such a test on time-series data for 14 LDCs and found support for a supply-leading direction of causality in most cases, but there were also cases of demand-following and two-way causality. Jung (1986) performed a similar test on time-series data for 56 developed and developing countries and came to the conclusion that for the LDCs in his sample, the causal direction from financial development to economic growth is observed more often than the reverse pattern. This conclusion was strengthened when he narrowed down his sample to rapidly-growing LDCs.[7]

Such tests, however, are of limited value. Both financial development and economic growth have to be reduced to one or two summary indicators, and the concept of causality is reduced to short-term lags between them. It is unlikely that such summary indicators and short-term lags will provide much insight into what is, essentially, a long-term interrelationship in which both economic growth and financial development are influenced by other variables as well, such as changes in the world economy and shifts in domestic policies.

More importantly, tests that attempt to reduce complex interrelationships to simplistic unidirectional causality fail to lead to useful policy conclusions. In deciding on an optimal time schedule for financial development, and on financial policies that may help to bring it about, a complex set of issues needs to be taken into account, such as the appropriate role for the government, the progress of monetization in the economy, the structure of corporate finance, the role to be given to banks, non-bank financial institutions and foreign financial institutions, and the need to maintain macroeconomic stability (Cameron et al. 1967; Patrick 1966).

Financial development is important to the speed and direction of economic growth because it breaks down the limitations of self-finance. Without financial intermediation investments can be only undertaken by economic units that have already accumulated the savings necessary to finance their projects or that can borrow such funds directly from nearby savings surplus units. In an underdeveloped world the limitations of self-finance and direct finance can be quite severe and can obstruct any substantial structural change in the economy. Financial development offers the possibility of an increasing role for indirect finance. In the financial development literature, it is claimed that a rise in financial intermediation can contribute to economic development in three ways (for example, Patrick 1966; Drake 1980).

(i)   Financial development enables individual economic units to allocate their given wealth more efficiently. Wealth may be allocated to productive and unproductive physical assets and to financial assets. Financial development, which provides a wider choice of financial assets, may lead to the formation of asset portfolios with higher returns and/or lower risks. This effect may be called the portfolio effect.

(ii) A greater role for financial institutions could also increase efficiency in the allocation of investment resources. Good savers may not always be good investors or may not always have good investment opportunities. Financial institutions allow a separation of saving and investing and can channel the funds to superior investors. They can also pool savings of small savers and use them to finance large and indivisible investment projects that could never be financed through self-finance. Moreover, they can perform maturity transformations between deposits and loans and achieve economies of scale and benefits of specialization. A well-developed financial system facilitates access to the international capital markets. In short, financial development has a number of 'institutional' effects.

(iii) Financial development could not only affect the allocation of wealth over alternative assets. It could also increase the amount of wealth if it would stimulate economic units to save more. Financial institutions offer a wide choice of saving instruments which have, in the absence of inflation, an attractive and certain return and a high liquidity. The availability of such assets could induce people to save more. But the higher and certain returns could also enable units to save less and still obtain the same (target) income from their assets. The direction of this 'saving' effect is therefore theoretically ambiguous and empirical studies have not found much support for it.

The main effects to be expected from financial development may thus result from the portfolio and institutional effects, which will be briefly analysed in the next two sub-sections. The saving effect will be discussed in more detail in Chapter 3.

1.4.1 Portfolio effects of financial development

Any economic unit can hold its accumulated wealth - and additions to that wealth (that is, its savings) - in the form of a number of assets. For the present purposes, the following assets may be distinguished: [8]

(a) productive physical assets, such as land, machines, inventories;
(b) unproductive physical assets, such as gold and precious metals, excess (uncultivated) land, excess inventories;
(c) financial assets:
　　(i) non-income-earning assets, basically M1 (currency and demand deposits)
　　(ii) income-earning assets, the main form of which is, in most LDCs, time and savings deposits with commercial banks (M2).

In the absence of financial development only (a) and (b) are available. The emergence of the wider portfolio choice is the outcome of two closely related historical processes that lie at the base of both financial development and economic growth: the monetization of the economy and the commercialization of production.

Monetization of the economy can be defined as the enlargement of the sphere of the monetary economy (Chandavarkar 1977). This implies a reduction in relative size of subsistence activities in total economic activities. It implies an increasing use of money, although it cannot be measured by a simple indicator, such as the M1/GDP ratio, since in the process of monetization, the financial structure and the velocity of circulation of money may change (Chandavarkar 1977). The process of monetization manifests itself in phenomena such as the increased marketing of output and the increase in cash transactions (rather than payment in kind) on labour, land and credit markets.

The term commercialization is generally used to describe a process in which production decisions become more market-oriented and more sensitive to market signals. It may result in the cultivation of cash crops next to subsistence crops, or in diversification of crops in response to changes in relative prices, and in an evaluation of investment projects in the light of available alternatives.

Monetization and commercialization are processes that, in an historical perspective, were enforced in many LDCs by colonial powers; they forced farmers to produce for (export) markets and ensured that the foreign exchange so earned would be spent on imported consumer goods. The financial institutions that arose in that context were engaged in trade financing. After independence the mandate of these institutions became the development of the domestic economy.

The processes of monetization and commercialization give scope for financial development as they introduce the use of money and other financial assets and of economic calculation in the allocation of available resources over consumption, physical investment or the acquisition of financial assets or liabilities. With the emergence of financial institutions some economic units may prefer to hold financial assets as the return on them is higher or more certain than the physical investment opportunities available to them. Other units that have investment opportunities with returns in excess of the loan rate on financial liabilities will try to obtain funds from these institutions.

According to the portfolio theory, a utility-maximizing economic unit would allocate its wealth over available assets according to (i) the expected returns, (ii) the risk related to that asset, and (iii) the transaction cost related to moving into and out of that asset, that is its liquidity (see, for example, Tobin 1958, 1965).

The process of monetization could be interpreted as an increasing use of money, that is asset (c)(i) above. It seems irrational though to hold M1, which has no return, when other assets with returns are available. One way to explain the demand for M1 balances is to argue that the return on money is the service enjoyed from it in the process of circulation, but in portfolio theory the standard approach has been to explain the demand for money through transaction cost and uncertainty. If, for every transaction for which one needs money, one has to transfer non-money income-earning assets into money, transaction costs will be incurred. Such transaction cost can be partially avoided by holding an amount of money balances. The optimal level of money balances is the level where the gains in transaction cost equal the opportunity cost of earnings foregone (Baumol 1952).

To this transaction demand for money a precautionary demand may be added if the timing of transactions cannot be foreseen with certainty. If the timing of transactions is uncertain, one could be surprised by sudden transactions with the related need to incur unforeseen transaction cost. These can be avoided by holding somewhat larger money balances (Tsiang 1969).

In the Keynesian tradition one would expect that, besides the transaction and precautionary demand, there would be a speculative demand for money. If the prices of non-money income-earning assets are uncertain, people may hold on to money to reduce the risk of capital losses. It can be shown, however, that if there is a relatively liquid income-earning asset with no greater risk of capital loss than money, there will be no speculative demand for narrow money (Hicks, 1967; Tsiang, 1969). Such an asset is, for example, the savings deposit, and one could conclude that there will be no speculative demand for money narrowly defined. All speculative balances, if any, would then be held as savings deposits.

The theoretical conclusions on the demand for M1 balances are:

- Demand for M1 increases with output (as a proxy for transactions). The pure transaction demand will probably rise less than proportionally with output as there may be economies of scale in the use of money. The relation between the demand for precautionary balances and income depends on whether, with an increase in production, the irregularity and unpredictability of the timing of transactions rises or falls (Laidler 1977). If uncertainty rises, the demand for precautionary balances will increase. Tsiang (1969) suggested that it is likely that the increase will be less than proportional, with the result that the overall demand for M1 balances will also rise less than proportionally with the increase in income.
- In the portfolio theory the demand for narrow money balances is sensitive to changes in the rate of interest. If the rate of interest increases, the opportunity cost of holding M1 balances will rise and this will reduce the demand for money.
- More importantly, the demand for money is sensitive to changes in transaction cost. The process of financial development may lead to increased access to income-earning financial assets and so lower the transaction cost related to them. This will tend to reduce the demand for non-income-earning M1 balances.

The implications for developing countries of the theory of demand for money are far from simple. One would expect that the gradual processes of monetization and commercialization would result in an increasing use of and demand for M1 balances. On the other hand, the increased use of money may lead to economies of scale and may increase the velocity of circulation of money when, for example, production becomes more concentrated in large units which intensively use checking accounts for transactions. The overall impact on the M1/GDP ratio is ambiguous.

The spread of financial institutions may lead to increasing access to income-earning financial assets (such as time deposits) and a reduction of transaction costs of moving into and out of such assets. This effect will tend to reduce the demand for M1. Empirical studies on the demand for M1 balances in LDCs only partially confirm the theoretical expectations (see, for example, Laidler 1977; Crockett and Evans 1980; Drake 1980; Ghatak 1981). They suggest that:

- The elasticity of the demand for M1 with respect to income is around one or just above it.
- The elasticity of the demand for M1 with respect to the rate of interest is insignificant. Most studies fail to find any statistically significant relationship.
- The elasticity of the demand for M1 with respect to the rate of inflation has not been convincingly established. When significant results were obtained, the direction (sign) of the relationship was sometimes positive and in other cases negative. The level of the rate of inflation, and past experiences with inflation which determine inflationary expectations, obviously influence the results strongly. High rates of inflation have a clearly negative impact on the demand for money.
- There are no studies available on the relationship between the level of financial development and the demand for M1.

The analysis of the demand for broad money, M2 balances, is more complex. The holdings of time and savings deposits could, as suggested above, be partly explained as a demand for speculative balances. In the Keynesian analysis of the demand for money, speculative balances are held as an alternative to bonds. In this context, bonds can be seen as representative for all assets that earn an income subject to uncertainty. The speculative demand for money should then be interpreted as a temporary abode, to be held until expectations with respect to the other assets have improved sufficiently (Davidson 1978). The nature of the speculative demand for money thus implies that it will go up and down with the expectations people hold about incomes to be earned on alternative assets. As such, the speculative motive in the demand for money cannot explain the substantial increase in the M2/GDP ratio that is observed in quite a number of LDCs over time. This increase is generally explained by the fact that in LDCs, where there is no active security market and few non-bank financial intermediaries, time and savings deposits in commercial banks are virtually the only income-earning financial assets available. The shift into M2 balances, in the context of the process of financial development, is not so much a speculative demand with respect to alternative assets with fluctuating prices but a shift out of other assets with low returns.

Empirical studies have shown that in LDCs the income elasticity of demand for M2 balances is greater than that for M1 (Thirlwall 1974b, Chapter 5; Drake 1980, Chapter 4). Crockett and Evans (1980) found, in a sample of 19 countries, a central tendency for the income elasticity of M2 demand between 1.25 and 1.50. Income elasticity in excess of 1 implies that, with economic growth, there is rapid growth in the demand for M2 balances. At higher levels of income, the income elasticity of demand may level off when alternative financial assets become widely available. But in countries like Thailand M2 balances, that is savings and time deposits with commercial banks, are still the major financial asset available to all.

In general, the elasticity of the demand for M2 balances with respect to the deposit rate of interest is positive, and that to the rate of inflation negative. But these findings are far from uniform; much seems to depend on the specification of the equations, in particular on the way in which (expected) inflation is introduced (see Ghatak 1981). Most money demand functions include expected inflation. This variable is, of course, unobservable and the ways in which estimates of it are formed differ. These differences affect the role played by the variable in the regressions. It should be noted that the findings on the impact of the interest rate and the rate of inflation are often interdependent. Many studies use the real deposit rate as the explanatory variable in the equation. The real deposit rate is formed by deducting (expected) inflation from the nominal deposit rate. Since in most countries the nominal deposit rate rarely changes, the real deposit rate variable really is the same as the rate of inflation.

Studies to be reported in Chapter 4, section 4.5.1 suggest a positive relationship between the demand for M2 balances and the level of financial development. Financial development results in the increased availability of financial institutions and therefore in the reduction of the transaction costs related to income-earning financial assets.

An important question is whether the increase in financial savings (that is M2 holdings) reflects an increase in overall savings or is the result of a substitution within a portfolio of a given size. There are several possibilities for substitution. Going back to the alternative assets listed previously, it is easy to see that financial development, defined as the increased availability and use of financial assets and reduced transaction cost, stimulates a shift out of unproductive physical assets, which have no returns and no liquidity, into financial assets. The only exception to this could be in situations of rapid inflation when in fact the flows could be in the reverse direction.

It could also be that financial development induces a shift from productive physical assets into financial assets. This could be the case when low or risky returns on real investment cannot compete with the certain returns on financial assets.

Another form of substitution occurs when funds that were previously used in the unregulated money market are now deposited with banks. If, over time with the expansion of the official financial system, resources were to be shifted from the unregulated market segment to banks this could be recorded as an increase in the holdings of financial assets by households.[9] This has certainly been the case in Thailand. As Chapter 4 will show, over the last 25 years, the unregulated money market has grown little, if at all, whereas the official financial market has grown rapidly.

There could also be a short-term substitution of funds between the unregulated market and financial institutions in response to changes in the real deposit rate. Such short-term substitution plays a role in recent short-term macroeconomic models and will be further discussed in section 1.5. It is of importance, therefore, to give some attention to the nature of unregulated financial intermediation in LDCs.

The unregulated money market is mainly relevant for households and unincorporated enterprises. Most studies have concentrated on rural financial markets. The economic aspects of rural, and in particular agricultural, credit markets have been the subject of elaborate debate. A major concern in that debate has been to explain the high interest rates observed on these markets.

An obvious explanation for the high rates could be the exploitation of rural households by monopolistic money-lenders imposing usurious interest rates, but other reasons have been suggested. Bottomley (1975) provided a number of reasons for the high interest rates other than monopoly powers. If money-lenders themselves borrow the money from banks, at for example 10 per cent, they will have to charge more than that to earn the basic rate. If in addition there is a demand only for short-term loans, extending over a part of the year, the interest payments must cover returns on the idle period as well. Furthermore, the risk of default could mean a loss of principal and a loss of interest income and this has to be compensated for by the income earned on performing loans. If, finally, one adds the high administration cost, the interest rate can easily become very high without any monopolistic element being introduced.[10]

Others have maintained that the monopolistic element is more important. The default risk, for example, is absent if the money-lender has collateral. Through monopoly power the money-lender can even undervaluate the collateral so that the default risk is more than fully shifted to the borrower (Bhaduri 1977).

In judging whether the unregulated credit market is monopolistic or not, it is important to recognize the lack of specialization in this market. The main suppliers of funds are landlords, neighbours, traders, shopkeepers, rice millers; the specialized money-lender may be a rare phenomenon. It has been observed that factor markets in rural areas are intensively interlocked, with farmers obtaining credit from landlords from whom they also rent land and to whom they may sell labour (Bardhan 1980). The credit market can also be related to commodity markets, with suppliers of inputs extending credit and purchasers of output (traders, rice millers) providing pre-harvest credit. In such a complex web of interlocking market relations the price on one of these markets, the interest rate on the credit market, is an inadequate indicator of the existence of monopoly power. These conditions also affect the analysis of substitution processes between the unregulated money market and the official financial system. In terms of a portfolio model, changes in the relative rate of interest would call for such substitution. But if, for the main suppliers of funds in the unregulated market segment, money-lending is derived from their main function, say as a landlord, shopkeeper or trader, their willingness to extend credit will be determined by the returns on their main activity as well as changes in interest rates.

It should be observed that the relationship between the unregulated and the official market segments may be complementary rather than competitive. When suppliers of funds at the unregulated market are themselves borrowers from banks, financial development could go hand in hand with the growth of the unregulated market. Taking these arguments together, one could suggest that the forces for substitution between the unregulated and the official money markets are unlikely to be very strong at the supply side. The substitution that has been observed in Thailand will then have to be explained mainly from the demand side of the unregulated market. The spreading of official financial institutions and the increased access of unincorporated economic units (household businesses) to their (cheaper) credit may have reduced the demand for informal credit and so force lenders there to shift their resources. This argument is further elaborated in Chapter 4.

There is, then, scope for substitution between physical and financial assets and between official and unregulated financial market segments. As argued in more detail in Chapter 4, the rise in financial savings in Thailand cannot be satisfactorily explained by an increase in aggregate savings. The substitution processes help to explain the rapid growth of financial savings (M2/GDP ratio) observed in Thailand and in many other developing countries. The finding that the increase in financial savings accompanying financial development is mainly due to substitution within a given portfolio is important. The substitution in question is at the level of the individual economic unit, where the act of saving is disconnected from the accumulation of physical assets, that is investment. These units obtain, instead of physical assets, assets from financial institutions which, in turn, use these funds to finance investments elsewhere. At the macro-level, therefore, the levels of savings and investment need not change, but their allocation over economic units will change. It is quite likely that the units that obtain financial assets are not randomly distributed over the economy but will be concentrated in certain sectors and regions where the prospects for investment are not so attractive, or in areas where income growth has been very rapid or where savings are high for some other reason. Whatever the reasons, it is likely that an increase in financial intermediation will have consequences for the sectoral and regional allocation of resources and will thus influence the restructuring of the economy (see Chapter 4).

The separation between savers and investors also raises questions on the short-term macroeconomic stability; these will be discussed in section 1.5 and in Chapter 5.

1.4.2 Institutional effects of financial development

The shifts in the asset portfolio analysed in the previous section imply that financial development brings with it a shift of resources to financial institutions. These resources come from economic units that otherwise would have used these funds for investments with lower or riskier returns. Assuming that the financial institutions allocate these resources to loans according to the rate of return on the projects to be financed with them, an increase in the efficiency of investment resources occurs (see, for example, Galbis 1977). Similar gains can be made when the official financial system takes over resources from the unregulated money market.

In addition to this, financial development may have other benefits. With the expansion of the financial system, economies of scale in intermediation may be reaped as financial institutions can pool risks of insolvency and illiquidity more than an individual saver or the unregulated money market can and they can perform maturity transformation between deposits and loans. Financial development may also allow increased specialization among financial institutions, bringing the benefits of division of labour and increasing special expertise (Patrick 1966). A well–developed financial system may also be conducive to attracting foreign investment and foreign loans.

These potential institutional benefits of financial development must be balanced, though, against some cost and potential disadvantages. First of all, the alleged increase in the efficiency of investment may too easily identify private with social returns. Returns may be higher only because financial institutions extend credit to the modern sector, where returns are high because of oligopoly powers or tariff protection. Financial institutions do also extend credit for less productive uses, such as consumer credit or credit to the government. In addition the returns on physical investment, that were reduced by the units that obtained the financial assets, may not be so much lower on average but may be subject to great uncertainty and fluctuation (for example, due to weather conditions and variations in world market prices), or they may be low because of government intervention.

This raises a further, obvious point about the 'efficiency' of financial institutions. Efficiency in the allocation of investment resources is not the only objective in economic development: the government may have objectives with respect to employment creation, regional balance of economic activities, income distribution, and so on, the attainment of which sometimes requires the stimulation of investments with lower direct private returns. It should also be noted that financial development is not an exercise without costs. Bank buildings, and certainly prestigious bank buildings, are expensive to build and banks use scarce high-level manpower.

Finally, financial development may facilitate the attraction of funds from abroad, but it may make capital flight easier too. Generally speaking, integration of the domestic financial system into international capital markets reduces the effectiveness of domestic monetary policy.

It could also be questioned whether financial institutions are such good examples of economic rationality. The sociological study of bank behaviour is underdeveloped; it is not recognized that banks have a strong tendency towards concentration and the formation of monopolies.

23

Hilferding observed, in a book originally published in 1910, how, at the beginning of this century in European countries, the increasing use of bank credit contributed to the concentration of capital (Hilferding 1981). In the first place, some firms had better access to bank credit than others and the firms with best access also tended to have the best access to the Stock Exchange for share capital to expand their capital base further. And in the second place, the concentration among financial institutions was also encouraged. Banks cannot compete easily on the basis of interest rates – where margins are small – or on the basis of technology – which is rather uniform – and thus can only compete on the basis of their size.[11] Hence banks will try to increase their size through mergers, take-overs, etc. These concentration tendencies lead to the abolition of free competition, as banks are not interested in free competition under which the gains of one are the losses of another. So banks cooperate to establish monopolies. The end result of these processes was summarized by Hilferding as

> Finance capital signifies the unification of capital. The previously separate spheres of industrial, commercial and bank capital are now brought under the common direction of high finance, in which the masters of industry and of the banks are united in a close personal association. The basis for this association is the elimination of free competition among individual capitalists by the large monopolistic combines. (Hilferding 1981, p. 301)

This description comes very close to the concept of the 'Group' that has emerged in development literature. A 'Group' may be defined as a multi-firm conglomerate that draws its capital widely from sources beyond the single family or group of families that control the group and often through its own bank. It is likely to be engaged in investing and producing in several product markets (Leff 1976, 1979).

Groups are held together by interpersonal and interfamily links of ownership and management positions. The strongest groups are those organized around banks because the latter provide access to external resources. This industrial organization is certainly also found in Thailand. Studies, to be quoted in Chapter 4, have shown that each of the big commercial banks in Thailand is owned or controlled by one or a few families and forms the centre of a network of corporations extending over the financial, industrial and trading sectors of the economy. Viewing banks as the centres of groups of firms held together by family links and operating in protected markets leads to the question whether efficiency criteria will be dominant in their allocation decisions. Strategic considerations related to the growth and diversification of the group as a whole may override profit-maximization rules. The groups with activities stretching over many sectors may serve as another mechanism through which intersectoral flows of funds can be directed.[12]

1.4.3 Financial policies

Those who argue in favour of a positive effect of financial development on economic development generally base their argument on the propositions that (i) financial development enables economic units to form more efficient portfolios, and that (ii) financial institutions ensure an efficient allocation of their resources, so that even if aggregate savings do not increase, the efficiency of investment increases and economic growth improves. These issues were raised at an early stage by Patrick (1966) who argued on the basis of these expected effects for a 'supply-leading' financial development policy. Elements of such a policy are the active stimulation of the growth and spread of financial institutions and assisting financial development by keeping the rates of return on financial assets attractive and avoiding inflation.

Financial issues moved into the centre of attention in development policy debates after the publication of the books by McKinnon (1973) and Shaw (1973), often mentioned in the same breath as the fathers of the 'financial repression' or the 'financial liberalization' school, despite significant differences in their original contributions. Both observed that capital markets in LDCs, like many other markets, are segmented so that clients face different prices for credit, and have different access to it. Two segments can be identified in the capital markets of most LDCs. One is the official credit market consisting of formal financial institutions catering to large firms in the modern sector of the economy. This market segment is generally subject to intensive government intervention and regulation. This intervention takes various forms: interest rate ceilings, selective credit controls, subsidized credit for priority sectors, etc. The effect of these is that the institutions can offer only low deposit rates, which makes their assets unattractive and discourages financial development. This is called 'financial repression'. The other segment is the unregulated money market which deals with the medium- and small-scale firms. This unofficial market can easily evade government intervention.

McKinnon and Shaw made a detailed theoretical analysis of saving and investment in developing countries and of financial policies that could contribute to economic growth. Both argued against standard neoclassical monetary models in which the accumulation of financial assets is seen as a substitute for, and thus competing with, real accumulation.[13] They argued that this need not to be the case in LDCs, although the way in which they argued this point is quite different.

McKinnon assumed that in LDCs, investments are self-financed as capital markets are narrow and imperfect. The markets are too small to generate the funds required for investment projects and, more importantly, the risks related to an investment project in the early stages of development may be too large for financial institutions to participate in long-term financing. Given the fact that many investment projects have significant indivisibilities (that is a substantial minimum size), firms have to accumulate money balances until they have enough to finance the planned investment project. The liabilities of the financial system, in particular their time and savings deposits, are often the only means of holding such temporary balances. As 'the average time interval between income and expenditures is longer in the case of investment than it is in the case of pure consumption' (McKinnon 1973, p. 57), the demand for M2 balances will thus rise with an increase of the investment ratio. Financial savings and real investments are therefore complementary and not substitutes. This finding has come to be known as the 'complementarity hypothesis'. It has been captured in the following demand function for real M2 balances:

(7) $(\frac{M2}{P})^d = f(Y, I/Y, i_d - p^e)$

$(M2/P)^d$ = demand for real M2 balances
P = price level
p^e = expected rate of inflation
i_d = nominal deposit rate of interest

The demand for real M2 balances is a function of the level of income Y (positive), the investment ratio I/Y (positive), and the real deposit rate of interest $i_d - p^e$ (positive). If firms want to invest more, they will also demand more broad money balances. But this argument is also turned round: if the demand for M2 balances is increased in other ways, for example through an increase in the deposit rate, this will induce more real investment as the opportunity cost of holding savings in money balances is reduced (McKinnon 1973, p. 60). This, however, is not immediately obvious. One could interpret McKinnon's model as implying that the total income earned on a particular investment project is composed of (i) the interest earned on the M2 balances during the time that savings were accumulated until they were large enough to finance the investment, and (ii) the returns earned on the project once completed. The decision to save in order to finance an investment project must be determined far more by the returns to be expected on that project than by the interest income over the time during which funds were accumulated to finance the project. As the returns on the investment project are independent of the deposit rate, there is little reason to believe that a change in the deposit rate would induce significantly more investment and thus more financial savings. An exception may be when the real deposit rate is being kept down by a very high level of inflation. Such high inflation may simultaneously discourage financial savings and real investment. Although moderate levels of inflation would theoretically reduce the demand for money, they are possibly a sign of strong overall demand and could increase the willingness to invest.

Shaw followed a quite different route to show the absence of a substitution between the accumulation of physical and financial assets. Self-finance is not assumed: savers and investors are different units; and financial markets are necessary to bring them together – hence the name of his model: the 'Debt

26

Intermediation View' (Shaw 1973). In this view, M2 balances are not part of net social wealth: they are the assets of some units and the liabilities of others.[14] Thus an increase in M2 holdings need not be at the expense of real investment, as financial institutions pass these balances on in loans to investors.

Empirical tests of the 'complementarity hypothesis' have concentrated on estimating the sign and significance of the coefficient of the variable I/Y in the money demand equation (7). The results did not lead to confirmation of the hypothesis (Fry 1978; Galbis 1979; Gupta 1984). These studies generally concluded that in the countries included in the test samples, financial development has progressed to a stage where firms are no longer confined to self-finance. Of course, firms finance a significant part of their investments from their own funds even in financially highly developed countries. The access to credit, though, means that the timing of investment is no longer dictated by the accumulated savings and that firms need not finance their entire investment from their own funds. Thus most subsequent work has been based on Shaw's debt intermediation view, where financial institutions intermediate between savers (who are sensitive to the level of the real deposit rate) and investors (who are constrained by the availability of credit).[15]

The basic message of McKinnon and Shaw is meant for financial policy-makers. They argued that financial repression keeps the level of financial development low and thus slows down economic growth. Financial repression takes many forms and is generally the outcome of well-meant, but ineffective, government intervention in allocation decisions (Fry 1982; McKinnon 1973, 1980; Shaw 1973). The main forms financial repression takes are:

(a) The imposition of ceilings on the loan rates of financial institutions. The argument for this policy may be that the low cost of credit will either stimulate private investment or keep the interest burden on domestic public debt low.

(b) The imposition of high reserve requirements on financial institutions, some of which may have to be kept as non-interest earning deposits in the central bank, and some in low-interest government securities.

(c) Selective credit controls that force financial institutions to allocate part of their loans to specific uses, often at lower loan rates.

(d) Special financial institutions may be set up to channel cheap credit to priority sectors. The other financial institutions are often forced to provide cheap funds to these special agencies.

(e) As a result of points (a)-(d), loan rates of interest will be low and financial institutions will need a wide spread between loan and deposit rates to cover the subsidized activities. Therefore with low loan rate ceilings and with wide spreads the deposit rate becomes very low indeed.

(f) The level of the deposit rate may be further lowered in real terms once the impact of inflation is taken into account. These low rates undermine the saving mobilization efforts of the financial institutions.

It is clear that financial repression arises from attempts to increase investment and to shift investment resources to the public sector (for example, through obligatory bond holdings of commercial banks) and to selected priority areas in the private sector (for instance through selective credit controls) (Fry 1982). But it is claimed that the outcome of these attempts is to keep the official financial system small, so that all sectors have fewer investment resources available to them than they would have in the absence of the repression. Financial liberalization, that is the removal of the various forms of repression, would make financial savings more attractive and thus increase credit availability.

Fry (1980) ran a regression explaining the savings ratio S/Y using a number of variables, among them the real deposit rate, for seven Asian countries. He found a significant positive coefficient for this variable.[16] At the same time, he ran a regression for the investment ratio I/Y for 61 LDCs and found a significant coefficient for the variable representing credit availability. On the basis of this evidence he suggested that an increase in the real deposit rate would increase aggregate savings and thus make more credit available for financing investments.

Logically, this argument is not without problems. It is asserted that savings are a positive function of the interest rate and that there is no shortage of investment projects with high returns. But, even if one accepts that the willingness to save depends on expected returns, it is clear that the deposit rate of interest is only one return on one asset. If there are so many good investment projects with high returns then it is possible for economic units to save and to channel funds directly to the investment projects, thereby benefiting from the high returns on these projects. One would expect such a direct link particularly if one assumes, as this study does, that most savings are made out of profit income by enterprises in the corporate and unincorporated sectors.

One gives an incomplete picture if one paints financial repression as just another case of ineffective government intervention. It is rather a logical construct at the early stages of development. Colonial financial institutions were designed for import/export financing; how could such institutions be turned into agents that would contribute to the financing of economic development? The first stage of development planning consisted generally of import-substituting industrialization in which substantial investment needed to be made in often fairly capital-intensive production processes. In such early stages, the contribution of self-finance was limited as the profits of the new corporations were still low and as there were no domestic capital markets where share capital could be placed. In addition to the financing needs of industry there was a great and urgent need for public investment in the physical and social infrastructure which could hardly be financed from the narrow tax basis.

In several LDCs a significant part of the financial needs were covered by capital inflows, but these were generally not sufficient; the demand for domestic finance was great at a time when per capita income was still very low so that aggregate savings were small, and when financial development was still limited to a few bank offices mainly in the capital city. Under these conditions a system with low interest rates, with government intervention in the allocation of credit and with specialized institutions to channel foreign capital inflows, seems to be a logical outcome. It is certainly not clear that in such a phase of economic development, a more liberalized financial system would perform better. There are very few historical examples of countries, certainly in the Third World, that have gone through that phase with a fully free financial system.

In the assessment of financial liberalization policies two separate questions need to be addressed. Firstly, does financial liberalization increase total savings? Some have argued that an increase in the real (deposit) rate of interest increases aggregate savings (Fry 1982). In Chapter 3, there will be a brief review of the evidence on the relationship between the real rate of interest and aggregate savings. This evidence is mixed: some studies arrive at a positive relationship while many others fail to establish significant results. It may thus be wise not to expect too much from financial liberalization in this respect. There is more support for the finding that the real deposit rate influences the level of financial savings, that is holdings of M2 balances.

If total savings do not increase but financial savings do, a second question arises: which assets are transformed into financial assets? Seen in that light the argument for financial liberalization becomes an argument for a different allocation of resources. Financial liberalization may shift the balance between the official financial system and the unregulated credit market and may affect the sectoral allocation of investments. These substitution and re-allocation processes were already discussed previously in sections 1.4.1 and 1.4.2. Under financial repression, the funds available on the official market are limited, so that firms have to depend on the unregulated market in which interest charges are high. Credit in these markets is expensive, not so much because of monopoly powers, but because of the large cost of administration and high risks (Shaw 1973). Financial liberalization may increase the resources available at the official market at the expense of the unregulated market and of own investments in the unincorporated sector.

The sectoral implications of the shifts of financial resources as a result of financial liberalization and their impact on the efficiency of investment have been summarized in extremely simplified form by Galbis (1977). His model described a fragmented economy with a backward sector in which investments are absolutely self-financed as the rates of return are too low for credit financing. The modern sector has much higher rates of return but is constrained to self-finance because financial intermediation is underdeveloped. Financial liberalization will increase the deposit rate and make it attractive for units in the backward sector to substitute financial assets for real investments. With these financial savings, banks can help to finance a greater volume of investments in the modern sector. The shift in assets does imply a different allocation of real investment over economic units. The assumption is that this reallocation increases efficiency.

Of course, the process in which an increased deposit rate results in increased financial savings which allow banks to provide more credit, is founded on the assumption that investments are more finance constrained than cost determined. However, financial liberalization may also increase the cost of credit and, if the willingness to invest depends on that cost, this may discourage investment (Taylor 1983).

This long section on the financial development literature may be summarized in three points.

(i) This literature deals, often implicitly, with the same fundamental questions as the classical development literature reviewed in section 1.2, namely, does financial development help to make more resources available for investment and does it help to allocate these resources to the modern sector? It is observed that in most developing countries financial institutions and the role of financial intermediation has grown more rapidly than the economy. But there is no convincing evidence that the growth of financial institutions or that financial policies (of high interest rates) have had an effect on the level of the aggregate savings ratio.

(ii) The main contribution of the financial system to economic development should be expected to be its role in the intersectoral flow of resources. The previous analysis of the portfolio effect and the institutional effect suggested that financial development might induce shifts in the asset portfolio of individual economic units; it could also shift resources from the unregulated to the official money market; and might bring about a different sectoral allocation of investment resources. Financial institutions may be seen then as an alternative channel for intersectoral flows, together with the involuntary channels discussed in section 1.2. This makes it important to analyse the allocation preferences of the financial institutions. It would be somewhat naive to believe that rates of return would be their only guiding principle. For economic and other reasons, banks have a preference for large loans to modern sector firms engaged in trade and industry.

(iii) The call for financial liberalization should be interpreted as an attempt to increase the role of financial institutions in the allocation of resources. In this study it is not accepted that the call for financial liberalization can be based on the alleged superiority of 'undistorted' prices. An assessment must be made of whether the outcomes of financial liberalization agree with the wider economic, social and political priorities of society.

The instruments of financial repression all have the intention of influencing the allocation of resources, for example in favour of the public sector. The relevant policy questions are whether these allocative priorities are well chosen and whether the instruments applied are effective or whether other instruments could do the same job at less cost. The attack on price 'distortions' caused by financial repression is not convincing. In a world characterized by institutional rigidities, monopolistic firms and regulated international commodity markets, all prices are 'distorted' and removing some government interventions in the Third World would not change that. So, what is needed is not an ideological debate on the role of the market but a pragmatic analysis of which prices to distort, and how and why (see Jansen 1983, Chapter 1). To do this one would have to analyse carefully the origin and direction of the funds flowing through financial institutions and their consequences for overall economic development. Chapter 4 will attempt to do that.

1.5 Stabilization policies

The previous sections dealt with the long-term and more structural aspects of the relationship between financial development and economic growth. Growth and sectoral change (industrialization) can lead to macroeconomic instability. When the supply of necessities such as food cannot keep pace with the growing demand from the industrial labour force, inflation results (Kalecki 1976). And when rising import demands are not matched by export supplies, balance-of-payments problems arise. Many developing countries have experienced such macroeconomic imbalances and these problems have raised the need for short-term stabilization policies. In theoretical models for stabilization policies, monetary variables and monetary policies generally have a central role.

The explanation of inflation and balance-of-payments problems out of sectoral bottlenecks was the central argument of the Latin American 'structuralists' (for a summary of their views, see Seers 1983). The structuralists argued that the desire for rapid economic growth and structural change in developing countries ran into inelastic supply conditions, institutional rigidities and market imperfections, narrow tax bases and declining international terms of trade which inevitably resulted in inflation and balance-of-payments problems. Strict monetary policies under these circumstances would reduce inflation, but would do so only at the cost of lower rates of growth. The balance-of-payments problems resulting from domestic demand pressures could be contained through import controls, which were needed anyway to help industrialization.

One problem that the structuralists could not cope with was that inflation, if not controlled, had the tendency to accelerate. They did not really have a concept, or a programme, for stabilization. The history of many Latin American countries shows then how periods of rapid growth and accelerating inflation were followed by sudden shifts in policy – sometimes induced by change of government – to monetarist policies including huge devaluations and attempts at monetary control.

Such shocks have not been the experience of Thailand. The analysis of growth and stability in the Thai economy in Chapter 5 will show that, in general, the supplies of food and exports have coped easily with growing demand and import requirements. The only 'structuralist' bottleneck that has been felt is the narrow and inelastic tax base which led to the tendency for the fiscal deficit to widen.

This experience justifies the analysis of short-term instabilities, as reflected in inflation and the current-account deficit, as reflections of macroeconomic imbalances between aggregate supply and demand rather than the outcome of more fundamental disequilibria. Financial development increases the opportunities for such macroeconomic imbalances. The growing role for financial intermediation reflects an increased separation of decisions to save and to invest. Discrepancies between planned savings and investment are the root of short-term imbalances.

Since Keynes, saving and investment behaviour and financial intermediation have played a central role in the analysis of short-term economic imbalances. Financial intermediation implies the separation of saving and investment decisions. The combination of an interest-inelastic saving function with an interest-elastic investment demand and money demand sets the scene for an effective monetary policy. A change in the money supply would change the interest rate and affect the desired level of investment and would bring about an equilibrium between saving and investment. In the case of sluggish investment demand and hoarding of money in speculative balances, an unemployment equilibrium is possible where monetary policy is ineffective and fiscal policy required (Keynes 1936). The latter case, however, has not been so dominant in recent writings on stabilization policy, certainly not on LDCs. Typically, the analysis of excess demand has dominated. It can be defined as an *ex ante* excess of planned expenditure over expected output or income, or of planned investment over planned savings. The question is whether there are adjustment mechanisms operating in the economy that correct such imbalances. If not, a stabilization policy is required and the question arises: what type of policy instrument is most effective? The answer partially depends on the stage of development of the financial system.

In macroeconomic theory a number of adjustment mechanisms are suggested that could correct an *ex ante* excess demand situation in a closed economy (see, for example, Dornbusch and Fischer 1981; Leff and Sato 1980; Taylor 1983):

The real output effect. If there is excess capacity in the economy an increase in demand can result in an increase in real output and income, out of which additional savings will flow which, *ex post*, will make savings and investment equal.

The real balance effect. If there is no excess capacity, excess demand will result in price rises. The attempt by the public to restore the value of their real money balances will result in a fall in expenditure. It has also been argued that inflation will redistribute income to groups with higher saving propensities.

The interest rate effect. The excess demand and the increase in real output or in prices will increase the money demand, which will push up the rate of interest. This may discourage investment and encourage saving and the inflow of foreign savings.

Unfortunately, these effects are not necessarily effective in an open economy and even in a closed economy the direction of all these effects is ambiguous: for example the real income effect influences not only saving, but also – through the accelerator principle – desired investment. If the latter effect is greater, the initial excess demand gap will become even wider. Similarly, if inflation shifts income to capital income, these higher profits may stimulate investment as much as or more than saving. The excess demand may also lead to increased imports rather than to increased output or prices. If the monetary authorities sterilize the resulting loss of reserves (in an effort to keep the interest rate from rising), excess demand might widen rather than narrow. Also the interest rate might only have a mild effect on investment, but a much stronger one on the inflow of foreign funds. The increased availability of funds could stimulate investment if investment is constrained by the availability of credit more than by its cost, as might often be the case in developing countries.

The condition for stability is that an *ex ante* excess demand, through the adjustment mechanisms, creates more additional real savings than investments (Leff and Sato 1980; Taylor 1981, p. 473). The observations above suggest that this need not be the case. Of course, one would expect that sooner or later it will no longer be possible to finance the increasing gap between savings and investments – the rate of interest or the rate of inflation will increase too much or the government will intervene with credit ceilings. But in countries where the investment-savings gap is financed by capital inflows from abroad, the imbalances could become considerable before any action is taken.[17] The central importance of this condition makes it worthwhile to analyse the determinants of saving and investment behaviour, and of the channels of financial intermediation between savers and investors, in more detail. Leff and Sato (1980) did this, at the aggregate macroeconomic level, for six countries. They found that aggregate saving is not sensitive to the growth of real output and to inflation, but that investment does increase with these. They assumed that the interest rate effect is not so relevant in LDCs. Hence their conclusion was that the conditions for stability are not fulfilled and that government intervention, through credit controls, is necessary to prevent excess demand or to restore equilibrium.

The policy conclusion drawn by Leff and Sato is similar to the recommendations emanating from the models based on the monetary approach to the balance of payments that guides much of the IMF's advice to LDCs (see IMF 1977). In these models it is argued that in LDCs, there is no open capital market for bonds and shares, and few other liquid assets exist that the public can hold as alternatives to money. Hence the demand for money is stable and not sensitive to the rate of interest. In the first short-term macro-models specifically designed for LDCs, a very simple money demand equation was used:

(8) $\quad M1^d = a\,Y$
$\quad\quad M1^d$ = demand for M1 balances.

The demand for money is a stable function of the level of output (Polak 1957). Saving and investment are not explicitly included in this model, but given the assumed absence of a capital market and the stable money demand function, the implicit assumption is that all domestic savings are directly and fully transferred into investments. Under the assumption of full employment, excess demand, caused by investments financed through monetary expansion cannot result in a rise in income and savings, as in the Keynesian model, but rather leads to a balance-of-payments deficit and a loss of reserves.

The policy variable in this model is the domestic credit expansion. An increase in domestic credit will, in the first instance, increase nominal output. This increase in nominal output could be the result of a rise in real output if excess capacity exists, or of an increase in prices, or of both. The increase in nominal output will push up the demand for imports which will lead to a loss of reserves and thus to a fall in the money stock. In the end, money and nominal output are back at their original levels. This is the fundamental monetary approach to the balance of payments result (Polak 1957).

The model was subsequently further developed and refined (see IMF 1977). Khan and Knight (1981), for example, presented a money demand function with the level of real income and inflationary expectations as variables. The innovation in this model is the splitting-up of nominal income Y in equation (8) and in the rest of the model into a real income and a price-level segment. Their analysis shows that monetary expansion can generally have a small effect on real output and income, but usually results in higher prices. Higher prices feed inflationary expectations, which have a negative effect on the demand for money and, if they lead to an increase of domestic prices relative to international prices, on the balance of payments as well. Here again, the basic conclusions of the monetary approach are maintained.

In Khan and Knight's model neither the rate of interest nor the analysis of saving and investment processes plays a role, but there are equations on government revenue and expenditure and thus on the fiscal deficit. The implicit message, as in most IMF models, is that the fiscal deficit is the main source of short-term disturbance in LDCs. In the absence of well-developed capital markets such a deficit can only be financed through monetary expansion, with disturbing effects on the balance of payments. The assumed absence of capital markets is probably also the reason for the neglect of saving and investment behaviour: if there are no capital markets one may assume a direct link between savers and investors and hence there is less scope for disturbances arising from the private sector.

Saving and investment were included in an interesting version of the Polak model in which the saving and investment process is more explicitly introduced and the money demand function widened (Polak and Argy 1971). Compared to Polak (1957) the money demand function becomes:

(9) $\quad M1^d = a\, Y - b\, i$
$\quad\quad$ i = rate of interest.

The demand for money is now dependent on the rate of interest.

An investment function is introduced in which desired investments are sensitive to the rate of interest. The saving equation is Keynesian. This model is representative of a more developed financial system which is partially integrated into the international financial markets. Excess demand, expressed as an increase in domestic credit, leads, in addition to the adjustment process analysed above, to an adjustment through the interest rate mechanism. The increase in the money supply will result in a fall in the interest rate which will increase the demand for money, increase desired investment and reduce the inflow of capital. The combined effect of the increase in domestic credit, through its effects on nominal output and on the interest rate, is somewhat ambiguous. But if the positive effect of the interest rate fall on the demand for narrow money is not large, the conventional monetary approach result, in which nominal output and the money supply and the interest rate return to the original levels, may be reached even more quickly than in the model without the interest rate mechanism. A more developed financial system would thus render monetary policy even less effective.

The Polak model and its subsequent elaborations have become known as the 'monetary approach to the balance of payments' and underlie the IMF's thinking on stabilization in LDCs. The basic message is that control of domestic credit expansion is a necessary – and it is sometimes suggested also sufficient – condition for reducing inflation or solving balance-of-payments problems. The monetary approach models have been criticized for their inadequate analysis of the impact of credit controls. It is asserted that credit control will reduce aggregate demand, but other authors (for example, Keller 1980; Taylor 1981) have argued that:

(a) Not all elements of aggregate demand are equally affected. In LDCs there is relatively little consumer credit, thus the direct effect on consumption is limited. But the effect on investment can be strong if reduced credit availability or higher cost of credit discourages investment and so undermines future growth of output.

(b) Much of the credit may be used to satisfy the working capital needs of productive firms. A fall in credit availability can, through the working capital nexus, reduce current output more than it reduces aggregate demand so that the demand gap widens.

These criticisms could be paraphrased by saying that in the monetary approach models, too much attention is paid to the money demand and supply processes and too little to the processes of production, saving and investment which in the end determine macroeconomic balances.

The interest rate mechanism received more emphasis and another role in short-term stabilization models based on the ideas of McKinnon and Shaw. Kapur developed a stabilization model, using a wider definition of money, M2 (Kapur 1976). He postulated the following money demand function:

$$(10) \qquad (\frac{M2}{P})^d \ = \ f\,(Y, \ i_d - p^e).$$

The demand for money is dependent on the level of income and the expected real deposit rate of interest. An increase in the real deposit rate would lead to an increase in M2 balances. This should be contrasted with the analysis in the Argy/Polak model where the demand for money balances (M1) was a negative function of the interest rate. Now the demand for M2 is positively related to the interest rate. The differences between these two models reflect different theoretical perspectives but also different phases of financial development. The concentration on M1 is logical in a phase of financial development where time and savings deposits are still unimportant. The recent emphasis on M2 demand reflects the progress in financial development that occurred in many developing countries.

The Kapur model goes on to assume that financial institutions will use these deposits to extend loans to businesses, who will use these loans for working capital purposes. The basic assumption is that excess capacity exists so that the increased availability of working capital funds does have a positive effect on output. The model can be used to show that standard monetary policy measures, such as lowering the growth rate of the money supply, have only a slow, and in the short-term perverse, effect since (i) the impact on the demand for money is slow: slower money growth will reduce the inflationary pressures but the demand for money will increase only once the inflationary expectations decline, which will take time when expectations are sticky; and (ii) the effect on current output, through the availability of working capital, will have an immediate and negative effect on aggregate supply. It is suggested that, for reasonable values of the crucial parameters, the rate of inflation will eventually fall, but the adjustment process will be painful and possibly long. Kapur suggested that an alternative adjustment policy would be to increase the nominal deposit rate, so that the real deposit rate would rise immediately. This would have a direct and immediate effect on the willingness to hold M2 balances, so credit could even expand and supply could rise, thus closing the *ex ante* demand-supply gap from both sides. The rate of inflation would subsequently fall as it is determined by the degree of excess demand. A subsequent gradual decline in the growth rate of the money supply could further help to reduce inflation. As the fall in inflation is gradual but the increase in the nominal deposit and loan rate is immediate, the real cost of credit increases, but as long as that cost remains below the rate of return on working capital there need not be any concern that it would undermine production. Hence this alternative route to stabilization is far less costly than the traditional 'monetary approach' measures (Kapur 1976).

The contrast between this approach and the monetary approach is sharp. In the monetary approach it is assumed that existing capacity is fully utilized; this seems to be a reasonable assumption when analysing excess demand problems. Using that assumption a further rise in demand will lead to inflation or balance-of-payments problems. The financial liberalization approach rather optimistically assumes idle capacity so that output can grow.

The analysis of production and growth in Kapur's model is somewhat unsatisfactory. Output can be continuously increased by adding loan-financed working capital to existing (infinite?) excess fixed capital. Saving and investment play no part in the process of growth. This is unrealistic even in a short-term model (Fry 1982).

Mathieson (1980) partly corrected this by assuming that bank loans finance a part of both working and fixed capital, the rest being financed by the firm's own savings. In that model the rate of investment, and the rate of growth of output, fall when the real loan rate rises (Mathieson 1980; Fry 1982). However, even this model is based on a relatively simplistic analysis of saving and investment behaviour of the corporate sector.[18]

The neo-structuralists (see, for example, Taylor 1981, 1983) stand in the tradition of the Latin American structuralists mentioned above in that they have an eye for how the structure and institutions of an economy affect its behaviour. They have further criticized the financial liberalization approach and expanded the analysis of stabilization patterns by introducing:

- A portfolio analysis in which total wealth is given, so that an increase in a holding of one asset (for example M2) occurs at the expense of another asset; and
- A cost function which determines the price level, so that for instance an increase in the cost of working capital credit will have a direct effect on the price level.

The portfolio approach, as used by the neo-structuralists, typically assumes that the private sector can allocate its given wealth over (i) deposits with banks and (ii) direct loans to firms through the unregulated credit market (Taylor 1981). In that case an increase in deposit holdings, for example, as a consequence of an increase in the real deposit rate, would be at the expense of direct loans without adding any new funds. In fact, as banks have to hold a part of the new deposits as reserves, the total loan supply falls (Buffie 1984). These results would be somewhat changed if there were a third type of asset, say gold, which is unproductive (Taylor 1983, Chapter 5; Buffie 1984). An increase in the real deposit rate could then lead to a fall in the holding of gold (which may stand for all unproductive assets such as currency, jewellery, excess inventories, foreign currency). If that occurred, the total loan supply would increase. The combined effect would depend on the strength of the different substitution processes, but even with 'gold' an overall contraction of the loan supply is possible.[19]   Van Wijnbergen (1982) observed that, at least in South Korea, savings deposits and loans on the unregulated credit market are much closer substitutes than deposits and currency. There is no significant substitution between the latter two.

If firms use credit mainly for working capital purposes, and if they have some discretionary market power to set their prices based on cost of production, then an increase in the cost of credit will have an inflationary effect (Bruno 1979; Taylor 1981, 1983; Van Wijnbergen 1983; Buffie 1984). This effect could be quite strong in developing countries where modern sector firms are often heavily indebted. But the neo-structuralists may well have over-emphasized the inflationary effects of financial liberalization.

An increase in the loan rate on the official credit market would make loans on this market more expensive, although still cheaper than unregulated market loans. Given the wide spread between loan rates and returns to lenders at the unregulated market, due to high risks and administration cost, an increase in interest rates on the official market could draw funds from the unregulated market to the official one. The supply of funds on the official market would increase and a greater share of overall credit demand would be satisfied in this market segment. The supply of funds on the unregulated market would fall, but so too would the demand, because a greater share of credit demand is now satisfied on the official market. The net effect on the unregulated market loan rate is therefore ambiguous. The overall effect on average cost of credit also depends on the shares of both markets in total credit supply. Cole and Park developed a simple model of the interaction between the official and the unregulated credit market in South Korea and came to the conclusion that an increase in the deposit rate on the official market could easily lead to a fall in the interest rate on the unregulated market (Cole and Park 1983, p. 149). The average cost of total credit would also change because the share of the official market increases and the share of the unregulated market falls, although the increase in the former may be smaller than the fall in the latter. The overall impact on average interest cost is uncertain.

Clearly these neo-structuralist approaches give a better insight into the channels of financial intermediation. The main element is that an increased holding of one financial asset (for example, time deposits) may be at the expense of other productive assets as much as, and probably even more than, at the expense of consumption or unproductive assets.

The sectoral implications of the reallocation of assets has received little attention in these models though. Van Wijnbergen (1982) postulated that the official credit market caters primarily to the export sector and the unregulated market to the domestic sector. But that seems to be a special feature of the South Korean situation and is also contradicted by Cole and Park who reported studies suggesting that the industrial distribution of loans of the two market segments is quite similar (Cole and Park 1983, p. 166).

In other countries the effects may be different, but in general one could hypothesize that a change in the composition of the asset portfolio will shift resources between public and private sectors, between large-scale and small-scale units or between unincorporated and corporate sectors, and between rural and urban areas.

The analysis of saving behaviour in the stabilization process remains unsatisfactory even though the stability outcome depends strongly on it. Taylor (1981, 1983) gave some attention to it, but this discussion remained at the simple level where (i) saving is mainly from corporate profits, so that inflation can force saving through a reduction in real wages; and (ii) the profit rate of corporations depends, with a fixed mark-up rate, on the level of capacity utilization; by pushing up the latter excess demand can increase profits and savings.

Other authors have suggested that aggregate savings may be sensitive to the deposit rate of interest (Buffie 1984) or more specifically to the rate of interest on the unregulated market (Van Wijnbergen 1982).

This section on stabilization models may be concluded with three comments.

(i) The models reviewed partially reflect an historical sequence in which they were developed. This sequence could be interpreted as a gradual catching-up of theory with the realities of financial development: for instance, there was little point in debating the effectiveness of the deposit rate as an instrument of monetary policy at a time when the financial system was hardly developed. Of course, this interpretation of the variations between the models should not ignore the important theoretical differences that exist between the various contributions.

(ii) The problem of short-term macroeconomic management can be summarized by the question how an *ex ante* disequilibrium between planned savings and investments will lead to an *ex post* equilibrium. Crucial to the answer is an analysis of how saving and investment react to the adjustment mechanisms and policies to which the disequilibrium gives rise.

There seems to be a fair degree of agreement on the reaction patterns on the investment side. Excess demand results in an increase in nominal income, and income growth generally stimulates further investments. On the other hand, excess demand may lead to an increase in the interest rate and investment is generally found to be sensitive to interest cost. The outcome of these automatic adjustment mechanisms is thus uncertain, but it is found that investment can generally be influenced through monetary policies. The level of investment is sensitive to the level of interest rate and to the availability of credit and these instruments can thus be used to bring investments back to the level that can be financed. The reaction patterns on the saving side have been less satisfactorily studied. Savings are less sensitive to price increases or interest rates, and no policy instruments have been suggested that could be shown to have a clear and positive effect on aggregate savings. The conclusion of these findings is unsatisfactory because it suggests that the only solution to short-term imbalances is to cut back on investment and thus on growth. Given this unpleasant conclusion, it is surprising that no attempts have been made to analyse saving behaviour in more detail. An attempt to do this will be made in Chapter 3 of this study and its implications for stabilization analysis will be drawn in Chapter 5.

(iii) The models reviewed here analyse adjustment through increases in real income or in prices, through changes in the interest rate and through monetary policies. As argued in section 1.3, the international capital flows have become much more endogenous with the internationalization of the world's financial markets. This has the result that, for example, in a country like Thailand, with easy access to international capital markets, short-term imbalances are accommodated through capital flows rather than through other adjustment mechanisms. This severely limits the effectiveness of monetary policy. Credit ceilings can be evaded by borrowing abroad and interest rate policy is only effective if the domestic interest rate is below the international one. The implications of this will be further analysed in Chapter 5.

1.6   The approach of this study

The comments made in reviewing the literature in the sections above have already suggested the approach that this study will take. It may be useful to summarize explicitly its purpose and method in three brief points:

(a) This study aims to analyse the causes and effects of financial development. It will do that in the framework of the fundamental questions related to financing development, that is the questions on the speed, direction and stability of economic development.

(b) The main effect of the development of the financial system is that an additional channel for the intersectoral flow of resources is created. The difference between this channel and others is that the decision to channel funds through financial institutions is voluntary. Hence it is necessary to analyse the determinants of the sources and uses of the funds that flow through this channel.

(c) The growth of financial intermediation also implies a separation between the acts of saving and investment. This has consequences for the sectoral allocation of investment and for the equilibrium between aggregate savings and investments. Both elements will be analysed.

The emphasis in these three points is on the structural, or sectoral, implications of financial development. In the early development planning literature sectoral considerations were central: a surplus had to be appropriated from agriculture to finance industrialization. In this study, though, it is recognized that the process of development is not just characterized by industrialization and by a relative decline of the agricultural sector, but rather by a changing organization of production in *all* sectors of the economy. Gradually small-scale, family-based production using traditional techniques is being replaced by larger-scale modern production organizations. In some sectors these processes of change may have proceeded rapidly and be almost completed. In others they may still have to start.

Schimmler (1979) suggested that a breakdown of economic activities into a modern and a traditional sector requires clear criteria – for example, the organization of production or the intensity of technology use – but that in most of the productive sectors of the economy traditional and modern activities exist side by side, so in the absence of detailed data, a breakdown will always be somewhat arbitrary.

The dichotomies mentioned above are often used to define the process of economic development. Development is taken to mean a relative decline of the agricultural sector and growth of the industrial sector, or an increasing use of modern technologies and of formal ways of organizing production, or a shift from small household firms to large corporations. But it is useful to note that such shifts have their limits. Even in an advanced country like the United States a substantial sector of small-scale, family-operated businesses still exists. The reason for this is that the nature of the commodity or service provided (for example, personal services or retail trade) and the available technologies do not allow it, or do not make it profitable, to concentrate these activities in large units.

Galbraith (1975) distinguished, for the United States, a 'Planning System' composed of large corporations planning their own production, investment and prices, and a 'Market System' of small firms based on the exploitation of own and family labour. O'Connor (1973) used a similar breakdown for the United States: in his 'competitive sector' prices and wages are set by market forces, whereas in his 'monopolistic sector' they are determined by firms and by bargaining. Galbraith considered the market system inherently stable since its expenditures adjust quickly to changes in prices and incomes. But the planning system is unstable because its saving decisions (emanating from price setting) and its investment decisions do not necessarily match (Galbraith 1975).[20] These studies of an advanced economy suggest that an analysis of the behaviour of the unincorporated sector in LDCs would not be for temporary use only.

On the basis of these arguments this study will make a basic distinction between, on the one hand, the 'household sector' or 'unincorporated sector' and, on the other hand, the corporate sector.

The unincorporated sector consists of small-scale production units, generally based on family labour and operating on competitive markets. This type of production organization is dominant in the agricultural, trading and services sector of developing countries. The corporate sector is dominated by large firms, using hired labour and operating on more oligopolistic markets.

National Accounts and Flow-of-Funds statistics present economic data by an institutional breakdown distinguishing a sector of 'households and unincorporated enterprises', a sector of 'corporations' and a government sector. In this study it is assumed that the unincorporated sector can be identified, by approximation, with the National Accounts sector 'households and unincorporated enterprises'. The corporate sector is then identified with the sector 'corporations' as presented in these data sources. This procedure is justified because in many developing countries, and certainly in Thailand, most households are self-employed unincorporated production units. Only a relatively small proportion of households are pure wage earners. Obviously, not all large firms need to be incorporated and some corporations may be quite small. The corporate form is a legal concept as well as an economic one. Sometimes very large firms prefer to remain family businesses and a small firm may prefer to register as a corporation. In the absence of detailed data one has to ignore these niceties and concentrate on averages.

The breakdown by production organization is crucial to this study because the two sectors differ markedly in (i) the way profits are earned and savings are made; (ii) the physical investment opportunities and incentives available to them; and (iii) their access to official financial institutions. These differences in saving and investment behaviour have important implications for the patterns of financial development as well as for the analysis of short-term stabilization processes.

The sectoral breakdown enables the analysis of the saving behaviour of the unincorporated sector, an aspect neglected in the development finance literature. These savings – of a sector with limited investment opportunities and incentives – are the root of financial development. Household firms earning profits and making savings place these savings increasingly with financial institutions, who use these funds to extend credit to all sectors, although on a net basis the corporate sector benefits more than others. In this way the institutions provide an important channel for the intersectoral transfer of resources. Flow-of-Funds Accounts of Thailand will be used to indicate the magnitude of these flows.

This study will establish clearly that the fundamental cause of financial development is the increase in transfers between individual economic units and between economic sectors through the mediation of banks. It is not caused so much by an increase in total savings, nor does it lead to this. The net outcome of the increase in financial intermediation is a change in the sectoral allocation of resources. In Thailand, on balance, the corporate sector benefited from this. It is not unlikely that in other developing countries that have gone through a process of financial development a similar shift of funds occurred.

The detailed study of the saving behaviour of household firms also has important implications for the analysis of stabilization processes. In most stabilization approaches saving behaviour is ignored or analysed only at the aggregated level. Aggregate private savings are made up of household savings and corporate savings. A disaggregated analysis shows that household saving behaviour can be very destabilizing. The household savings ratio can be very volatile, as is to be expected of a (predominantly agricultural) sector operating at competitive markets where prices (and thus incomes) fluctuate with exogenous factors (like weather or world market conditions). The savings ratio of the corporate sector is far more stable – again, this is to be expected from a more oligopolistic sector – so that the fluctuations in aggregate savings generally follow the pattern of household savings.

In the past, Thailand's access to international financial markets has made it possible to accommodate the fluctuations in domestic savings through foreign borrowing. This suggests that the inflow of foreign capital is far more determined by fluctuations in domestic savings than that such capital inflows would determine domestic savings, as was suggested by some studies reviewed in section 1.3.

These issues, discussed at the theoretical level here, will now be elaborated at the empirical level in subsequent chapters. The next chapter, though, will first give a brief historical introduction to the economic and financial development of Thailand over the last 25 years.

Notes

1. In presenting equations in this study the same symbol for a variable will be used throughout. The definition of symbols is not continuously repeated in the text. Time subscripts are not given unless the equation contains variables referring to different time periods.
2. Nurkse pointed out that investment projects typically require more resources than just food for the workers. Additional finance is required to pay for material inputs, transport, etc. This increases the need to control consumption through taxation or to acquire additional funds from abroad (Nurkse 1953). Kalecki also considered it important that the consumption of high-income groups be taxed (Kalecki 1976).
3. The proceeds of such an 'inflation tax' depends on the extent to which inflation affects the demand for money. At high rates of inflation the public may move out of money so that the tax base for the inflation tax narrows. But at modest levels of inflation, there will be a shift of real resources to the public sector (Newlyn 1977). These calculations on the proceeds of the inflationary tax should be used carefully. They ignore important aspects of inflation, such as whether inflationary financed public investment 'crowds out' private investment in

the real sphere (for example, through claims on scarce foreign exchange), or what the impact of inflation is on exports and imports.

4. These arguments are placed in a closed economy context. In an open economy the industrial sector could import inputs and export surplus production thereby escaping the limitations set by the agricultural sector. Mundle argued that such industrialization would be fragile and precocious as it would lack an indigenous basis (Mundle 1985, p. 77).

5. There are serious data and interpretation problems with these regressions. First of all, some capital inflows are recorded on the current account of the balance of payments (for instance, transfers and interest payments). Secondly, it is unclear whether it is a capital inflow that 'causes' a fall in savings, or a shortfall in savings that makes an inflow necessary (Weisskopf 1972). In cross-country analysis it may be that countries with low savings ratios receive large amounts of aid because they tend to be the poorest countries (Papanek 1973).

6. Throughout this book, where necessary, the money stock will be accompanied by a number: M1, M2 or even M3. The definitions follow standard practice in which M1 consists of currency in circulation and demand deposits; M2 consists of M1 plus time and savings deposits with commercial banks; and M3 of M2 plus deposits with savings banks, finance companies, etc.

7. Jung (1986) included Thailand in his sample of countries. On the basis of data covering the 1953–81 period he concluded that the only significant relationship that could be established was that of the M2/GDP ratio following economic growth.

8. Note that portfolios may also contain liabilities (or negative assets). In fact, banks can only accept deposits if other units are willing to accept liabilities. The demand for liabilities (say, bank loans) can also be treated in the portfolio context.

9. The monetary consequences of this substitution are complex. If a substantial part of the unregulated market activities are in kind, the substitution to official channels will imply an increase in the monetary variables. If all transactions on the unregulated money market are in cash, the substitution may imply a fall in currency in circulation and an increase in M2 balances and bank loans. If these bank loans are taken out in cash the total money supply could fall as banks need to hold back some cash as reserves. This point arises again in section 1.5 (see note 19 below).

10. For example, if the basic interest rate is 10 per cent and 20 per cent of the loans default, the performing loans will have to carry an interest rate of 37.5 per cent just to earn the basic rate over the initial outlay and to recover the losses.

11. Some banks may try to compete through specialization in a special type of business. In that case they will tend to remain small and often become subsidiaries of major banks.

12. Leff (1976) argued that a group may function internally as an efficient (segment of the) capital market. Profits of the member firms and the funds obtained from outside, for example through banks, are pooled together and allocated to the superior investment opportunities in the group. If the group would see good opportunities in new lines of business outside its current pattern it could easily marshall the resources to enter such a field.

13. McKinnon (1973) argued that neo-classical models are prone to inflation. If money holding and investment are seen as alternatives, inflation will be considered useful as it will reduce the demand for money and thus free resources for investment. In McKinnon's analysis inflation has a negative effect as it intensifies the financial repression.

14. To use terminology of Gurley and Shaw (1960), Shaw considered M2 balances as 'inside' money. McKinnon used the 'outside' money approach.

15. McKinnon himself, in more recent work also seems to have left his complementarity hypothesis as he discussed the M2 balances more in a loanable fund approach (see McKinnon 1980).

16. Giovannini (1983) criticized Fry's result. He updated the sample period and found that the significance of the real deposit rate disappeared.

17. This story could also be told in an IS/LM framework, in the way that, for example, Taylor (1981) and Leff and Sato (1980) did. If investments react more strongly to income growth or price increases than savings, the IS curve will be upward sloping. Whether the system is stable and will reach a new equilibrium then depends on whether the slope of the LM curve is steeper than that of the IS curve. If it is, the money market will force the system back to equilibrium. But capital inflows could shift the LM curve outwards.

18. Mathieson (1980) assumed that investment is determined by income and by the savings ratio. The savings ratio, in turn, is determined by the rate of return on capital and by the real loan rate.

19. Taylor (1983) Buffie (1984) and Van Wijnbergen (1982, 1985) used balance accounts to make this point clear.

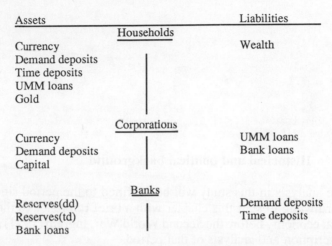

Assets	Liabilities
Households	
Currency	Wealth
Demand deposits	
Time deposits	
UMM loans	
Gold	
Corporations	
Currency	UMM loans
Demand deposits	Bank loans
Capital	
Banks	
Reserves(dd)	Demand deposits
Reserves(td)	Time deposits
Bank loans	

It is argued that the demand for M1, currency and demand deposits, is insensitive to changes in the deposit rate. Thus the substitution in the household portfolio can only take place between gold or loans on the unregulated market (UMM loans) and time deposits. If a certain amount of UMM loans is transferred into time deposits banks can extend more loans, but the increase in bank loans is less than the decrease in UMM loans since banks need to hold some of the funds back as reserves. It is argued that the size of the UMM relative to the bank system is large, so the contractionary effect can be significant.

20. Other authors argued that the planning nature of the corporate sector results in great stability because investment plans are drawn up for the medium term and not continuously adapted to new conditions (for example, Eichner 1985).

2 Economic and financial development in Thailand

2.1 Historical and political background

The analysis in this study will be confined to the period since 1960, but it is worthwhile to start this chapter with a brief reference to the structure of the Thai economy before the Second World War. Ingram (1971) gave an excellent description and analysis of that period.

The Thai economy in that period was an open economy. Rice, both the main staple and the main export crop, was produced by small-holding peasants. The surplus generated by them was appropriated by the urban elite which consisted of two groups: firstly the indigenous elite of the Court and bureaucracy, and secondly the foreign commercial interests. As there was almost no domestic industry, non-food consumption needs of the urban elite were catered for through imports.

The main foreign element in the economy was in trade. Residential Chinese and Europeans dominated both internal and external trade. The surplus they earned was not invested but sent abroad. A surplus on the trade balance served to finance the accumulation of international reserves and the remittances of foreigners.

Although Thailand remained independent, it had to accept a significant degree of foreign intervention, particularly in affairs of trade and economic policy. The Bowring Treaty of 1855 between Thailand and Britain had set rules for trade and for public revenue. The fear of more active (possibly even military) foreign intervention in the case of dissent led to a very strict adhesion to these rules on the part of the Thai authorities: public investment was hardly undertaken and fiscal and monetary policy was passive and cautious. The low level of private and public investment kept the economic growth of the system very low, basically determined by the growth of the rural population and by the availability of new land, and thus the economic structure remained unchanged.

After the disruptions of the Second World War and the recovery period, a more nationalistic economic policy was pursued in Thailand, initially relying largely on the public sector and state enterprises but later – after 1956 – increasingly depending on private enterprise.

There were three political processes responsible for this shift in economic strategy. The first was that the Revolution of 1932 had replaced the traditional monarchy with a more modern leadership. On top of this came a major change in the international political environment with the post-war decolonization process: this created international political and economic dynamics in which such non-colonies as Thailand also participated. Although Thailand was never a colony, it had certainly seen its freedom of choice limited in matters of economic policy, particularly by Britain. Decolonization, therefore, opened options, for example, in matters of fiscal and trade policies. Finally, the third process was the result of the Revolution in China which cut off the Chinese merchant class in Thailand from its motherland. Capital remittances to China dropped sharply and resident Chinese became more interested in investing in Thailand (Siamwalla 1975).

Thus it was almost simultaneously that the international context changed, state power shifted into more modern hands, and a potential local bourgeoisie emerged. These three elements have subsequently dominated Thai economic development. The state and the local bourgeoisie of mainly Chinese origin formed a close coalition that steered economic development policy; they created the preconditions for rapid growth and structural change in Thailand. In the 1950s and 1960s this coalition took the form of military and bureaucratic leaders serving on the board of directors of major firms. This ensured the political leaders of an additional income and gave the bourgeoisie political protection and influence (Skinner 1958). However, the rapid integration of the Chinese in Thai society gradually made protection less necessary and allowed the bourgeoisie a more independent political role through its political parties.

The breaking point was the 1973 student-led revolt which, temporarily, discredited the military and which more permanently increased the role of political parties. It appeared at first that that revolt challenged the ruling coalition. The movement protested against the political role of the military, against the influence of Japanese multinationals, against the exploitation of farmers and workers: in short, it protested against the whole complex on which the Thai development model rested. In the subsequent 1973–76 'democratic period' there was indeed an increase in workers' activities: the number of strikes rose dramatically. Farmers also came to Bangkok to protest against government neglect of their problems (Morell and Samudavanija 1981). The post-1973 movement, though, was quickly taken over from the students by political parties representing bourgeois interests. The culmination of this process came in 1976 when, in a bloody coup, the military reasserted its role and the old coalition was restored.

2.2 Growth and structural change

Thailand has experienced high and sustained economic growth over the last two-and-a-half decades. The average annual growth rate of real GDP was 8 per cent in the 1960s, almost 7 per cent in the 1970s, falling to 4.7 per cent during 1980–86. This growth was carried by a strong expansion of agricultural production and a rapid industrialization.

Economic growth in Thailand has been rapid, also from a comparative perspective. The growth record does not match that of the star performers among developing countries, such as South Korea or Taiwan, but it is very respectable. Of the 100 non-oil and oil-exporting developing countries listed in the 1987 *World Development Report* of the World Bank, only 13 had higher rates of growth of the per capita GNP over the period 1965–85 (World Bank 1987, p. 202) and few of these could match the macroeconomic stability that had accompanied Thai growth: inflation has always been moderate in Thailand and, by 1988, the external debt was still easily manageable. The exchange rate between the US dollar and the Baht did hardly change from the 1960s up to 1981.

In Table 2.1 some indicators of growth and structural change are presented.[1] Economic growth was rapid and the production structure of the economy changed significantly. The industrial sector was certainly the leading sector in this growth process, but the growth performance of agriculture was also remarkable. Agricultural output, measured at constant prices, grew by 5.6 per cent, 4.2 per cent and 2.9 per cent in the 1960s, 1970s and early 1980s respectively.

Growth in the industrial sector was even faster. This sector first concentrated on the production of goods for the domestic economy but gradually started to export more. The indicators of foreign trade in Table 2.1 are very telling of the change that occurred. Over time the Thai economy has become more open: both the export/GDP ratio and the import/GDP ratio increased significantly. The composition of imports changed – as one would expect from a country going through an import-substituting process – away from the importation of consumer goods and towards intermediate inputs. The export composition also changed, with an increasing share of exports originating in the manufacturing sector.

Thailand's rapid economic growth and structural change was accompanied by an increasing rate of investment, as Table 2.1 shows. The pattern in the overall investment ratio and its major elements are shown in Chart 2.1. The ratio of investment to GDP, which had been very low in the pre-war years, reached a much higher level. Gross private investment as a proportion of GDP

48

increased from around 11 per cent in 1960 to almost 16 per cent by 1970, and to an even higher level of 18 per cent in 1974/75. After those years there was no further increase; the ratio fluctuated from year to year and declined sharply in the 1980s.

Table 2.1   Indicators of structural change in the Thai economy, 1960–86

	Averages over the period (percentages)					
	1960–64	1965–69	1970–74	1975–79	1980–84	1985–86
Production:						
Agriculture/GDP	37.1	33.4	30.4	28.9	22.6	16.9
Manufacturing/GDP	13.6	14.7	16.9	18.9	19.6	20.4
Trade:						
Import/GDP	19.5	21.1	22.2	26.3	27.7	25.8
Export/GDP	17.9	18.7	19.4	21.7	24.2	27.1
Import composition (%)						
consumer goods	31.6	24.0	15.9	12.0	11.6	9.8
intermediate goods	18.2	21.4	28.9	27.5	24.7	32.5
capital goods	27.8	33.1	32.0	28.4	26.7	31.2
other (incl. oil)	22.3	21.4	23.3	32.1	36.9	26.4
Export Composition						
share manufactured goods	1.8	12.0	19.3	24.8	38.9	52.7
Protection						
import duties received/	21.6	19.6	17.5	12.9	11.0	12.6
total imports						
Accumulation:						
GDCF/GDP	18.1	23.4	23.9	26.2	24.0	22.5
Gross National Savings/GDP	18.6	22.7	23.7	23.2	19.8	17.9
Current Account Deficit/GDP	0.5	1.3	1.6	5.0	5.6	1.8
Statistical Discrepancy						
(I-S-CAD)/GDP	–1.0	–0.6	–1.4	–2.0	–1.4	–2.8
Stability:						
Government Expenditure/GDP	13.2	15.4	16.4	16.6	17.9	18.9
Government Revenue/GDP	12.8	13.7	13.4	13.6	14.5	15.5
Treasury deficit/GDP	0.5	1.7	3.0	3.0	3.4	3.4
Inflation (CPI)	1.7	2.7	9.0	7.0	8.5	2.1

Private investment consists of investment by households and unincorporated enterprises and by corporations (I_{pr} in Chart 2.1). The Flow–of–Funds Accounts data, which will be analysed in greater detail in Chapter 4, show that the household investment ratio was very stable over the years, the increase and fluctuations in the overall private sector investment ratio are the result of the activities of the corporate sector.

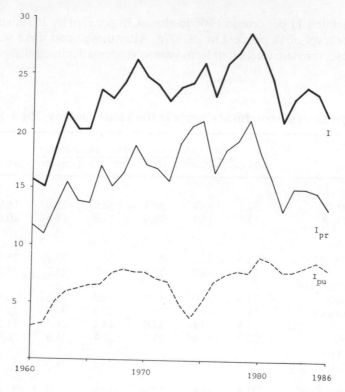

Note:
Total Investment is Gross Domestic Capital Formation and thus includes increases of Stocks. Private investment includes the Gross Fixed Capital Formation by private Households and Corporations. Public investment is the Gross Fixed Capital Formation by Government and State Enterprises.

Chart 2.1 Investment ratios (as % of GDP)

The public investments are made up of investments by the central and local government and by state enterprises (I_{pu} in Chart 2.1). The increase in the 1960s reflected the growing activities of the government. The deep dip in the period 1973–75 was the result of the restrictive fiscal policies of those years; a recovery followed in the years afterwards. The high level of public investment in the late 1970s and early 1980s was due to the increased activities of the state enterprises: their investments started to rise very rapidly after 1976. This development will be analysed in more detail in Chapter 4.

The ratio of overall investment to GDP, presented in Chart 2.1, seemed to show, in a long-term perspective, an upward trend from 1960 to 1979. Since then, however, there has been a considerable fall.

Could the high level of investment be matched by domestic savings? Chart

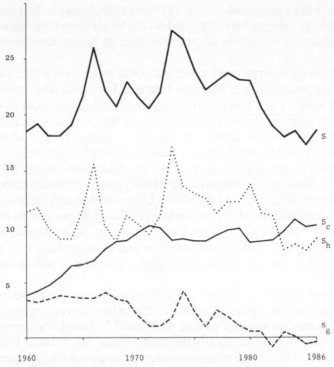

Note:

S_h = savings by Households and private non-profit organizations
S_g = savings by General Government
S_c = savings by Corporations and Government Enterprises, including provision
     for consumption of fixed capital
S = Gross National Savings

Chart 2.2   Savings ratios (as % of GDP)

2.2 shows the aggregate savings ratio and the ratios of the main sectors, and traces the patterns in the ratios over the years. The determinants of the savings ratios of the various sectors will be analysed in detail in Chapter 3. Here it will suffice to identify the main trends.

Corporate savings (S_c) consist of the net savings of private corporations and of state enterprises, and of depreciation allowances.[2] From 1960 to 1971 there was a continuous increase in the ratio of gross corporate savings to GDP. This was to be expected, as the share of the corporate sector in the economy was expanding. But the share of the corporate sector continued to expand after 1971, when the savings ratio stabilized. It is thus likely that the growing savings ratio in the 1960s also reflected the high profits that the corporations earned on the protected markets of a rapidly growing economy. And the

51

stagnation in the savings ratio in the 1970s and 1980s may reflect the declining rate of profit as competition increased on the larger domestic market and as a growing share of corporate output was sold at highly competitive export markets.

The corporate savings were never sufficient to finance all the investments made by corporations; the rest was financed by the savings surplus of the household sector (S_h). The ratio of household savings to GDP showed wide fluctuations over the years but no clear trend. But within household savings, a significant shift in the allocation did occur, with a greater share of these savings being held in the form of financial savings. If financial savings are defined as the increase, in a year, in holdings of time and savings deposits with commercial banks and holdings of promissory notes of finance companies, the share of financial savings in total Gross Domestic Savings increased from 11 per cent in the 1960s to 24 per cent in the 1970s and 46 per cent in the first half of the 1980s. The impact of the financialization of household savings on financial development in Thailand will be analysed in section 2.3 below; the implications for the intersectoral transfers of resources will be analysed in Chapter 4.

With these financial savings the deficits of the corporate sector and the government could be financed, and the balance between aggregate investment and savings was maintained so that, as Table 2.1 shows, the current account deficit remained very small till the mid-1970s. Since then, however, the stagnation and decline of domestic savings, combined with the continued high levels of corporate investment and fiscal deficits, have led to increasing imbalances.

The contributions reviewed in Chapter 1 (section 1.2) raised three general questions on economic growth and its financing. Firstly, will economic growth endanger macroeconomic stability? Secondly, can sectoral balances be maintained during the process of structural change? And thirdly, how will economic growth and structural change affect the income distribution and employment? The analysis of these three questions will be dealt with in the remainder of this section.

2.2.1 Economic growth and macroeconomic stability

The most frequently used indicators of macroeconomic stability are the rate of inflation and the current account deficit.

Thailand's record of inflation is remarkable for two reasons. The first is its low level. In the 1960s there was very little inflation, and even in the 1970s, when the world's inflation rate went up substantially, Thailand followed only moderately.[3]

The second notable characteristic of Thai inflation is its sharp fluctuation. From one year to the next the rate of inflation can sharply increase but also sharply decrease: for example, it rose from 4.9 per cent in 1972 to 15.5 per cent in 1973 and even to 24.3 per cent in 1974, but then fell back to 5.3 per cent in 1975. A similar pattern may be observed around 1981.

In small open economies with fixed exchange rates and free trade and capital movements, the domestic prices will be strongly influenced by international trends. In the case of Thailand these considerations are all the more important due to the particular composition of its international trade, which makes the impact of foreign prices very direct and strong. Domestic prices are directly and indirectly influenced by international prices, both on the import and on the export sides (Chaipravat, Meesook and Ganjarerndee 1976).

On the export side, it is important to recognize that Thailand is a major exporter of basic consumer items, such as rice, sugar and maize. The domestic prices of these main agricultural crops follow world market prices. In a few cases (rice and sugar) there is some government intervention in pricing, but these interventions aim to soften the domestic impact of international price movements rather than to remove it. Thus world market prices directly influence the domestic price of a number of basic consumer goods. There is an

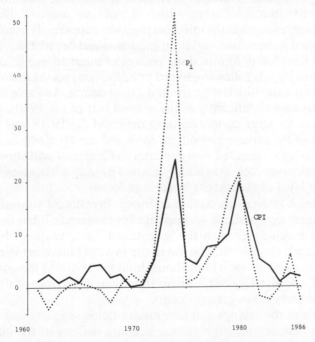

Note:
Pi (the dotted line) gives the annual rate of increase of an index of international prices.
CPI (the solid line) gives the annual rate of increase of the Thai Consumer Price Index.

Chart 2.3   International and domestic inflation

indirect effect of international inflation on the export side, when a rise in export prices increases the income of the unincorporated firms in the household sector that produce these goods, and this leads to an increase in aggregate demand in the economy.

On the import side, an increase in the price of imported goods directly affects the cost of all goods and services. Most imports are not final consumer goods but intermediate inputs and capital goods for the corporate and public sectors. The corporate sector, as a price-setter, will immediately transfer these increased costs into higher output prices. The higher domestic prices have an indirect effect on aggregate demand through the real balance effect.

The Thai economy has a particular structure in which most export goods are also domestically consumed, the corporate sector is very sensitive to the cost of imports, and there is relatively little government intervention in price setting. There is therefore great sensitivity to international price movements. These relationships are reflected in Chart 2.3 in which the rate of increase in the Consumer Price Index of Thailand is plotted against a composite index of import and export prices.[4] The chart shows that in the 1960s, Thai inflation was in step with international inflation, which at that time was low. During that period the (minor) changes in the inflation rates were apparently unrelated. But since 1971, when international inflation increased and became more volatile, Thai inflation has closely followed the pattern of international prices.

With inflation largely following world price movements the main indicator of macroeconomic stability is the current account deficit. As Table 2.1 shows, the deficit increased significantly in the second half of the 1970s. Chart 2.1 makes clear that the large current account deficit of the 1970s was related to the high level of the private investment ratio and the acceleration of public investment. The more detailed analysis later in Chapter 4 will show that the growth in public investment was mainly caused by state enterprises financing a much higher level of investment by foreign loans.

In the 1980s, however, the picture changed. Investment slowed down as public investment consolidated and private investment fell, but the savings ratio declined much faster than the investment ratio, keeping the current account deficit at its high level. The fall in the savings ratio was mainly due to the decline in the savings ratio of the household sector and of the government (see Chart 2.2; see also Chapter 3 where the saving behaviour of the various sectors will be analysed in greater detail).

The analysis of the savings and investment ratios suggests that domestic excess demand created the high current account deficits of the late 1970s, when there was a high level of investment, and in the early 1980s, when there was a high level of consumption (or low level of savings).

One can also look at the current account deficit from the trade side. Despite the disincentives – such as export taxes and premiums and the relatively overvalued exchange rate that, as usual, accompanied import substitution – the output of traditional export crops (for example, rice and rubber) continued to grow. According to some authors, taxation of the traditional crops had the (unintended) effect of stimulating the diversification of agricultural output (see, for example, Ingram 1971). Others have argued that this diversification was forced by the increasing cultivation of dry lands where rice could not grow (Van de Meer 1981). Whatever the cause, agricultural output, and with it agricultural exports, increased and diversified. In addition, the contribution of the manufacturing sector to exports increased rapidly (see Table 2.1) and Thailand also became a major tourist destination.

In terms of volumes, the export performance is outstanding. In the period 1960–72 the volume of exports increased by 8.8 per cent per year, whereas real GDP increased by 7.6 per cent. In the subsequent period, 1973–82, the volume of exports increased even faster, at 12.1 per cent, while real GDP growth fell to 6.5 per cent. And even in the recent years (1983–86), with greater macroeconomic problems, the average of the export volume growth rate at 6.4 per cent exceeded the average real GDP growth of 4.5 per cent. The good export performance was undermined by two factors: (i) the terms of trade, and (ii) changes in the non-trade items in the current account.

Terms of trade Since the boom in commodity prices in the early 1970s, the terms of trade have moved against Thailand. If export and import prices had remained at their 1975 level, actual export and import volumes in 1982 would have led to a trade balance surplus of Baht 25 billion rather than the actual Baht 36 billion deficit. But, of course, such terms-of-trade losses are real losses to which the economy has to adjust. The decline in domestic savings (see Chart 2.2) suggests that consumption remained too high in the face of falling terms of trade.

Non-trade items There are three elements of importance here. Firstly, US military spending in Thailand and official transfers to Thailand related to the US involvement in the war in Indochina dropped quickly in the early 1970s. Such receipts were equivalent in 1972 to about 25 per cent of merchandise exports by 1977 they had fallen to less than 2 per cent.

A second element is the increasing debt-servicing burden because of higher interest rates. Thailand does not have an excessive external debt, but it is growing. Payments on investment income in the current account were equivalent to 9 per cent of merchandise exports in 1970, to 13 per cent in 1980 and to 20 per cent in 1986.

These negative trends were to some extent compensated by a third element: the remittances of Thai workers in the Middle East. Estimates made by the Bank of Thailand put these transfers in 1986 equivalent to 7 per cent of exports of goods and services.

These factors meant that the export growth could not keep pace with the growing import demand. The growing current account gap was financed through increased external borrowing. Direct foreign private investment was never very high and did not increase to fill the growing gap.[5] Government borrowing abroad did increase after 1975 but was not very high. As will be discussed in greater detail in Chapter 4, borrowing abroad by state enterprises increased significantly after the mid-1970s. Private corporations did not borrow much abroad until then and when they did start to do so in later years, their demand fluctuated strongly from year to year.

The public and private external debt of Thailand was estimated at around US$ 5 billion in 1980 (World Bank 1983b). Compared to that of neighbouring countries this external debt and the debt-servicing burden are relatively modest, but the worrying aspect is that the debt is growing so rapidly (World Bank 1984). By 1986 external debt service (repayment of principal and interest payments) amounted to 20 per cent of the exports of goods and services.[6]

As Charts 2.1 and 2.2 show, two of the domestic factors behind the growing import demand leading to the current account deficit were the increasing level of public investment and the declining government savings. Chart 2.1 cannot, though, be directly compared with Chart 2.2, because public investment in Chart 2.1 includes government and state enterprise investment, whereas state enterprise savings in Chart 2.2 are included in corporate savings. In Table 2.1 the government expenditures and revenues as a percentage of GDP are given, and these figures clearly show that the government deficit appears to be increasing.

The development efforts led to a strong expansion of government activities: government expenditure as a percentage of GDP went up from around 13 per cent in the early 1960s to close at 18 per cent in the early 1980s.

The Revenue/GDP ratio was stagnant at around 13 per cent and seems to have increased only slightly in recent years. Such a pattern is not unexpected: the political and economic elite exerts strong pressure on government to maintain and increase expenditure and it resists tax increases. In a comparative perspective, the expenditure and revenue ratios of Thailand are not exceptionally high.[7] This is an indication of the moderate role the government assumes; development efforts rely to a great extent on the private sector.

Historically, a significant part of the tax burden has been on the agricultural sector in the form of export premiums and export taxes. With the fall in the share of agriculture in GDP, the contribution of these taxes to government revenue declined, although the taxes remained a heavy burden on the agricultural sector (see World Bank 1983a). As it was apparently quite difficult to find alternative taxes to fill the gap and increase revenue, government savings fell (see S_g in Chart 2.2) and the budget deficit widened.

2.2.2 Economic growth and sectoral balance

The theories reviewed in Chapter 1 (section 1.2) interpreted the problem of sectoral balance mainly in terms of the agriculture-industry interaction. The rate of industrial growth that can be 'financed' depends on the real resources that can be made available: workers for the factories, food for the workers, raw materials for industry and foreign exchange to import intermediate and capital goods. Many of these resources have to be generated by the agricultural sector.

The first factor that needs to be emphasized is the special nature of agricultural development. In the 1950s Thailand was still basically a 'rice economy', but since then growth and diversification in agriculture has been rapid. Thailand is a country rich in natural resources and, probably more importantly, it is a land surplus economy. Agricultural growth could thus be achieved by a growing rural population taking more land under cultivation to grow an increasing variety of crops.

Over the period 1960–85, the annual growth rate of agricultural value added at constant prices was 4.3 per cent per year, the area cultivated expanded at 3.4 per cent and agricultural employment at 1.6 per cent per year. These figures suggest a growth in the yield per acre at only 0.9 per cent per year and of the agricultural labour productivity at 2.7 per cent. This implies that the main factors behind agricultural growth have been the expansion of the area cultivated and the more intensive use of rural labour. The growth in productivity per acre (yield) is due to a shift to crops with a higher value added (diversification) rather than to new technologies and varieties: the yields per acre of most crops have been stagnant.

The success and the nature of agricultural growth have a number of important consequences for overall development of the Thai economy.

Firstly, the high rate and extensive nature of growth kept a high proportion of the population in the rural areas; open unemployment is very small. The available new lands enabled most households to benefit from growth and the incidence of poverty fell from the early 1960s to 1980. But as there was little growth in productivity, the supply price of labour for urban employment was kept low.

The growth of agricultural output provided a ready stream of food supplies for the urban labour force. Government price interventions (mainly in rice marketing) aimed to keep the prices of these goods low, so that industrial wage levels could remain low and competitive internationally.

The extensive nature of agricultural growth also implied that growth could be achieved without major financial investments in agricultural activities being undertaken. Public funds could be concentrated on industrial growth and the agricultural sector could generate a substantial surplus that helped finance industrialization.

A final effect worth mentioning, of the growth and diversification in the primary sector, is that it provided a growing stream of inputs for processing in the manufacturing industry. Thailand is rich in natural resources and the processing of these has been an important aspect of the industrialization process.

Although agricultural growth has been rapid in Thailand, there can be no doubt that industry has been the leading sector in the development process. At the end of the Second World War, Thailand lacked an indigenous bourgeoisie that could lead the process of industrialization. The Thai elite was engaged at the Court or in the bureaucracy. There was, though, a sizeable Chinese community, engaged mainly in commerce, but willing and able to shift to industrial activities. An acceptable position was reached between the Thai political élite and the Chinese bourgeoisie, whereby the latter were allowed to take the lead in the economic sphere.

It is interesting to contrast this Thai experience with that of neighbouring countries, like Malaysia and Indonesia, where there was also a Chinese capitalist class which was not allowed to play its role as freely as in Thailand. Probably as a result of this, the role of multinational corporations in these two countries (see Asian Strategies Company 1982) and of the state in the economy is much larger than in Thailand. It was estimated that the stock of foreign direct investment (in 1974 US dollars) was 1350 million in Malaysia, 2100 in Indonesia and only 550 in Thailand (Wong 1979, pp. 177–9). Direct foreign investment accounted for less than 5 per cent of total private investment in the 1970s (Prasertset 1981). The ratio of government expenditure to GDP in 1984 was 18 per cent in Thailand, 30 per cent in Malaysia and 24 per cent in Indonesia.

The alliance between the political elite and economic bourgeoisie in Thailand was strongly biased in favour of modern industries in urban areas and against the agricultural sector and urban workers. This bias showed in various policy interventions, such as tariffs and other forms of industrial protection; an overvalued currency favouring the import-dependent industrial sector at the expense of the exporting agricultural sector, agricultural pricing policies, and labour policies aimed at keeping wages low and trade unions powerless.

Industrialization began in the 1960s; in 1961 the first Development Plan was published. The early attempts followed the usual pattern of import-substitution. Tariffs and import controls, together with other investment incentives, aimed at creating an industrial sector producing for the domestic market. In the analysis of the pattern of industrialization in Table 2.2, manufacturing production is broken down by two criteria. Natural-resource-based industries (NR) are processing domestically produced primary commodities for export or home consumption. Import-dependent industries (ID) import raw materials and intermediate goods for final processing or assembling into goods that are then exported or consumed locally. Both NR and ID industries may substitute local production for importation of final goods. The classification applied here has the advantage of showing more immediately the extent of linkages between the various sectors of the economy and the balance-of-payments consequences of industrialization.

The main impetus for industrial growth in the 1960s came from the industries producing for the domestic market, but even at this early stage of industrialization the rich natural resource base of the country provided a competitive advantage for some export-oriented industrial activity (for example, food processing).

As Table 2.2 shows, the growth rates of the ID industries surpassed those of the NR industries in all periods presented. A main reason for this may be that the growth of the NR industries is constrained by the supply capacity of the primary sector, mainly agriculture. Agricultural growth has been based on area expansion and product diversification. The slowdown of agricultural growth over time may be due to the fact that gradually less fertile lands are taken under cultivation and the limits of diversification and specialization reached. A more rapid growth would then require an increase in agricultural productivity which can only be achieved when investments in agriculture would increase.

Table 2.2   Pattern of industrialization
(Growth rates of manufactured valued added at constant (1972) prices)

	1960–70	1970–80	1980–86	Share in 1986 MFG GDP
Natural resource-based industries:				
Export-oriented	5.9	6.5	4.5	25
Domestic market-oriented	10.1	7.4	1.6	11
Total	8.1	6.8	3.6	36
Import-dependent industries:				
Export-oriented	–	13.8	6.9	37
Domestic market-oriented	15.2	12.1	4.5	24
Total	15.2	13.1	5.9	61
Total manufacturing	10.9	10.1	5.3	97*

* The total does not add up to 100 per cent because of an unclassified category of 'miscellaneous manufacturing'.

Note:
ID industries are those that in 1975 had an import requirement per unit of output of 25 per cent or more; for NR industries that requirement was below 25 per cent.
Export-oriented industries exported in 1980 10 per cent or more of their output and domestic market-oriented industries exported less than 10 per cent of output.
Of course, over the years export orientation and import dependency may have changed so that the classification inevitably has an element of arbitrariness. It should, therefore, be used with caution.
Data to make these classifications are obtained from the 1975 and 1980 Input-Output Tables of Thailand (as reported in TDRI 1987, t.2.53; and Ajanant et al. 1986, p. 71).

In the 1970s the export-oriented NR industries grew slightly faster than in the 1960s and a number of ID sectors (for example, textiles, basic metals and metal products, electrical machines and appliances) were able to shift from an exclusive orientation on the domestic market to export markets. And in the 1980s, the export markets had become the leading force in the growth of the industrial sector.

This rapid shift towards and growth of industrial exports is quite remarkable. Generally, import-substituting industrialization is criticized for leading to inefficient industries not capable of competing on export markets. Two structural reasons may be suggested for Thailand having been able to escape that fate and be successful in becoming an exporter of manufactured goods. The first reason is the natural-resource base mentioned previously. Thailand has a natural advantage in the processing of its primary commodities for exports (for example, leather and wood products, canned fruits and fish). A second reason could be that Thai industries in general were never very inefficient; the size of the economy is important here. Thailand has, in the comparative perspective of LDCs, a large economy. In terms of the size of 1985 GDP Thailand ranked 16 in the list of 100 LDCs for which data are given in the *World Development Report 1987* (World Bank 1987, p. 206). Although the size of an economy is not a sufficient condition for efficiency, the large size implies that domestic-market-oriented industries can still benefit from economies of scale that industries in smaller LDCs cannot reap. In many sectors the size of the domestic market may even stimulate active competition forcing firms to be or become efficient. Under such conditions, import-substituting industries may be quite efficient and gradually capable of shifting to export markets.

It is remarkable that both types of industries and, in fact, most industrial subsectors in them, were able to develop some export activities. One factor that will have helped this export performance is the location of Thailand in the Asian/Pacific region of high economic growth. The major dynamic economies in this region (China, Hong Kong, Japan, Malaysia, Singapore, South Korea and Taiwan) are all major trading partners of Thailand, together accounting for over 50 per cent of merchandise exports.

The natural resource base is still the main export earner for Thailand; more than half of merchandise exports are resource-based commodities. One could also add two other main foreign exchange earners which are also 'resource'-based: tourism and workers' remittances. In 1986 tourism receipts were 12 per cent of the total exports of goods and services and workers' remittances were equivalent to around 7 per cent of it.

The ID industries have been very successful in shifting to export markets. This trend is dominated by goods like textiles, garments and integrated circuits. As primary commodities are also increasingly exported in some processed form, the exports of manufactures (processed NR goods and ID goods) have become the dominant feature of Thai external trade in recent years.

60

Industrial output growth fell sharply in the 1980s. In Table 2.2 this decline can be seen to be sharpest in the domestic market-oriented industries. The export performance of industrial goods continued to be satisfactory in this period, although not as good as in the 1970s. The main cause for the decline in growth was the fall in domestic demand. As a result of the low level of primary commodity prices worldwide, the nominal value of agricultural GDP actually declined and in 1986 was lower than it had been in 1983. The overvaluation of the Baht until the end of 1984 discouraged exports, and after 1984 the deflationary macropolicies further contracted demand. The period is analysed in greater detail in Chapter 5.

A logical question that arises after the description of growth and industrialization is to what extent public policy supported and steered this process.

As observed already, the political powers have always been in favour of the modern industrial sector and the main thrust of public policy has been to create the conditions for private industrial accumulation. That attempt has taken three main forms.

The first, and probably the least important, were the direct subsidies to industry in the form of investment incentives, tax deductions, etc.

Of far greater importance have been the attempts to shift the relative prices in favour of industrial activities. Tariffs and import controls protected the domestic market and allowed corporations to increase product prices. At the same time, input prices, particularly of labour and of imported inputs, were kept low. The government controlled food prices through export taxes, so that the real wage level did not need to increase. Only in 1986 was the rice premium and export tax abolished; as international prices were low at that time this had little effect on domestic prices. In addition, trade union activity was repressed, sometimes forcefully. The tariff structure and the overvalued currency helped to control the cost of imported inputs of the industrial sector. The significant appreciation of the real exchange rate (that is the rate corrected for inflation) of the Baht versus the US dollar since 1971 was incompletely corrected by the devaluation of 1981 and was only conclusively turned around with the devaluation of 1984 (TDRI 1987, p. 97). The devaluation of 1984 and the sliding down of the Baht, alongside the US dollar, against other major currencies since 1985 for the first time gave the export sector a competitive advantage.

A third form of public policy favouring industrial accumulation was the macroeconomic policies. Short-term monetary and fiscal policies were left to the technocrats who executed rather conservative policies: the fiscal deficit was generally small and monetary policies restricted to the defending of the exchange rate. With the exception of some periods, these policies were highly successful: inflation was generally low and largely determined by world inflation; up to the late 1970s the current-account deficit was modest and up to the 1980s the exchange rate was exceptionally stable. These conditions helped to create an economic environment of stability and confidence which must have helped to stimulate domestic and foreign investment.

The absence of government attempts to regulate the economic cycles also meant that Thailand largely followed the ups and downs of the world economy. This affected mainly the agricultural sector of which the product prices and income followed the world market. One of the results of this was that investment in agriculture became unattractive. Not only were output prices generally low, because of government manipulation of prices and the exchange rate, but they also fluctuated widely. Probably because investments in agriculture were unattractive, rural surplus income (for example, of rich farmers, rice millers, traders) was massively deposited with financial institutions which could channel it to industrial investment.

So, the three strands of public policy directly and indirectly favoured industrial accumulation. They helped to increase industrial profits, to attract foreign industrial investment and to steer domestic savings to industrial credit: on average, in the 1960s and 1970s, around half of all corporate investments were financed out of own profits, one third out of transfers from the household sector, and the rest by foreign funds.

As observed in Chapter 1, a crucial aspect of economic development is the changing sectoral balance in the economy. This aspect is usually captured by the decline in the contribution of agriculture to GDP and the increase in the contribution of industry. In Table 2.1 it can be seen that, despite the impressive growth of agricultural production, the share of agriculture in GDP fell sharply over the years. The very sharp fall during the most recent years is also due to the poor world market prices for agricultural products. Table 2.1 also shows that the share of the manufacturing sector has increased.

In Chapter 1 it was suggested that the agriculture-industry breakdown significantly overlaps, but is not identical to, the breakdown of productive activities into a competitive sector of small-scale household enterprises and an oligopolistic or monopolistic corporate sector. Differences in the organization of production and in market conditions determine price and income formation and have direct implications for saving and investment behaviour. As Chapter 3 will show, savings arise out of profits of the production units in the corporate and household businesses. The large differences in market conditions and in the organization of production between the corporate sector on the one hand and the unincorporated household sector on the other, requires a separate analysis of the two sectors. The question arises as to whether the two sectors can be identified from available statistics.

They may be located by interpreting the Household Sector, as measured in National Accounts and Flow-of-Funds Accounts, as the sector of unincorporated, small and competitive firms, and the Corporate Sector as the sector of organized, large and monopolistic firms. The labour force data (see Table 2.3) and the National Income data (see Chart 2.4) show that most households are self-employed and that the major part of household income is earned in unincorporated enterprises. But would these data provide an adequate basis for the estimation of production in the two sectors?

National Income data include also income earned from wage employment and property income (dividend, interest and rent) under the heading of Household Income, the major part of which is earned in the corporate sector. One way to measure the production of the unincorporated sector would be to take the Household Income derived from Farms and from Professions and Other Unincorporated Enterprises as an indicator of the production in the unincorporated sector and assume that the rest of GDP originates from the corporate sector. An alternative way of measuring the two sectors would be to break down GDP data into production that takes place in small family enterprises with low capital intensity and facing competitive markets, and production organized in large corporations with higher capital intensity and more market power. In the formulation of Social Accounting Matrices (SAMs) such detailed allocation of production activities over unincorporated and corporate sectors is sometimes made. But such breakdowns are typically made for a single year and are therefore only partially helpful when one is attempting time series analysis. To make time series analysis possible, one needs to be able to link the sectoral breakdown of GDP (over agriculture, manufacturing, etc.) to the breakdown of activities into a corporate and an unincorporated sector.

The National Economic and Social Development Board (NESDB) together with the World Bank prepared a Social Accounting Matrix for Thailand for the year 1975 (see NESDB and IBRD 1982). The 'informal sector' is assumed to (i) behave neo-classically, that is, have flexible wages and prices (against a formal sector with sticky prices); and (ii) be financially constrained (against a formal sector with free access to domestic and international credit). It was concluded that, in terms of value added, all of agriculture was informal, 73 per cent of trade, 32 per cent of services, 31 per cent of transport and communications and 28 per cent of manufacturing. The other economic sectors were fully formal.

In formulating another SAM for Thailand, Amranand and Grais (1984) used the following criteria to allocate activities to the formal and informal sector. Activities that were (i) owned and managed by the same household, (ii) facing flexible wages, and (iii) financially constrained, were considered informal; and activities that were managed by different people from the owners, facing fixed nominal wages and able to borrow whatever funds they required, were formal. On the basis of these criteria they allocated all of agriculture to the informal sector and most of manufacturing and all of construction and the energy sectors to the formal sector. Services were allocated to both the formal and informal sector.[8]

In all productive sectors, both unincorporated and corporate forms of production exist side by side, but in most sectors one form dominates: for example, in the manufacturing sector it was estimated that in 1978 small establishments (with less than ten employees) accounted for 58 per cent of employment but only about 20 per cent of value added (World Bank 1984). Capital intensity and labour productivity may be indicators of the form of organization that dominates in a sector. The labour productivity of productive sectors like Construction, Transport and Communications and Manufacturing in Thailand is high and this may suggest the predominance in them of large, capital-intensive units. In sectors like Agriculture and Services, on the other hand, labour productivity is lower.[9]

These considerations have been used to come to an approximation of the shares of the corporate and unincorporated sectors in GDP. Agriculture, Wholesale and Retail Trade, Ownership Dwellings and Services are the sectors assumed to constitute the unincorporated sector. The other sectors (with the exclusion of Public Administration and Defence) are taken as the corporate sector. This breakdown largely follows that of NESDB and IBRD (1982) and of Amranand and Grais (1984) in their SAMs for 1975; the sectors assigned by them to both the corporate and the unincorporated sector are now allocated to one of these depending on their level of labour productivity. By making this rough breakdown of GDP, it is possible to identify the trend in the shares of the corporate and unincorporated sectors. The share of the unincorporated sector in GDP fell from around 67 per cent in the early 1960s to around 60 per cent around 1970 and around 52 per cent in the early 1980s.[10] These estimates of the sizes of the two sectors will be used in Chapter 3 in analyzing saving behaviour and in Chapter 5 in tracing the effects of macroeconomic disturbances.

2.2.3 Income distribution and employment

It would be useful to study how the growth and structural change described previously has affected employment and income levels and distribution. With rapid population growth the labour force increased rapidly,[11] as shown in Table 2.3. The proportion of wage and salary employees in the labour force increased to about one-fifth in the 1980s. This trend is not surprising, given the process of urbanization and the growth in the corporate sector of the economy. But it should be emphasized that employment in Thailand continues to be dominated by family labour: own account workers and unpaid family workers still account for three quarters of the labour force. Seen in a comparative perspective the proportion of self-employed labour is exceptionally high in Thailand.[12]

Political control of wage labour is very strict: workers are generally not allowed to organize freely (Tritasavit 1978). Even in the absence of such controls workers may have few opportunities to organize, as there is an ample supply of labour. On the other hand, the ready supply of relatively cheap wage goods, particularly food, makes organization for wage demands less necessary.

64

Trends in wage levels are difficult to assess, since there is no complete and continuous system of data collection. One has to rely on occasional studies, but these are seldom fully comparable. Real wages were probably rather stable during the 1960s.[13]   The real wage of unskilled workers in Bangkok fell between 1970 and 1974 under the impact of inflation (ARTEP 1982). The high rate of inflation in those years, and particularly the high food prices, may have been one of the reasons for the great popular support for the student movement and revolt in 1973 (Morell and Samudavanija 1981).

Table 2.3   Labour force by status

| | (percentage distribution) | | | | |
	1960	1970	1975	1980	1984
Employer	0.4	0.4	0.4	1.2	1.2
Employee					
Government	3.6	4.7	4.7	5.3	6.6
Private	8.3	10.9	13.6	16.6	18.3
Total	11.9	15.6	18.3	21.9	24.9
Own account workers	29.6	29.6	33.8	30.2	29.6
Unpaid family workers	57.3	53.7	47.6	46.6	44.4
Total	100.0	100.0	100.0	100.0	100.0
(Total in '000)	(13 781)	(16 652)	(18 181)	(22 463)	(25 700)

Source: National Statistical Office: Population Census and Labour Force
          Surveys

After the political changes of October 1973, there was a period in which organized labour was allowed a more active role. The number of strikes increased significantly although their impact was less than may have appeared; work time lost through strikes in municipal areas never amounted to more than one half day per worker per year (Bertrand and Squire, 1980, p. 497). The effects of these political changes on the real wage level are difficult to assess precisely, but it is likely that there was a small increase in real wages after 1974. A legal minimum wage had been introduced in April 1973 and this was subsequently increased in January and May 1974 and January 1975. It has been argued that the wages actually paid in this period were often in excess of the legal minimum and that, where lower wages were paid, no attempts were made to enforce the legal minimum rate. Morell and Samudavanija (1981) reported a 1974 survey in which 44 per cent of the employers were found not to pay the legal minimum wage. The wage share in National Income remained low throughout these years. Thus, although the real wage may have increased slightly in this period, there are no indications that wage pressure was a destabilizing factor and caused the acceleration of inflation that occurred in the early 1970s.

Data from the annual Labour Force Survey of the National Statistical Office (see World Bank 1986; TDRI 1987) show that real wages stagnated between 1978 and 1982 and increased thereafter between 1982 and 1985. But this overall picture is the outcome of a quite mixed pattern. Agricultural wages do far worse than non-agricultural wages; in fact, the real wage in agriculture declines from 1978 to 1985. As the agricultural wage, in absolute terms, is about half the non-agricultural wage, this implies that income disparities have widened in recent years. Also when one looks at wages rates per region it can be seen that wages in the Bangkok region do far better than those in provincial areas, so the rural–urban gap is widening.

Rapid economic growth and structural shifts in production and employment had a significant impact on income distribution in Thailand. With the changes in the structure of the economy and labour force came a change in the distribution of National Income. Chart 2.4 shows the trends in the income shares of the major categories. The share of Farm Income (F) fell, which is as one would expect when, with economic development, the share of the agricultural sector declines.[14] The fall in the share of Farm Income was interrupted around 1966 and 1973 by two periods of high international prices for farm products. The macroeconomic conditions in these two periods will be analysed in detail in Chapter 5. Until 1980 the fall in the Farm Income share dominated the trends in the other income categories. The income shares of Property Income (PROP) and Net Corporate Savings (PROF) and even of Wage Income (W) were relatively stable. The tendency of the share of Income from Professions and Other Unincorporated Enterprises (SE) to increase is the logical counterpart of the decline in the Farm Income share, as all shares have to add up to 100. This also explains why the share of Income from Professions and Other Unincorporated Enterprises seems to fluctuate in opposite directions to those of the Farm Income share.

The trends after the late 1970s show another pattern though. The fall in the Farm Income share is sharp due to poor world market prices. The income share of Professions and other Unincorporated Enterprises also falls, but the share of Property Income increases with the high interest rates. The increase in the Wage share is partly due to the remittances received from workers abroad and partly the mirror image of the very poor conditions in the other income categories and is less due to sharp increases in wages. Despite the stable Wage share in National Income and the falling share of Farm Income, rapid economic growth meant that the incomes of most people could increase.

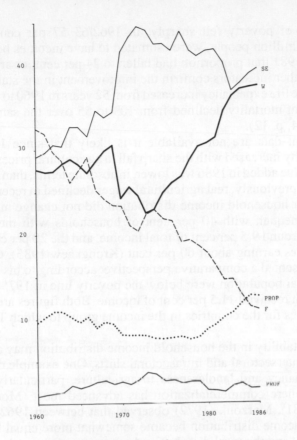

Note:

W	= compensation of employees
F	= income from farms received by households
SE	= income from professions and other unincorporated enterprises received by households
PROP	= income from property received by households and private non-profit institutions
PROF	= savings (net profits) of corporations

There was a change in statistical series in 1970. The sharp increase in SE and the sharp drop in W in that year is therefore more a result of a change in definition and coverage than to real income changes.

Up to 1969, F and SE were only presented together as one total referring to the income received by households from farm, profession and other unincorporated enterprise. The data on F before 1969 have been approached using the data on GDP originating in the agricultural sector. That estimate was then used to derive SE as a residue. These rough approximations are only made to give an impression of trends before 1969 and should not be used as firm estimates.

Chart 2.4   Distribution of national income (% shares)

The incidence of poverty fell sharply. In 1962/63 57 per cent of the population, or 16 million people, were estimated to have incomes below the poverty line. By 1981 that proportion had fallen to 24 per cent, or around 11 million people. Other indicators confirm the improvement in the standard of living: for example life expectancy increased from 52 years in 1960 to 63 years in 1980, and infant mortality declined from 103 to 55 over the same years (World Bank 1984, p. 12).

Although recent data are not available it is likely that since 1981 the incidence of poverty increased with the sharp fall in agricultural prices. In fact the agricultural value added in 1986 was lower, in absolute terms, than in 1983. Also, as observed previously, real agricultural wages declined in recent years.

The personal or household income distribution did not change much and remained quite unequal, with 40 per cent of households with the lowest incomes earning around 9.5 per cent of total income, and the 20 per cent with the highest incomes earning about 60 per cent (Krongkaew 1985). Chenery (1979, p. 460) presented a comparative perspective: according to his data, 23 per cent of the Thai population were below the poverty line in 1975 and the poorest 40 per cent received 11.5 per cent of income. Both figures are almost exactly the averages for the countries in the income group to which Thailand belongs.

This apparent stability in the household income distribution may disguise quite substantial intersectoral and intrasectoral shifts. One example of this is the increasing tenancy and landlessness in agriculture, particularly in the Central Region where commercialization has advanced most (Morell and Samudavanija 1981). Marzouk (1972) observed that between 1962/63 and 1970, the urban income distribution became somewhat more equal but was still very distorted, and the rural distribution became more unequal.

2.3   Financial development

The first banks were established in Thailand at the end of the last century; they were branches of foreign banks engaged in trade financing. The first domestically-owned bank, the Siam Commercial Bank, was established in 1904 (Ingram 1971, p. 150). By 1940 there were three Thai-owned and six foreign-owned banks and by the end of the 1950s these numbers had increased to 12 and 9 respectively. In 1982 there were 16 Thai and 14 foreign banks (Bangkok Bank 1982).

The banks were generally established by merchants involved in international trade and branching out to banking. Before the Second World War the banks' activities were confined to import/export financing and arranging the remittances of Chinese and other foreign residents (Rozental 1970, p. 104).

The rapid increase in the number of banks in the 1940s and 1950s was due to the external changes brought about by the war and the post-war boom. Since the mid-1950s the authorities have been unwilling to issue new bank licenses, arguing that the number of banks was adequate.[15]

The role of foreign-owned banks has become quite minor and considerably less important than in many other countries: they represent only 5 per cent of total commercial bank assets.[16] Foreign banks typically have only one office, in Bangkok (Vongvipanond 1981).

Domestically owned banks have branched out very rapidly. In 1960 there were 352 commercial bank offices (or 652 offices if the offices of the Government Savings Bank (GSB) and the Bank for Agriculture and Agricultural Cooperatives (BAAC) are included). By 1970 that number had increased to 647 (1032) and by 1986 to 1891 (2418). The number of bank offices in the provincial areas, that is outside Bangkok, increased rapidly.[17] As the deposits collected by these rural offices exceed the credits given by them, they are a channel through which a financial surplus leaves the rural areas (see Chapter 4).

Over the years a number of non-bank financial institutions, such as Finance Companies, Government Housing Bank, Life Insurance Companies, etc., has emerged. The commercial banks are still the dominant type of financial institution though, accounting for over two-thirds of total assets (Aphimeteetam-rong 1980).

Through the rapid branching of banks the density of financial institutions has increased. The density index used by Cameron is defined as the number of bank offices per 10,000 population. This index was 0.13 for commercial banks in 1960 (or 0.25 when the GSB and BAAC were included). In 1970 it was 0.18 (0.28), and in 1980 0.31 (0.41). The 1980 density index is comparable to the figure for Japan around 1880 (Cameron et al. 1967). The index of 0.31 for 1980 compares to figures in that year of 0.40 for Malaysia and 0.28 for the Philippines (Lee and Jao 1982, p. 294).

Other indicators confirm the impression of rapid extension of the financial system. Cameron also used the ratio of Commercial Bank Assets to National Income as an indicator of financial development. Applying this indicator to Thailand gives 21 per cent in 1962, 37 per cent in 1970 and 54 per cent in 1980. By 1980 the Thai figure was comparable to that of England and Japan around 1900 (Cameron et al. 1967). Around 1980 this ratio was 61 per cent in Malaysia, 26 per cent in Indonesia and 52 per cent in the Philippines (Lee and Jao 1982, p. 295). Cole and Patrick calculated the ratio of financial claims to GNP. Financial claims include currency, all deposits, any negotiable financial instrument with maturity of one year or less and the market value of bonds and shares. In 1980 that ratio stood at 59 per cent in Thailand compared to 18 in Indonesia, 48 in the Philippines, 51 in South Korea, 200 in Singapore and 240 in Japan (Cole and Patrick 1986, p. 47). When making an international comparison of such indicators care is needed for these indicators are sensitive to differences between countries in the organization of financial institutions, the role played by non-bank financial institutions, the ownership structure in

69

the economy, and so on. For instance, in some countries firms may depend more on direct finance through bonds and shares, whereas in other countries the security markets are smaller and investments are supported more indirectly through financial institutions.

Aphimeteetamrong (1980) presented some evidence on the financial asset ratio (that is the ratio of all financial assets, including money, bonds, shares, etc., to GDP) which rose from 0.55 in 1962 to 1.25 in 1977. The ratio of financial assets of financial institutions to GDP rose from 0.24 to 0.69 over that period, showing that an increasing share of financial assets was being held by financial institutions. The ratio between the growth of domestic credit and gross private investment also rose, from 12.5 per cent to 58 per cent, during this period (Aphimeteetamrong 1980). This suggests the increased institutionalization of savings and investment. Other studies show different figures because of differences in the coverage of the indicators, but the trends are always in the same direction (see, for example, Cole, Chunanuntathum and Loohawenchit 1986, p. 147).

In Table 2.4 the assets and liabilities of the consolidated monetary system are presented as percentages of GDP.[18] Five-year averages are given to indicate the prevailing tendencies. The trend in the total assets/GDP ratio confirms the increasing trends in the other indicators of financial development. This trend extends further back: in 1947 the assets/GDP ratio was 18 per cent and in 1955 34 per cent (Trescott 1971, pp. 62–3).

The growth pattern of the total assets/GDP ratio was not uniform. The ratio increased steadily and rapidly from 1960 to 1972, mainly as a result of the swift growth in the holdings of quasi-money (that is, time and saving deposits). In the period 1973–81 there was consolidation rather than further growth; again this trend was due to the stagnation in the quasi-money ratio. After 1981 the ratios of total assets and of quasi-money to GDP increased again very rapidly.

Why did the growth of the quasi-money ratio slow down in the 1970s? One reason is institutional: since 1969 there has been rapid growth of a new type of non-bank financial institution, the finance companies. As these were not subject to the same controls as commercial banks, they could offer somewhat higher deposit rates (Panitchpakdi 1981). In the absence of control they also provided a way for foreign financial institutions to enter Thai financial markets. Finance companies do not create fierce competition with the banks, as many of them are in fact owned by banks, but they were able to draw savings funds away from banks. The credit allocation by finance companies over the various economic sectors is similar to that of commercial banks: the credit shares of agriculture, import/export trade and wholesale/retail trade are somewhat lower and those of manufacturing and personal consumption somewhat higher (Go 1984; Viksnins 1980).[19]

When the holdings of promissory notes of finance companies are added to the time and savings deposits of the commercial banks, most of the stagnation in the financial savings ratio (defined as quasi-money plus promissory note

Table 2.4 Consolidated statement of the monetary system: assets and liabilities

(as % of GDP; five-year averages)

	1960–64	1965–69	1970–74	1975–79	1980–84	1985–86
Assets:						
Foreign assets	15.3	16.9	11.2	7.6	4.0	5.5
Claims on government	8.3	10.9	17.7	12.7	15.6	18.2
Claims on private sector	12.3	16.0	22.0	29.3	34.9	46.0
Other assets	1.9	1.9	2.4	3.2	4.8	5.8
Total assets = Total liabilities	37.8	45.5	53.3	52.8	59.3	75.5
Liabilities:						
M1 Total	17.1	14.6	14.0	11.7	9.5	9.2
Currency	10.4	9.1	8.6	7.3	6.4	6.3
Demand Deposits	6.7	5.5	5.4	4.4	3.1	2.9
Quasi-money	9.4	14.9	23.1	26.1	34.7	50.3
Capital account	6.1	6.6	8.3	11.3	12.6	14.4
Other liabilities	5.2	9.4	7.9	3.6	2.5	1.7

Note:
The Monetary System includes the Central Bank, the Bank of Thailand and the commercial banks. Claims on Government and on the Private Sector include the credits given by the monetary institutions to these sectors in various forms. Quasi-money consists of the Time and Saving Deposits of commercial banks.

holdings) in the 1970s disappears. But even then the slowdown in the rate of financial development in the years 1973–81 remains. It is not unlikely that this slowdown can be attributed to the economic shocks that occurred in this period. The very high level of export prices in 1972 resulted in exceptionally high financial savings in that year. The oil shocks of 1973 and 1979 led to an acceleration of inflation in Thailand beyond levels known in the past (see Chart 2.1) and to uncertainty, which may have reduced financial development. The macroeconomic trends in these years are analyzed in greater detail in Chapter 5.

Another 'source' of funds for the monetary system has been the growth of 'capital accounts': the newly issued shares and the retained profits of the financial institutions. The significant increase of these is an indirect indicator of the profitability of banks.

Certainly, the rapid increase in funds in the official monetary system has been partly at the expense of the unregulated money markets. More detailed analysis in Chapter 4 will suggest that the unregulated market segment continued to grow in absolute terms but at a much slower rate than the official market.

A remarkable trend, emerging from Table 2.4, is the decline in the M1/GDP ratio. The studies on the demand for money in developing countries, briefly reviewed in Chapter 1, generally suggest an income elasticity of the demand for narrow money balances of around one and thus a more or less constant M1/GDP ratio. Indeed, for the period 1947–60, Trescott found for Thailand an income elasticity of money demand of just above one (Trescott 1971). The decline since then certainly cannot be interpreted as a process of demonetization. Chandavarkar (1977) quoted an estimate suggesting that in 1969/70, subsistence activities accounted for about 10 per cent of Thailand's GDP. This is a low proportion given the fact that around three-quarters of the labour force is active in agriculture and the same proportion self-employed. Another indicator of the significant extent of monetization is the fact that the great majority of transactions in the unregulated money market is in cash rather than in kind (see Chapter 4). Thus the process of monetization has probably been completed in Thailand and there is no reason for it to have reversed. The rate of inflation has, in general, been low and cannot have been the reason for a flight out of money.

Why, then, is there a decline in the M1/GDP ratio? Trescott (1971, pp. 86-7) ascribed the fall in this ratio in the 1960s to the increase in the interest rate on government bonds since 1956, which led to an increase in the interest rates for savings and time deposits. This resulted in a switch from non-income-earning financial assets (currency and demand deposits) to interest-earning deposits. This substitution was facilitated by the rapid expansion of financial institutions.

It should be recognized that saving and time deposits in Thailand are quite liquid. Money can be immediately withdrawn from saving deposits and withdrawals from time deposits can be made for a small fee. Over time the withdrawals became less costly in terms of time lost, through the expansion of bank branches.

Bank credit is predominantly extended in the form of overdrafts. The ready access to these credit lines has limited the need of firms to hold narrow money balances for transaction and precautionary motives. In some cases firms even use their saving and time deposits as collateral for the overdraft line. Rather than cashing in their time deposits they take credit and pay as interest only the spread between deposit and loan rate (see Cole, Chunanuntathum and Loohawenchit 1986).

The other part of the explanation lies in the increased intensity in the use of money. The turnover rate of demand deposits (that is the amount of debits against demand deposits divided by total outstanding deposits) increased from 3.5 in 1965 to 22.4 in 1984, so the outstanding demand deposits were much more intensively used. The increased popularity of cheques meant that one could do with far less demand deposits (Panitchpakdi 1981). If one were to express the amounts of debits against demand deposits as a percentage of GDP, one would observe an increase from around 16 per cent in 1965 to over 40 per cent in the early 1980s.[20]

The increased resources available to the monetary system have been used to accumulate foreign assets and extend credit to the public and private sector.

The main asset of the monetary system used to be the foreign assets. The foreign assets reported in Table 2.4 present the net position of the monetary system, which results from: (i) the gold and foreign exchange reserves of the Bank of Thailand, which are always positive; and (ii) the net foreign position of commercial banks, which is generally negative as the banks are net borrowers abroad. Over the years, the net position of the commercial banks, as a percentage of GDP, has remained constant on average. The decline in the overall foreign assets/GDP ratio is thus fully due to a fall in the foreign reserves holdings of the central bank. The Bank of Thailand has traditionally kept high levels of reserves. This was in keeping with the cautious monetary policy which was very much concerned with the stability of the Baht and the confidence of foreign investors. Rozenthal (1970) argued that the foreign reserve holdings were excessive and that the money could have been used to finance investment, although he conceded that the high level of reserves may have created the confidence needed to attract foreign investment. Panitchpakdi (1981) argued that the foreign exchange reserves of the Bank of Thailand help the country to (i) deal with short- term economic fluctuations, and (ii) maintain the stability of the Baht, which in turn promotes exports and foreign investment. The rapid decline of the foreign asset/GDP ratio since the late 1960s seems to have rendered this debate less relevant, but see Chapter 5).

The financing of the government deficit has gradually shifted from the central bank to the commercial banks. In the 1950s the Bank of Thailand played a prominent role in financing the government (Rozenthal 1970): indeed until 1955 even the entire government debt was held by the central bank (Trescott 1971). An increase in the interest paid on bonds and the possibility of holding bonds as required reserves made it attractive for commercial banks to acquire government bonds. In 1960 the Central Bank still held 80 per cent of the domestic government debt and commercial banks only 5 per cent (the GSB held 9 per cent). By the early 1980s the share of the central bank had dropped to around one-third and that of the commercial banks had increased to about one-third. The GSB held one-fifth.

The private sector has benefited most from the increase in resources available to the financial institutions. The credit extended to the private sector as a percentage of GDP has increased very rapidly. It is generally argued that in extending credit to the private sector, commercial banks follow the demand for credit (Trescott 1971; World Bank 1983b). If the demand for credit increases, banks reduce their excess reserves or borrow additional funds abroad. But that does not imply that *all* credit demand is satisfied by the banks: in particular, the demands of less established, smaller firms are not honoured (Rozenthal 1970; World Bank 1983b).

The commercial banks could have extended more credit than they have. Rozenthal argued that in the 1960s commercial banks held substantial excess reserves (Rozenthal 1970), and Vongvipanond (1980) provided data to show that this continued to be the case in the 1970s, although at a much smaller scale. Why should banks hold excess reserves rather than maximizing profits? Rozenthal (1970) argued that the main reason was that bankers do not fully identify with banking since they have other business interests as well. As a result, they are less concerned with maximizing their banks' profits than with keeping excess reserves which increase their flexibility. Thai banks are generally part of a wider 'group' of companies owned by a family or a few families (Hewison 1981; Phipatseritham and Yoshihara 1983). The interests of the bank are considered in terms of the group's interests. This particular form of 'industrial organization' of large corporations is also found outside Thailand (see Chapter 1) and gives rise to strong concentration in the activities of the commercial banks.[21] In 1980, 70 per cent of all private sector credits from commercial banks were extended to less than 20,000 customers. Big loans (in excess of 1 million Baht) accounted for 69 per cent of the total, superbig loans (of more than 50 million Baht) still for 24 per cent (Vongvipanond 1980, p. 48). A somewhat different breakdown is given in the World Bank's report:

Size of loan (Baht)	Number of customers	% share of total loans
< 1 million	125,393	28
1-5 million	15,446	14
> 5 million	5,590	58

Source: World Bank (1983b, Statistical appendix).

The same concentration can be observed on the deposit side, where less than 5 per cent of the total number of accounts with deposits of Baht 100,000 or more made up three-quarters of all deposits. The remaining 95 per cent of accounts held the remaining quarter of the deposits. Accounts holding more than Baht 500,000 represented only 1 per cent of all deposit accounts but brought in about half of all deposit funds. These concentration figures present a picture of commercial banks doing business with large corporations. The Flow-of-Funds Accounts analysed in Chapter 4 indicate that the financial institutions obtain their deposits from the household sector and extend their credit mainly to the corporate sector. Given the figures on the concentration of deposits, it is clear that these deposits do not represent the small savings of middle-income groups. Most deposits are from rich households that are probably engaged in business and holding deposits to earn attractive interest returns or to ensure access to bank credit for their businesses, or to channel funds into the pool of the 'group' to which they belong.

The World Bank report asserted that, besides the group links between banks and large corporations, the interest rate policy is also responsible for the concentration of bank activities. Loans to smaller firms bring higher administration cost and higher risks, but commercial banks are not allowed to charge them higher interest rates. If they were allowed to do so, they would certainly be willing to extend more credit to the smaller firms (World Bank 1983b). That argument is not fully convincing though: if banks were willing to extend more credit to smaller firms, they would be able to find ways round the loan rate ceilings, for example by imposing service charges or by demanding that clients should hold compensating deposits.

There has been some debate in the literature (see Chapter 1) on whether bank credit is used as working capital or to finance investment. McKinnon's emphasis on the self-financing of investment and the resulting complementarity between investment and financial savings seems to imply that bank credit is mainly used as working capital (McKinnon 1973). In other models the use of credit for working capital purposes has been stressed in order to show that credit controls have negative effects on output or that increases in the cost of credit would have inflationary consequences (for example, Taylor 1983).

In Thailand most commercial bank credit is extended in the form of short-term overdraft loans; the use of term loans is very limited. But that does not imply that the loans cannot be used to finance investments. First of all, it is quite usual for short-term loans to be rolled over, so that in effect they become long-term loans. And within the corporation funds are fungible. It seems reasonable to assume then, that firms make use of credit to finance their investment and working capital needs, to the extent that their own savings are inadequate to finance desired levels of investment.

2.4   Financial policies

A number of financial policies have helped to stimulate financial development in Thailand. Competition among banks was restricted by the regulations on the entry of new banks and on the expansion of bank offices, which have served to strengthen the position of Thai banks *vis-à-vis* foreign-owned banks. Over the years there has been increasing concentration among banks,[22] with the market share of the Bangkok Bank growing (Rojpibulsit 1976). The introduction of the finance companies did not increase competition since the most important of them were owned by the main banks.

Competition among banks was further restricted by the imposition of ceilings on the main market prices: the deposit and loan rates. The spread left between the two ceilings was wide enough to ensure high profitability. In the absence of price competition, banks could only increase their market share if they could increase their resources by mobilizing deposits, borrowing abroad or retaining profits and acquiring share capital.In recent years the monetary authorities have tried to stimulate competition among banks by keeping the deposit and loan rate ceilings far above market clearing and international levels. This has placed the profitability of banks under pressure. The effective lending rate is, in fact, below the imposed ceiling as banks have to offer credit to prime customers at competitive rates to prevent them from going to foreign capital markets. But individual banks cannot lower their deposit rate for fear of losing deposits to other banks, therefore the deposit rate ceiling continues to operate as the effective deposit rate. As a result the spread between deposit and loan rates has narrowed considerably. And the liquidity of banks has increased substantially as the high interest rates attract deposits and funds from abroad but reduce the demand for credit or induce domestic firms to borrow abroad. The profitability of the commercial banks has declined drastically since 1983 (Nidhiprabha and Arya 1987). It is not surprising that the banks keep on pushing the central bank to adjust the deposit rate ceilings.

Supervision of financial institutions by the Bank of Thailand was aimed at building confidence in them. This implied that when these institutions were in trouble, the Bank organized rescue operations rather than allowing weak institutions to default.

Monetary policy before the Second World War was passive, as international trade and finance determined the domestic money supply in a one-to-one relationship because deposit money was hardly used. High foreign exchange reserves were maintained to safeguard international confidence and national economic autonomy (Ingram 1971).

After the interruption caused by the war and the subsequent adjustment period, the conservative monetary policy based on high levels of foreign reserves was continued, and changes in the domestic money supply continued to be determined by the balance of payments. Table 2.4 may be used to show the factors determining the money supply,[23] which are roughly:

$$\Delta M1 = \text{Domestic credit expansion} - \Delta \text{Quasi-money} + \Delta \text{Foreign assets.}$$

Silcock (1967, p. 198) and Ingram (1971, p. 311) showed that over the period 1956–69, the net impact of domestic factors (credit expansion minus increased holdings of quasi-money) is small and that changes in the money supply are almost fully explained by the accumulation of foreign reserves. Since then this situation has changed drastically: in more recent years, the domestic factors have dominated the expansion of the money supply and foreign reserves have had only a small influence. Some years even showed a decline in foreign asset holdings. In itself this is a healthy trend, as it is costly and unnecessary to 'finance' the money supply with foreign assets. But, of course, the rapid expansion of domestic credit creates the potential for economic instability.

In general, the rather cautious monetary and fiscal policies and the high level of foreign reserves helped to avoid inflation and maintain the stability of the Baht (Silcock 1967; Trescott 1971; Panitchpakdi 1981). The low level of inflation helped financial development, as it made people willing to hold financial savings. It was only during a few years when international inflation was excessive that the real deposit rate was negative. The stability of the Baht has helped to integrate Thailand with the international financial markets.

The success of these policies has, however, undermined the effectiveness of monetary policy. Commercial banks have generally had considerable liquidity with the rapid growth of time and savings deposits and their tendency to hold excess reserves. Furthermore, attempts by the Central Bank to control the expansion of domestic credit can be evaded by commercial banks or large corporation borrowing abroad directly (Panitchpakdi 1981; Go 1984). Obviously, smaller firms do not have access to the international capital market and suffer from domestic credit controls, as events in 1984, for example, showed. One of the few central bank instruments remaining is the loan rate at which commercial banks can borrow from the central bank, and this rate is changed quite frequently. But commercial banks borrow more abroad than from the central bank, so even this instrument is not very effective. Nontapunthawat (1973) made a detailed analysis of the portfolio behaviour of commercial banks and concluded that in the 1960s the Thai banks gradually increased their access to borrowing abroad as their knowledge of international opportunities increased and their own creditworthiness improved. The level of borrowing abroad by banks in that period was mainly determined by the financing needs of imports. A later study by the same author suggested a shift to a more general use of funds borrowed abroad as banks started to use these funds to satisfy more generally domestic credit demands (Nontapunthawat 1978).

Integration with international financial markets limits control over domestic interest rates. The Thai interest rate has to follow the international ones so as to avoid capital outflow or excess inflows. Therefore, if the domestic bank rate is increased to reduce borrowing from the Central Bank, the differential between the domestic rate and the international rate may make it worthwhile to borrow abroad, thus increasing the liquidity of the banks, which was exactly what the initial increase in the bank rate was trying to prevent. The high level of domestic interest rates (relative to international rates) in recent years has led to a very high liquidity in the financial system. The credit/deposit ratio of banks, which had reached a maximum of 111 per cent in 1979, stood at 86 in 1986, the lowest level in more than ten years. As observed above, the Bank of Thailand expects that this situation would lead to more active competition among commercial banks, so making the interest rates more flexible and a more stabilizing factor.

An important element of financial policy has been the attempt by the authorities to shift financial resources to a number of priority sectors. Two types of instruments have been used: specialized agencies and selective credit controls.

Specialized agencies do exist, but are probably used less in Thailand than in many other LDCs. Some examples are the Bank for Agriculture and Agricultural Cooperatives (BAAC), the Industrial Finance Company of Thailand (IFCT), the Small Industries Finance Organization (SIFO) and the Government Housing Bank (GHB). The most important of these is the BAAC, founded in 1966, which deals with agricultural credit. The BAAC was never very successful in attracting deposits and relies on funds from other banks. In 1975 the commercial banks were forced to spend 5 per cent of their deposits on agricultural credit. This share was gradually raised to 15 per cent in 1980, of which 2 per cent could be loans to agri-business. In early 1987 the proportion was further raised to 20 per cent but the coverage was widened to the rural sector, including agriculture, agri-business and rural small- and medium-scale industries. As most commercial banks find it difficult to administer such loans, they fulfil their obligation by making deposits to the BAAC which has used these funds to expand its activities very significantly. In 1981 43 per cent of commercial bank credit to agriculture went directly to farmers and 57 per cent through deposits with the BAAC. The BAAC quite efficiently reaches 40 per cent of all farm households (World Bank 1983b).

The agencies designed to support the industrial sector are much smaller. The SIFO is alleged to be quite ineffective (Panitchpakdi 1981; World Bank 1983b); Vongvipanond (1980) concluded that both the IFCT and the SIFO are dependent on official funds and have underutilized their loan capacity.

The main selective credit control imposed on commercial banks is the obligation, mentioned previously, to lend to agriculture. In addition, there are a number of privileged rediscount facilities for loans extended to manufacturing, to agriculture and to exports. These rediscount facilities are not very popular with the banks, however, as the margin between the rediscount rate and the maximum rate that banks are allowed to charge on such loans is quite narrow (Panitchpakdi 1981).

It has been asserted that mainly richer farmers, large-scale exporters and large-scale manufacturing firms have benefited from these selective credit controls (Vongvipanond 1980; Panitchpakdi 1981; World Bank 1983b). Such clients may be the least needy of the subsidies involved, but given the overall preference of commercial banks for these clients, as observed before, it is not surprising to find that they are given preferential treatment for loans.

Notes

1. The statistical data underlying the tables and charts in this study have three major sources. These are the following periodical publications: Bank of Thailand, *Quarterly Bulletin;* National Economic and Social Development Board (NESDB), *National Income of Thailand;* Bank of Thailand and NESDB, *Flow-of-Funds Accounts of Thailand.* These three sources will not be listed in every Table or chart; other sources used will, however, be mentioned.

    The national currency, the Baht, is at present pegged to a basket of currencies. During most of the period under study, it was tied to the dollar in a very stable relationship. For the entire period 1960-84 an exchange rate of roughly 20 Baht to the dollar may be used. It was not until the devaluation of 1984, when the Baht also shifted to a basket of currencies, that this rate substantially changed. For these more recent years the rate of 27 Baht to the US dollar may be used as an indicator.

2. It may be useful at this stage to list the Thai National Account definitions of the various saving concepts used throughout this study. Household savings are estimated as the difference between household income and expenditure (the latter including consumption expenditure, direct taxes, interest on consumer debt, net transfers to the rest of the world). Corporate savings are defined as total profits minus losses, and minus income tax payments, dividends and profits accruing to foreigners. State enterprise savings are profits minus losses and minus the contributions made to the government. Government savings are defined as the difference between total current revenue (that is, taxes, other revenue, net transfer from households and from the rest of the world) and consumption expenditure by the government.

3. The Annual *World Economic Outlook,* published by the IMF includes Thailand in the group of 'other oil-importing countries', that is oil–importing LDCs with the exception of low-income countries and newly industrializing countries. In the period 1973–82 the average annual rate of inflation for that group was around 25 per cent; the rate for Thailand was less than half of that.

4. The international inflation index is a weighted average of the import and export price indices, using the shares of imports and exports of goods and services in GDP as weights.

5. The inflow of direct foreign investments as measured on the balance of payments averaged about 0.7 per cent of GDP without much fluctuation and without a trend.

6. The external debt of Thailand is still relatively modest. In 1980 it was estimated at 21 per cent of GNP, compared to 32 per cent for the Philippines and 34 per cent for South Korea (World Bank 1983b, statistical appendix).

7. In 1984, for example, the ratio of total government expenditure to GDP was 30 per cent in Malaysia and 24 per cent in Indonesia.

8. In his analysis of the operating surplus in Indonesia, Keuning (1985) classified the following as predominantly unincorporated: agriculture, trade, restaurants and hotels, transport and communications, banking, insurance, real estate, business services and services.

9. The ranking (from low to high) of sectors according to their labour productivity (value added per unit of labour) was as follows in 1976: agriculture, trade, services, manufacturing, transport and communications, construction, electricity and water, and mining (Meesook 1979).

10. The other way of measuring the unincorporated sector suggested earlier (that is, taking the Household Income from Farms, Professions and other Unincorporated Enterprises as the value added of the unincorporated sector, and considering the rest of GDP as corporate) would result in slightly different figures but the same trend.

11. Unemployment is difficult to measure when so many people are in self-employment, but it is generally asserted that unemployment in urban and rural areas is low (for example, Bertrand and Squire 1980). Grootaert (1986) also noted the low unemployment rate, but commented that the labour force survey on which it was based did not use proper definitions. When proper definitions were used he arrived at an unemployment rate of only 1.9 per cent for 1980 (Grootaert 1986, p. 119).

12. By comparison, in the Philippines the share is 54 per cent (1975), for Sri Lanka 32 per cent (1981) and for South Korea 53 per cent (1980) (*UN Demographic Yearbook*).

13. Bertrand and Squire (1980) observed that rural real wages in the Central Plain were stable in the 1960s. Hongladarom (1982) gave some data on annual wages of manufacturing employees which, when deflated, did not show any trend in that period.

14. Until 1969 the National Income Accounts grouped Farm Income and Income from Professions and other Unincorporated Enterprises together. The trends before 1969 have been estimated by using the GDP of the agricultural sector as a basis to approximate Income from Farms, and that estimate was then used to calculate the non-farm self-employed income. These rough estimates have been made only to obtain an impression of trends before 1969. In Chart 2.4 these estimated income shares are shown as a dotted line.

15. In 1978 an exception was made, forced by an exchange arrangement, for the European Asian Bank.

16. The role of foreign banks is also considerably smaller than in neighbouring countries: the share of foreign banks in total bank assets in 1981 was 13 per cent in Indonesia, 32 per cent in Malaysia and 12 per cent in the Philippines (Skully 1985, p. 128).

17. Although provincial branches have spread rapidly, distribution remains uneven. In 1977 the number of commercial bank offices per 10,000 population was 0.89 for Bangkok, 0.38 for the Central Region, 0.11 for the Northeast, 0.21 for the North and 0.30 for the Southern Region (Meesook 1978).

18. In interpreting Table 2.4, it should be noted that definitions and coverage have changed over the period. This does not affect major trends, but it may influence changes between particular years.

19. Finance companies are, on average, not typical consumer finance agencies: only about 20 per cent of their business is in consumer credit.

20. International comparisons of M1/GDP ratios are not very meaningful as monetary systems may differ. In 1981 the M1/GNP ratio was 13 per cent for Indonesia, 20 per cent for Malaysia but only 8 per cent for the Philippines (Skully 1985, p. 128).

21. Prasartset (1982) quoted figures collected by Krirkkiat Phipatseritham on 65 large business groups which together control assets worth Baht 420 billion (in 1978/79). The twelve groups among these which were grouped around a bank controlled Baht 309 billion or 73 per cent of the total.

22. The Bangkok Bank, Thailand's largest, is also the largest bank in Southeast Asia. It controls 33 per cent of total bank deposits in Thailand. In other countries bank concentration is not as high: the single largest bank in Malaysia holds 20 per cent of all deposits, in Indonesia 27 per cent and in the Philippines 23 per cent. The figures for the four largest banks taken together, in each of these countries and Thailand are, respectively, 50, 73, 40 and 65 per cent (Viknins 1980).

23. This equation gives only a rough impression, as it ignores elements such as Capital Accounts, Other Assets and Liabilities, etc., and is therefore only presented to study main trends.

3 Savings: theories and evidence

3.1 Introduction

Starting the analysis of processes of economic and financial development by studying the determinants of saving behaviour does not imply the acceptance of a prior-saving approach in which available savings determine the level of investment that is possible. In a Keynesian perspective, in which investment determines saving, an analysis of saving behaviour would also help to identify the ways in which this happens.

Early growth models defined the warranted rate of growth, g, as g = sk, in which s is the saving/output ratio and k is the incremental output/capital ratio (Harrod 1939). Subsequent developments in growth theory have led to more complex formulations (see Sen 1970), but they can still be summarized by the statement that the rate of growth of output depends on (i) the share of total output available for investment, and (ii) the efficiency of such investments.[1] This chapter will deal with the first factor; the efficiency of investment will receive some attention in the next chapter.

As was discussed in Chapter 1, a main problem in economic development theory is how to increase the resources available for capital formation, or how to control consumption and increase saving. The resources available for investment can be increased through more domestic saving or through a larger capital inflow from abroad. How can domestic savings be increased; what are the determinants of saving behaviour? Economic theory offers contradicting hypotheses on these questions. In section 3.2 of this chapter a review of the theory and empirical evidence on the determinants of saving will be presented as well as an assessment of their applicability to developing countries. In section 3.3 an attempt will be made to explain saving behaviour in Thailand, and section 3.4 will present the main conclusions.

3.2 The determinants of savings

3.2.1 The Keynesian saving function

Most theories of saving behaviour are derived from consumption theories. Keynes postulated a consumption function in which the amount of aggregate consumption is mainly dependent on the amount of aggregate income. Consumption increases with income, although not by as much (Keynes 1936, Chapters 8 and 9).[2] This can be summarized by the following consumption function:

(1) $C = a + bY$

Together with the definition of saving as $S = Y - C$, this leads to the following saving function:

(2) $S = -a + (1 - b)Y$

The negative constant may be seen as reflecting some assumed level of subsistence consumption. The coefficient $(1 - b)$ is the marginal propensity to save (MPS) which, because of the negative value of the constant a, is greater than the average propensity to save (APS), defined as S/Y. Keynes formulated the consumption function in the context of a short-term model in which macroeconomic fluctuations occurred because savings, made mainly by consuming households, need not coincide with investments, which are made by corporations. However, the ideas underlying this consumption function have also been used to analyse long-term trends in consumption and saving behaviour. If the MPS is greater than the APS one should see the APS rise as income grows. The theoretical justification for this is that at higher levels of income and consumption, the marginal utility of consumption declines.

Mikesell and Zinser, who brought together the results of studies on the saving behaviour in developing countries made during the 1950s and 1960s, concluded that time-series analyses generally suggest an MPS of between 10 and 15 per cent. There is no evidence that the MPS is greater than the APS; in fact the APS seems rather stable over time (Mikesell and Zinser 1973).

Given the shortage of data available for time-series analysis, it is not surprising that the test on the relationship between the level of the savings ratio and the level of income has been transformed into a cross-country test on the relationship between the savings ratio and the level of per capita income. Newlyn reported a test covering 70 countries in which a strong positive relationship was found. The ratio of Gross Domestic Savings to GNP increased from around 10 per cent at a per capita income of $90 to around 21 per cent at an income of about $3,000 (Newlyn 1977, p. 15). Mikesell and Zinser also reported cross-country studies which all seemed to indicate such a positive relationship (Mikesell and Zinser 1973). Thirlwall (1974b) tested whether the savings ratio increases with per capita income by running a regression on a group of 63 developing and developed countries. His results led to a parabolic function with the savings ratio increasing up to a per capita income level of around US$2,000 and falling thereafter.[3]

The apparent contradiction between the results of time-series studies and those of comparative analysis is less surprising than it may seem. Cross-country comparison suggests that the APS rises from 10 per cent to 12.5 per cent when per capita income increases from $90 to $190. But such a rise in per capita income, even at the high per capita growth rate of 3 per cent, takes 25 years, a longer period than is normally available for time-series analysis. So in the short periods for which data are available in most countries, increases in the APS, and differences between the APS and MPS, may not be discernible.

This finding that, on the one hand, the APS is relatively stable in time-series and, on the other hand, a positive relationship exists between the APS and per capita income in cross-country studies, has its counterpart in within-country studies. In many countries it has been observed that the overall savings ratio is more or less constant over time. At the same time, household budget surveys show that higher income groups have higher savings ratios. If households with higher incomes save more, and over time the average income of all households rises with economic growth, one would expect the aggregate savings ratio also to rise, but that does not occur. It is also observed that the savings ratio is relatively constant in the long run but shows considerable fluctuations in the short run. During recessions, consumption falls less than other spending categories (see Evans 1969; Modigliani 1986). A number of theories have been developed to deal with these paradoxes, two of which will be briefly discussed: the permanent income hypothesis and the life-cycle hypothesis. Rather than linking savings to current income, as in the Keynesian approach, the permanent income hypothesis relates them to permanent income and the life-cycle hypothesis to life-time income.

3.2.2 Permanent income hypothesis

The Permanent Income Hypothesis (PIH) assumes a rational household that maximizes utility through consumption decisions. Friedman (1957) postulated a household whose consumption at time t, C_t, depends on its permanent income Y^p,

(3) $C_t = a\, Y^p$

Permanent income may be loosely defined as the income which a household may expect to earn, on average, in the long run. More strictly, it was defined as 'the amount a consumer unit could consume (or believes that it could) while maintaining its wealth intact' (Friedman 1957, pp. 10–11). Under this definition:

(4) $Y^p = r\,W$

r = the long-run rate of interest and
W = total of human and non-human wealth.

The propensity to consume out of permanent income depends on the long-run rate of interest and on other factors, such as the ratio of human to total wealth, but such factors would change only little over time. Observed income is made up of permanent and transitory income, $Y = Y^p + Y^t$, in which transitory income Y^t may be negative. The main hypothesis of the PIH is that the ratio C/Y^p is independent of the level of income. The differences observed in the consumption ratio C/Y (and thus in S/Y) of various income groups are to be explained by the fact that higher income groups have a higher share of transitory income. The assumption is that transitory income Y^t is fully saved. This strict assumption could be relaxed, allowing for some consumption out of transitory income, without affecting the overall conclusions of the PIH very much.

These assumptions enable the PIH to explain (i) the long-run constancy of the APS, (ii) the observed differences in the APS of various income groups, and (iii) the short-run fluctuations of the APS; all phenomena observed in the United States (Evans 1969).

When it comes to empirical testing of the PIH, the main problem lies in finding an estimate of Y^p. Usually this is done by taking a weighted average of past values of observed income Y. After a Koyck-transformation, this results typically in a equation with the following form:

(5) $C_t = a\,C_{t-1} + b\,Y_t$

This general form, in which consumption in the current period is dependent on the level of consumption in the previous period, is consistent with other approaches to the explanation of consumption and saving. Duesenberry, for example, claimed that current consumption is determined by the highest level of previous consumption. In a growing economy that approach boils down to formulations like equation (5) above. Brown proposed a model in which the consumer slowly adjusts to changes in income; that approach can also be fitted into the equation above (see Evans 1969; Marglin 1984). These alternative approaches do not need the strict assumptions on which the PIH is based. Predictions of the values of the coefficients in equation (5) depend on the speed with which Y^p adjusts to changes in Y. The essence of the PIH is that this adjustment is rather slow, so that all past information on Y^p is contained in C_{t-1}.

Empirical tests of the PIH have also taken the form of running a regression like the following on time-series data:

(6) $S = a_0 + a_1\,Y^p + a_2\,Y^t$

84

in the expectation that the propensity to save out of transitory income will be greater than that out of permanent income. In theory, a_2 could even be equal to one. Studies reviewed by Mikesell and Zinser (1973) tend to confirm that the estimates for a_2 exceed those for a_1, but not that $a_2 = 1$. Gupta ran a regression of the aggregate saving function for twelve Asian countries. In nine cases the coefficients were statistically significant; in six of these the coefficient of transitory income exceeded that of permanent income; in three cases the reverse was true (Gupta 1984, p. 107).

An interesting aspect of the PIH is that it may help to explain the saving behaviour of different income groups. Self-employed persons, for example, generally have a greater transitory component in their income than wage and salary workers, and hence they are likely to show a higher ratio of savings to observed income. An interesting application of this aspect of the PIH is made by Knudsen and Parnes, who argued that export producers in LDCs face unstable weather and world market conditions, and thus relatively unstable incomes or a relatively large share of transitory income. In a sample of developing countries, they found a significant positive relationship between the degree of export instability and the domestic propensity to save. Countries with higher instabilities in export earnings have more savings available to finance investment and tend to have a higher rate of economic growth (Knudsen and Parnes 1975). It will be shown in section 3.3.3 that this is important in explaining saving behaviour in Thailand.

3.2.3 The life-cycle hypothesis

This approach to the explanation of consumption and saving behaviour is based on the assumption that consumers set their lifetime patterns of consumption and saving so as to maximize utility subject to a lifetime budget constraint. The underlying idea is that people want to spread consumption more evenly over their lifetime than their income will be spread. This leads to the conclusion that saving behaviour is dependent on age: during the income-earning period of life, assets are accumulated (that is savings) and on retirement dissaving takes place.

The life-cycle hypothesis (LCH) is clearly designed for industrialized economies where the following three assumptions may hold:

(a) Most individuals engage in wage labour.
(b) There is a perfect labour market where human capital (accumulated through both education and work experience) influences productivity, and thus income, and plays an important role in determining the pattern of income over the lifetime. The typical pattern of the age-earning profile shows an increase in annual earnings from the start of the working life till somewhere around middle age, due to accumulating work experience.

Later a decline sets in as productivity falls with old age. Income falls off upon retirement (see, for example, Evans 1969, p. 47).

(c) It is assumed that, on the basis of a utility function, individuals prefer to spread their consumption more equally over their lifetimes than their income. An assumed perfect capital market would enable them to do so. Hence the C/Y ratio would be high in the early years of household formation, when the household size is large due to dependants and thus when consumption needs are high and income relatively low. There could even be debt accumulation in this period. At middle age, when income reaches its peak and the number of non-income-earning dependants falls and consumption needs are less, saving would be high to repay possible debts from the earlier period and to accumulate assets for retirement. After retirement, the C/Y ratio would be high again and dissaving may take place.

At first sight the LCH appears to be of little relevance to LDCs, as in these countries employment conditions tend to be quite different. Certainly in most Asian countries a large part of the labour force is not in wage employment, but is self-employed and mostly engaged in farming. In these activities, human capital considerations may not play an important role: all farmers have, in principle, access to the same technology. More importantly, the separation of the childhood, working life and retirement periods is far less marked. Young children may work on the family farm or in the family business and old people keep on working alongside their children as long as they can. The age-earning profile is quite different in that it is determined by the production capacity of the entire household, not just by that of its head. The fundamental difficulty in applying the LCH to developing countries is that the LCH sees the household primarily as a consumption unit. The life-time earning profile is taken as more or less given and fixed and saving is interpreted as the attempt to even the consumption pattern of the household over time. Most households in developing countries are production units as well as consumption units. Attempts to explain the saving behaviour of the household would therefore have to look more at what determines household production and income than is usually done in the LCH.

The per capita income of the household tends to go down up to the middle age of its head (between 40 and 49 years), because production capacity is reduced by the need for childcare. Later, as children become adult, this need declines, children start to contribute to production and income, and the per capita income of the household rises. It may decline again at an older age when children establish their own independent household. Available evidence confirms this expectation.[4]

This family cycle also determines the consumption needs of the household. On the basis of these patterns in production capacity and consumption needs, one would expect the saving potential to be concentrated in households with heads in the age beyond about 50 years.

Kelley and Williamson estimated a saving function for each age group separately and found that the MPS increases with age. They interpreted this as support for the LCH (Kelley and Williamson 1968).

Musgrove, looking at data for ten Latin American cities, observed 'a very slight tendency of young households to show a higher marginal propensity to consume than older families' (Musgrove 1978, p. 462), but this finding is far from uniform over the cities and is affected by measurement and estimation problems. Lluch, Power and Williams (1977) summarized their analysis of consumption patterns in a number of developing countries by concluding that there is some tendency for the marginal propensity to save to increase with age. However, these saving patterns are not consistent with the retirement motive that underlies the LCH. This motive leads one to expect low savings, or even dissaving, in old age, but Kelley and Williamson found the highest MPS in the oldest age group. It may be suggested, then, that the observed age pattern of saving reflects the production capacity of the household during the life-cycle of the family far more than attempts to equalize consumption over time. The earning profiles, particularly of rural households, are determined less by the trend in the labour productivity of the household head (as in Western countries) than by the quantity of labour available to the household.

Leff (1969) presented another way of linking age structure to saving behaviour. He observed that the high birth-rates in LDCs result in high dependency ratios. The dependent age groups add to consumption needs and do not contribute to production, so there is less scope for saving. Leff concluded that demographic factors are important and that rapid population growth presents a serious obstacle to saving and capital accumulation. He also suggested that his findings could be integrated into a saving theory that would maximize consumption over a lifetime, subject to the constraints imposed by expenditure for dependants.

Leff's analysis has not gone unchallenged. Gupta (1971) argued that the sample is too diverse; at very low income levels, saving is totally impossible; it is only above a certain minimum income level that one may expect saving to take place. He split the 47 LDCs of Leff's sample into three income groups and repeated the regressions for each group. No significant results were obtained for the two lower income groups; Leff's results were repeated only for the highest income group.

Ram (1982) repeated Leff's regression on a much wider sample of LDCs and for a more recent period. His results failed to confirm Leff's findings.

The conclusion from these studies must be that attempts to introduce age factors into the saving equation through dependency ratios are very sensitive to the sample of countries taken and the period covered. Such sensitivities should, in general, not increase confidence in the usefulness of the approach.

There is also a conceptual problem with Leff's approach. Does the dependency burden really determine the capacity to save? Many studies on population growth suggest another pattern of causation, which is that people with low incomes have many children because they need the labour power these children provide and because children are the only form of old-age insurance they can afford. In this interpretation, it is the low income that causes both low saving and high dependency ratios.

Hammer (1986a) concluded from his survey that the theoretical arguments and empirical findings on the link between the age structure of the population and savings are ambiguous. The results are weakest for the poorest countries.

Summarizing, there is some evidence that saving propensity varies over the life-cycle of the household head, but the patterns are not very distinct. It is likely that the variations are due more to fluctuations in the household's productive capacity and income than to attempts to equalize consumption throughout working life and retirement. Self-employed households generally have a high saving propensity. The actual savings they make are largely determined by fluctuations in income.

Before abandoning the LCH, it is interesting to take a look at the way in which the LCH – which is in principle a micro-level explanation of saving behaviour – has been tested using macro-data. For such testing to be possible it must be assumed that the saving behaviour of individual households can be aggregated, first within age groups and then over age groups. Ando and Modigliani (1963) claimed that this aggregation can be performed.[5] They arrived at the following aggregated consumption function:

(7) $\quad C_t = a\,YL_t + b\,YL_t^e + c\,A_{t-1}$
YL_t = current non-property (or labour) income
YL_t^e = expected annual non-property income
A_{t-1} = accumulated net worth.

This equation is, in fact, quite similar to equation (3) of the PIH above. In that equation consumption was made a function of permanent income, Yp, which was defined as $Y^p = rW$. Total wealth W includes human wealth (the return on which is labour income) and physical wealth (or accumulated net worth). The problem with equation (7) is that it contains two variables, YL_t^e and A_{t-1}, on which observations are generally not available, certainly not in LDCs. Further developments of the model have attempted to deal with these problems.

It has become a general assumption that expected labour income YL_t^e is proportional to current labour income YL_t. Hence $YL_t^e = dYL_t$, and equation (7) becomes:

(8) $\quad C_t = (a + bd)\,YL_t + c\,A_{t-1}$

(Ando and Modigliani 1963; Modigliani and Tarantelli 1975).

Ando and Modigliani (1963) argued that on the basis of an assumed form of the underlying individual utility function, an assumed growth rate of real income, an assumed constant rate of return on assets, and observed lifetime earning patterns, the expected values of the coefficients in equation (8) can be calculated. The value of the coefficient of YL should be between 0.61 and 0.73, and of A_{t-1} between 0.07 and 0.13. In their application of this model to the United States, Ando and Modigliani (1963) obtained results that are in keeping with the expected values for the coefficients. Evans (1969), who ran equation (8) on more recent, post-war US data, concluded that the LCH performs very poorly, but that this may be due to the disruptions in the immediate post-war period.

When testing equation (8) with data on Italy, Modigliani and Tarantelli (1975) used the aggregated value of financial wealth as a proxy for A_{t-1}[6].

Again, results were obtained that are in keeping with theoretical expectations. They went on to argue that the coefficient c of A_{t-1} in equation (8) is not really a constant but, among other things, a function of the rate of return on assets and the rate of growth of income. The impact of the rate of return r is considered to be particularly important and they proposed a simple linear relationship for 'c', that is $c = c' + hr$, so that equation (8) becomes:

(9) $C_t = (a + bd) YL_t + c' A_{t-1} + hr A_{t-1}$
r = rate of return on net worth.

The value rA_{t-1} is the indicator of the expected long-run return on accumulated property. Current property income, as measured in the National Accounts, YP_t, is not a good indicator for this, as it is subject to short-run fluctuations in the interest rates and in the valuation of assets. In principle, rA_{t-1} could be approximated by a lag function of observed YP. It is emphasized that the coefficient 'h' is not the marginal propensity to consume out of property income; it measures the 'strength of the substitution effect between current and future consumption' (Modigliani and Tarantelli 1975, p. 838). In the long run, rA_{t-1} changes with changes in A (which have a positive wealth effect on consumption) and changes in r (which have an ambiguous effect, since income and substitution effects work in opposite directions). In the long run, changes in the value of accumulated wealth are likely to dominate, so that the value of 'h' in equation (9) is likely to be positive, and might well exceed the value of the coefficient of labour income YL or even exceed one. Attempts to estimate the value of 'h' for Italy did indeed result in a value greater than one, but the authors warned that the results are unreliable due to the unavoidable multicollinearity[7] between A_{t-1} and rA_{t-1} in equation (9) (Modigliani and Tarantelli 1975).

In conclusion, empirical support for the LCH at the aggregated level is not convincing, as it is plagued by problems of multicollinearity and strongly dependent on the definitions applied. It should be noted that the formulation in equations (9) contains labour and property income separatedly, and is thus quite similar to formulations derived from neo-Keynesian theories.

3.2.4 Post-Keynesian saving theory

The post-Keynesian growth models already discussed in Chapter 1 include a saving function which goes back to the classical economists. There is a separation of households into wage-earners, who consume all the income they receive, and entrepreneurs, who earn profits which are saved and re-invested. The saving propensity out of profit income is thus much larger than that out of wage income. This hypothesis contrasts sharply with the expectations formulated by the LCH, where it is possible that the propensity to consume out of property income exceeds that out of labour income. This difference arises from the totally different theoretical perspectives of the two approaches.

According to the LCH, an individual household receives both current labour income and property income from previously accumulated assets. These assets are accumulated to spread consumption equally over the life-cycle and to ensure income after retirement. It is thus possible that there is substantial consumption out of property income, because the main purpose of asset accumulation is to look after consumption needs. In the post-Keynesian approach, property income is received by entrepreneurial households and constitutes a return on past productive investment. A large part of it is saved to satisfy further investment needs of the firm. In short, in the LCH perspective the share of property income in total income is determined by consumption decisions, and in the post-Keynesian models the profit share is determined by investment decisions.

One would expect that the different expectations with respect to the relative size of the saving propensities out of different types of income could be settled by empirical evidence. Modigliani and Tarantelli (1975) estimated a Kaldor-type saving function for Italy and came to the conclusion that support for the Kaldor-hypothesis is found, that is there is a lower saving propensity for labour income than for property income, but the result is very sensitive to the specification of the equation. They tested the LCH model on the same data and concluded that the outcomes – which show a significantly higher marginal propensity to consume for property income but suffer from multicollinearity – are in principle superior to those from the Kaldor specification. Marglin (1984) also conducted tests comparing LCH and post-Keynesian saving assumptions on USA data and concluded that the outcome depends strongly on the form of the equation chosen and the definitions of variables applied.

Song (1981) followed the approach of Modigliani and Tarantelli and calculated a set of different consumption or saving functions for South Korea. The Keynesian function (see equation (1) above), and the PIH function (see equation (6) above) performed equally well. A post-Keynesian saving function (see equation (1) of Chapter 1) gave satisfactory results once the income data are corrected by imputing a labour income for the self-employed and by accounting for the effect of unemployment. A LCH function was not estimated for lack of data. Song continued by arguing that for a country like South Korea, the breakdown between urban and rural households is as crucial as that between profit and wage-earners. The conditions of rural households are quite different from those of urban households: they tend to be extended families, engaged in production, and their tastes and preferences differ from their urban counterparts. Using rural and urban household survey data, Song estimated a consumption function which combines the urban/rural dichotomy with the post-Keynesian wage/profit breakdown. The marginal propensity to consume of urban wage-earners is found to be highest, followed by that of rural households and then that of urban property–income-earning households (Song 1981).

There is substantial evidence from household surveys (to be reviewed later in this chapter) that the propensity of self-employed households to save is greater than that of wage-earning households. This could be considered as support for the post-Keynesian hypothesis that households with entrepreneurial incomes save more. However, such surveys also suggest that the simple dichotomy between labour and property income is far from adequate. Saving propensities may differ significantly, for example between farming households and other self-employed households, as will be argued further in section 3.3.

3.2.5 Assessment of saving theories

The saving theories discussed above are developed in and for industrialized countries. In applying these theories to developing countries at least three problems have to be faced. The first of these is that developing countries are going through a process of rapid structural change. Secondly, most households are primarily production units and not only consumption units. The third problem is that the assumption of prefect markets, that underlies most of the saving theories, is not necessarily fulfilled.

Structural change: The simple Keynesian saving function linking the level of saving to the level of income is not very meaningful. In virtually all theories of saving, one would expect the level of saving to depend on income. Forms that attempt to explain the savings ratio S/Y are therefore more useful. Attempts to relate the savings ratio to the level of per capita income led to significant results in cross-country studies but not in time-series analysis. One explanation for this may be that increases in per capita income take time and will only be reflected in the APS in the very long term. But in that very long term also the structure of the economy is changing and these changes also affect the APS. In fact, the increase in the savings ratio may be not so much determined by the increase in income as by the long-term structural changes in the economy that occur with economic development. Such changes include the proletarianization of the labour force, the modernization of agriculture, the growing share of the corporate sector and the changing role of government.

Using 1950s data, Houthakker concluded for example that household savings are proportional to household income and that the higher share of corporate savings seems to be responsible for the higher overall savings ratio in rich countries. On the other hand, government savings tended to be somewhat higher in developing countries (Houthakker 1965). The analysis of the Thai savings ratios in Chapter 2 also suggested that the increase in the aggregate savings ratio in the 1960s was due to the increase in corporate savings. The impact of these processes of structural change on the overall savings ratio will be felt only in the long term and they may dominate any effect that a higher per capita income may have. The effects of structural change are not easily predictable; in fact, some processes of structural change may have opposite effects on the overall savings ratio.

Production units: Most saving theories analysed above are derived from consumption behaviour. In the Keynesian consumption function, consumption and saving are stable functions of current income. In other approaches the variability of income plays a greater role: in the PIH short-term variations and in the LCH life-time variations. In both cases savings arise from the desire of households to spread consumption more evenly over time than income. These theories, though, are less explicit about what *causes* the variation in income. In the PIH it is suggested that higher income groups experience more income variation. Knudsen and Parnes added that export instability leads to income variation. The LCH draws life-time earning profiles, but such profiles are less clear in developing countries. Income may fluctuate with age, but the patterns are vague and other factors may be far more important in explaining income variation and savings.

The fundamental fact is that most savings in developing countries are made by production units. A first problem with saving theories derived from a consumption perspective is that a large part of aggregate savings is made by economic units that do not engage in consumption at all: the corporations. And even the households are not all exclusively consumption units. Both the PIH and the LCH are based on the household as a consumption unit whose only task is to spread consumption evenly over time. Many, if not most, households in LDCs are simultaneously consumer and producer. Hence saving decisions and the acquisition of assets are determined not only by a desired consumption pattern over time but also – and probably more so – by the conditions of production in the household enterprise.

Does that imply that the post-Keynesian theory in which savings are made out of enterprise income is more applicable? The post-Keynesian theories discussed above are not really theories of saving: they are growth theories based on particular assumptions with respect to saving behaviour. The contrast with the LCH is sharp. In the LCH it is assumed that the propensity to save out of labour income may be greater than that out of property income, because property is accumulated with consumption needs in mind. In the post-

Keynesian approach the reverse is true, because property income is seen as the income of capitalists who have a great urge to re- invest their income. As such, this seems to be an easy matter to settle empirically, but the statistical problems involved are great and no satisfactory conclusion so far has been reached.

The very sharp distinction between labour and property income may be unrealistic in most developing countries, where many households receive income from various sources. But it may be assumed that households that receive a relatively large proportion of their income from own enterprises have different opportunities and incentives to save than households depending more on wage income (see also Bhalla 1978).

Imperfect markets: The Keynesian saving function, the PIH and LCH assume utility-maximizing households whose behaviour is not constrained by market imperfections. The assumption of a rational household is strong. As Marglin (1984) observed, households are assumed to maximize utility over their lifetime. However, over that period there is little scope to learn from experience, by trial and error, as there may be on daily markets. Hence the formation and adjustment of preferences (the utility function) is difficult. At the same time, lifetime earnings can be foreseen only imperfectly, hence the budget constraint is also uncertain. With unstable utility functions and uncertain budget constraints, the maximizing household finds itself standing in quicksand. Needless to say, these circumstances, which already apply in full force in advanced countries, will apply even more in rapidly changing developing countries.

The LCH is based on a Western model of the household where the head of the household has to look after his old age and where assets can be freely acquired to serve that purpose. Even in that context, the introduction of social security and pension funds has complicated the model. Attempts to include such institutions in the LCH have led to quite complex modifications (see, for example, Modigliani and Hemming 1983). But the nature of the household in LDCs and the income profile over the lifetime is quite different: there is no retirement, people work as long as they can; children contribute to household income after a certain age and often look after their parents in old age.[8] Capital markets are also far from perfect in LDCs and often hardly accessible. Is it realistic in such circumstances, to assume that the household can decide on an optimal saving-consumption pattern over time?

These points imply that, even as consumption units, households may find it difficult to come to optimal saving patterns. But this study emphasizes that households are also production units, so that one should not only look at consumption markets but also at markets for production inputs and outputs.

To deal with the three problems identified above, section 3.3 will try to explain saving behaviour in Thailand by:

(a) Separating aggregate savings into savings by households, corporations and government. By doing so an important aspect of long-term structural change is eliminated because, to a considerable extent, this change is reflected in the relative growth of these three sectors;

(b) Interpreting household and corporate savings as retained profits of the household firm and of the corporation, thus doing full justice to the production nature of the household;

(c) Assuming that household firms face competitive commodity markets, while corporations are assumed to operate on more oligopolistic markets. Of course, household firms may in fact deal on rather shaky markets with incomplete information, but still the difference in market power between the unincorporated household firm and the larger corporations is fundamental to the explanation of their rather different saving behaviour.

In the next section (3.2.6) there will be a brief review of aggregate saving functions that have been estimated for Thailand. Each of the saving theories discussed above led to rather specific forms of the saving function to be estimated, although the practice of econometric work on saving functions has been different. Actual econometric saving functions have tended to be rather eclectic, combining variables suggested from different theoretical perspectives and adding, on an *ad hoc* basis, other variables which could be expected to influence saving behaviour. It may be useful to list the variables that have been suggested by the different saving theories as determinants of saving behaviour, plus variables that have been frequently used in empirical attempts to fit saving functions, and to establish the expected direction of their influence. The following variables will be discussed: per capita income, permanent and transitory income, exports, income distribution, age structure, rate of interest, financial development, rate of inflation, growth rate and foreign capital inflows.

Per capita income This variable may have a positive effect on the savings ratio, but probably more as a result of the long-term structural changes that accompany income growth than of the higher level of income itself.

Permanent and transitory income The PIH suggests that the saving propensity out of transitory income is higher than that out of permanent income. At the level of aggregate income, this hypothesis is not very discriminatory: for example, it is quite compatible with the hypothesis of the link between the savings ratio and the rate of growth (see below). It becomes more interesting when one breaks down aggregate income into its components and shows that some categories of income or groups of income earners may have greater variability than others and thus a different savings ratio. One could apply this to, for example, the post-Keynesian breakdown of wage and profit income, where it is likely that profit income shows greater variation over time and

94

therefore has a greater transitory part, which may explain the higher saving propensity.

Exports The latter point is also relevant to the relationship that has been established between exports and saving behaviour. Maizels (1968) suggested that an increase in exports may lead to an increase in savings, because, for instance, the export sector has a greater propensity to save, or because exports add to government revenue and thus to government savings. He ran a regression of savings as a dependent variable and export income and the remainder of GDP as explanatory variables for a sample of developing countries and found that the coefficient of the export variable is significant and tends to be larger than that of the rest of GDP. Lee (1971) ran the same regression on a larger sample over a longer time period and confirmed Maizels' findings.

These findings also agree with those of Knudsen and Parnes (1975) who argued their case in the PIH framework, suggesting that export earnings tend to be subject to greater variations, making the share of transitory income in export earnings greater than that of other components of GDP. Hence countries with a higher export ratio will also tend to have a higher savings ratio as well.

Income distribution Both the LCH and the neo-Keynesian models make the aggregate savings ratio depend on the distribution of income between labour and property income. But the expectations with respect to the direction of the influence of the income distribution on the savings ratio differ, and empirical evidence has been rather unsuccessful in settling this matter.

Age structure The LCH also suggested the age structure of the population as an explanatory variable. There is weak evidence that older households save more and that countries with higher dependency ratios and thus with a relatively young population, save less.

Interest rates In a neo-classical framework, one would expect the 'price' of capital (that is, the rate of interest) to have an effect on saving and investment. In Chapter 1 the financial repression school was discussed, which asserted that financial liberalization (that is an increase in the real interest rate) would increase financial savings and might also increase aggregate savings. An increase in the rate of interest has two effects: firstly, it increases the present value of wealth, which has a positive effect on current consumption; and, secondly, it leads to substitution between current and future consumption, which has a negative impact on current consumption. These contradictory effects make it difficult to make theoretical statements on the effect of interest rate changes on aggregate consumption and saving. Empirical studies do not help in determining which of these effects dominates.

Mikesell and Zinser (1973) reviewed a number of studies and observed that many of them suffer from econometric problems. They noted that some of them conclude to a positive relationship between saving and the rate of interest and others to a negative one.

Gupta (1984) provided a more up to date survey. He concluded that 'while there is some evidence of a positive effect of the real interest rate on aggregate savings, the findings so far are too conflicting to warrant a definitive statement'. His own estimates, based on data on a set of Asian countries, did not help much. In the regressions trying to explain aggregate savings, the impact of the real interest rate was often statistically insignificant and, when it was significant, as often positive as negative (Gupta 1984, pp. 107, 108).

Using a set of pooled time-series data for seven Asian countries, Fry (1980) found a generally significant positive coefficient for the real deposit rate for most of his countries. Giovannini (1983) criticized Fry's results. He argued that the outcomes are sensitive to changes in the sample size. If two extreme values are eliminated, the significance of the coefficient of the real interest rate disappears. When he re-ran the regression on the same seven countries but extended the sample period to include more recent years, the sign of the real interest rate coefficient reversed and became negative, though insignificant.

It is also interesting to observe that, in his Nobel Prize lecture, Modigliani stated as his 'personal view that s (ratio of aggregate savings to income) is largely independent of the interest rate' (Modigliani 1986, p. 304).

Bhalla (1978) argued that the interest rate more generally reflects returns on investment opportunities. He made a direct estimate of the (physical) investment opportunities of farm households in India by measuring their access to high-yielding varieties. He found that poor households with such opportunities save more, but rich households less. This is explained by the fact that these rich households have access to credit markets, where they can obtain the funds to finance the investment. The wealth effect of the expected higher future income induces such households to save less with the prospect of profitable investment opportunities.

Financial development   These findings of Bhalla already indicate a possible role for financial development, which could stimulate savings in that it makes available more and more attractive saving instruments. But as with the interest rate, this may also reduce savings if the greater expected return or the lesser risk on the assets stimulates consumption.

In Chapter 1 the question was raised as to whether financial development induces an increase in overall savings or only a reallocation of existing wealth. Some research has been done on the relationship between financial development and the savings ratio. Wai (1972) found a positive relationship in some countries or regions, but not in all. Gupta (1984) criticized these results for improper specification of the equations. Gupta himself performed some simple tests comparing trends in the Financial Intermediation Ratio[9] and the ratio of private savings to private disposable income, and trends in the ratio of financial savings to real savings and the private savings ratio. The expected positive relationship exists in some cases, but no general and clear conclusion emerged. Gupta also estimated a saving function for nine Asian countries in which the level of financial development was one of the explanatory variables. In only four of these cases was the coefficient of this variable significant: in two cases it had a negative sign and in two cases a positive sign. Other regression results of Gupta also suggested that financial savings and real savings are substitutes, so that with a higher level of financial development and with higher real deposit rates of interest, the share of financial savings increases (Gupta 1984).

Inflation The post-Keynesian approach gave rise to the expectation that the rate of inflation would influence the savings ratio. Thirlwall (1974b) suggested two mechanisms through which inflation can stimulate savings. The first is the income redistribution towards profits, discussed in Chapter 1. The second is the inflation tax on money holdings. If the government increases the money supply to pay for its expenditures, prices will rise and private money balances will lose value. This forced tax shifts control over real resources from the private to the public sector, but it does not affect saving directly. The effect on saving occurs when one assumes that the private sector has a stable demand for real money balances, so that inflation which reduces the real balances leads to increased saving to restore them.

Howard (1978) argued that for private savers, unexpected inflation increases the uncertainty with which real income is expected. Increased savings would be one way to cope with this uncertainty. Inflation also reduces the value of real wealth, and this may result in reduced consumption.

Empirical findings have not been able to establish a clear relationship between inflation and saving. Weber (1975) failed to find a significant impact on the basis of US data. Howard (1978) argued that one has to look at unexpected inflation only, as people can take action against expected inflation. He did this and indeed found a positive relationship.

Thirlwall tested the relationship between savings and inflation but he failed to find significant results (Thirlwall 1974a, 1974b). He argued that the reasons for this may be that different countries may react differently to inflation - so that cross-country comparisons fail to lead to significant results - and that inflation may have different causes. The post-Keynesian theory argues that demand-induced inflation will lead to redistribution of income. In reality, inflation often has other causes (e.g. increased import prices), and domestic reactions to this may well have opposite effects on the income distribution. This makes it difficult to test the neo-Keynesian model on the basis of observed inflation.

In empirical studies of aggregate saving behaviour, the rate of inflation (or the expected rate of inflation) is often introduced together with the nominal rate of interest to establish the effect of the real rate of interest on aggregate savings.

Since in most countries, the nominal interest rate is administratively controlled and changed infrequently, most of the variation in the real interest rate is due to fluctuations in the rate of inflation. To a considerable extent, therefore, the conclusion reached above, that the real rate of interest cannot be shown to have a significant impact on aggregate savings, can be taken to imply that there is no relationship between the rate of inflation and aggregate savings.

The failure to show convincingly a relationship between inflation and saving does not imply that the assumptions underlying the neo-Keynesian theories are unrealistic. There may well be a differential saving behaviour related to different types of income. But there are good reasons to accept that in LDCs, credit-financed investments may not be able to shift the income distribution very much. Three points seem relevant here.

The first is that credit-financed investment in the modern sector of the economy has a high import component, as capital goods are not locally produced. So much of the demand pressure leaks away immediately through imports, without causing much inflation domestically. A second point is that a large share of investments is in the public sector. The resulting inflationary pressure are felt in commodity and factor markets by workers and capitalists. It is, a priori, unclear what the effect on the income distribution will be. It could be that the increase in public investment will crowd out private investment through the claims it lays on available foreign exchange, construction capacity, etc. The fall in private investment may have a negative influence on private savings. Thirdly and finally, when excess demand results in balance-of-payments problems, import controls are the usual response. The subsequent fall in consumption may be a form of forced savings, but the lack of foreign exchange could also undermine any further investment plans the capitalists may have, that is they may find it difficult to 'realize' their profits.

The rate of growth   Both the LCH and the PIH establish a link between the savings ratio and the rate of economic growth. In fact, the LCH predicts that in an economy with a zero growth rate and a stable population, the savings ratio is zero, as saving by those who work is balanced by the dissaving of the retired (Modigliani 1986). The PIH argues that in a growing economy, the share of transitory income is larger, as estimates of permanent income follow growth with a lag, and hence the savings ratio is higher.

The link between the rate of growth and the savings ratio, though, is not unique to neo-classical saving theories. In the post-Keynesian analysis, a higher investment ratio, which together with a constant capital-output ratio, results in a higher growth rate, also leads to an increase in the profit share and thus an increase in the savings ratio. Even using a very simple saving theory, whereby savings are determined by the level of income, they would be sensitive to the rate of growth if changes in income were to lead to changes in consumption only after an adjustment lag.

Empirical tests lend strong support to the rate of growth as a determinant of the savings ratio (Mikesell and Zinser 1973; Modigliani 1986), but these results should not be claimed as strong evidence in favour of any particular saving theory, because almost all the saving theories discussed could accommodate such a relationship.

Foreign capital inflows The hypothesis that an increase in the inflow of foreign capital may have a negative effect on domestic saving was discussed in section 1.3 of Chapter 1. A few tests were reported there that supported the hypothesis.

This list of variables that have emerged from the theoretical discussions and empirical testing of saving behaviour may be useful as a background for the brief review of attempts made by other authors to estimate an aggregate saving function for Thailand.

3.2.6 Some aggregate saving functions for Thailand

Attempts have been made from a number of theoretical perspectives to explain the aggregate saving behaviour in Thailand.

Gupta estimated the following equation for the period 1960–77:

$$(10) \quad S = -2.520 + 0.23\ Y^p + 0.20\ Y^t + 0.06\ p^e - 0.06\ p^u$$
$$(1.57) \quad (35.82) \quad (128.28) \quad (2.50) \quad (2.43)$$
$$+ 0.01\ i_d - 41.25\ FIR + 2.08\ VE$$
$$(0.07) \quad (3.16) \quad (2.70)$$

$R^2 = 0.999$; D.W. = 2.20; between brackets t-values

S = aggregate national savings deflated by the consumer price index

Y^p and Y^t = permanent and transitory real GNP respectively

p^e and p^u = expected and unexpected inflation respectively

i_d = the nominal deposit rate on 12-month deposits

FIR = financial intermediation ratio (see note 14, Chapter 1)

VE = uncertainty index, related to fluctuations in the rate of inflation (Gupta 1984, p. 107).

These results contain a number of surprising elements. The coefficient of transitory income is slightly lower than that of permanent income. This conflicts with the PIH's expectations and with the results obtained in many other studies. Another surprise is the highly significant negative coefficient for the financial development variable, FIR. It is likely that the negative sign is caused by the intercorrelation between FIR and real GNP, both of which have a strongly increasing trend. Such multicollinearity undermines confidence in the regression results. The effects of expected and unexpected inflation on aggregate savings seem to be small.[10] It is not surprising that the coefficient of the nominal deposit rate is insignificant: there have been very few changes in the level of the deposit rate during the period. Taking these observations into account, the only conclusion that seems to emerge from equation (10) is that the strongest determinant of aggregate savings is GNP, a rather obvious result.

Go (1984) provided a more useful formulation of the regression equation

(11) $S/Y = 0.2861 - 0.0023\ (i_d - p) + 0.0044\ g + 0.003\ y$

   (11.68)   (4.93)   (3.43)   (5.19)

               $- 0.2367\ F/Y - 0.7492\ B/N$
               (1.41)   (4.99)

$R^2 = 0.84;\ D.W. = 1.81$

y = level of real GDP

F/Y = foreign savings (current account deficit/GDP)

B/N = number of bank branches per 10,000 population (Go 1984, p. 120).

Go found a significant but negative relationship with the real deposit rate. Once again, the financial development variable also has a negative sign. The author suspected that this was due to intercorrelation with y. As expected the growth rate has a strong positive impact and the availability of foreign savings has a negative impact on domestic savings.

This latter effect is also analysed by Vongvipanond for the period 1960–78:

(12) $S = - 6.163 + 0.27\ y - 0.425\ F$
           (3.695)(18.96)   (2.27)

$R^2 = 0.98;\ D.W. = 1.34$

S = real domestic savings

y = real GDP

F = real foreign savings

(Vongvipanond 1980, p. 9).

Go cited the results of a two-stage least-square regression performed by Fry on Thai data covering the period 1961–81:

(13) $S/Y = -0.197 + 0.332(i_d - p^e) + 0.092TT - 0.553F/Y -$

           (1.70)   (1.91)   (2.50)   (2.03)
           $- 7.802D + 0.636g + 0.677(S/Y)_{(t-1)}$
           (2.81)   (3.63)   (6.08)

$R^2 = 0.80;\ D.W. = 2.98$

S/Y = national savings/GNP

F/Y = foreign savings/GNP

TT = log of the external terms of trade

g = growth rate of real GNP

D = dependency ratio

(Go 1984, p. 122).

The results obtained on the impact of foreign savings and of the growth rate conform to those of other studies. By contrast with Go's findings, the real deposit rate now has a positive impact. It is interesting that the international terms of trade emerge as one of the variables explaining saving behaviour. The precise definition of the terms used is not stated in the text, but presumably it was some index formed by dividing export prices by import prices. In the analysis of saving behaviour in section 3.3 export prices will also play an important role.

As the period covered in these regressions is more or less the same, one would expect similar results, but that is not the case. Only the growth rate and foreign savings have the expected sign in all the equations in which they are introduced. The dependency ratio, introduced in only one equation, also has the expected negative sign. The indicator of financial development has an unexpected negative sign in the equations in which it is included. And the results on the role of the rate of interest and the rate of inflation are mixed. Go and Fry found significant coefficients, but with opposite signs, for the real deposit rate. As the nominal deposit rate has changed very little, this variable mainly reflects the impact of inflation; Go therefore suggested a positive impact of the rate of inflation on the savings ratio, whereas Fry suggested a negative one. Gupta's findings cannot be compared because he used a rather unsatisfactory formulation of expected and unexpected inflation and its variability. It is very surprising that his regression suggests a lower saving propensity for transitory income.

These mixed findings suggest that the results of the aggregate saving function are very sensitive to the variables included in the regression and to their definitions. The rather diverse set of variables included in the various regressions also suggests the lack of a consistent theoretical framework from which regression equations may be derived. There is a tendency to lump together variables suggested in various approaches and just see what comes out.

A point which was mentioned earlier and will be developed further is that aggregate savings are made up of the savings of different economic groups. The saving behaviour of such groups may be sensitive to quite different variables, or it may react in opposite ways to a change in a given variable. If that is so, it is not surprising that attempts to explain the savings of all groups lumped together fail to come to a very meaningful conclusion.

3.3 Domestic savings disaggregated

3.3.1 Introduction

The theories of saving and the empirical evidence discussed in section 3.2 have not contributed much to a better understanding of saving behaviour in LDCs. It is possible that the failure to explain aggregate savings is due to the fact that these are made up of a number of elements that are relatively independent, which means that changes in one component may be cancelled out by changes in another. In order to understand the whole one must understand the

101

constituent parts. The aggregate savings in an economy are made up of the savings from many individual economic units, each of which is likely to face quite different conditions, and whose saving behaviour may be determined by quite different factors. Would it be possible to form a number of groups of units with relatively homogeneous conditions and behaviour, for which one could explain saving behaviour? The possible disaggregations were already indicated previously: one could disaggregate savings by the type of income from which they are made (wages and profits) or by the type of institution that does the saving (corporations, households, government). In the LCH theory, an economic unit receives current labour income and property income. In the post-Keynesian theory, the two types of income are received, in principle, by different types of economic units: wage-earners and entrepreneurs. In industrialized countries there may be a considerable overlap in the breakdowns by type of income and by institution, with corporations earning profit income and households earning predominantly wage income. But in LDCs the worker/capitalist distinction is less pervasive because much of the labour force is still in self-employment. The household sector there contains a large component of unincorporated firms earning profits.

National Accounts generally break down total savings into savings by households and unincorporated enterprises (h), by corporations (c) and by government (g). As a result the overall average propensity to save S/Y can be broken down into:

$$(14) \quad \frac{S}{Y} = \frac{S_h}{Y_h} \cdot \frac{Y_h}{Y} + \frac{S_c}{Y_c} \cdot \frac{Y_c}{Y} + \frac{S_g}{Y_g} \cdot \frac{Y_g}{Y}$$

in which the average saving propensities of the various groups are weighted with their income shares. If the APS of each group is different, the aggregated APS can change when, firstly, the APS of any of the groups changes or secondly, the income shares change.

This presentation suggests a search for the determinants of the saving propensities of the household, the corporate and the government sectors. But seeking separate determinants for each sector is justified only if the saving decisions of the units in these sectors are relatively independent of each other. The saving theories discussed above analyse saving behaviour as a choice between consumption and saving. However, a significant share of total savings originates from economic units that engage hardly at all in consumption, that is the corporations. The neo-classical saving theories normally look at total private savings (taking households and corporations together) as they assume that households own the shares in the corporations and that corporations decide on profit retention and investment so as to maximize the utility of the owners. In the end, therefore, when the utility-maximizing household decides on consumption and saving, it incorporates all forms of current income, wealth and expected future incomes into its considerations. In such a perspective, the saving decisions of households and corporations are closely related and offer no scope for separate analysis.

It has been pointed out that the modern corporation has separated ownership and management. Management controls strategic decisions with the aim of maximizing corporate objectives (for example, growth of sales or of market share) in ways that need not always correspond to the interests of the owners or even to the rules of utility maximization (Berle and Means 1967; Galbraith 1967). Of course, one could still maintain that the corporate retentions enter the consumption function of the shareholding households.

In LDCs, however, the ownership of corporate shares is generally less anonymous and the separation of ownership and management is less advanced. A relatively small number of wealthy families may own and manage most of the corporate sector. This in itself would suggest that there is less scope for separating the household from the corporate sector. But on the other hand, this small number of families would hardly be representative of the large majority of households, nor would it necessarily generate most of the household savings, as the savings made by their corporations are retained in the corporate sector. Most households in LDCs, and certainly in Thailand, are engaged in production on their own farms or in their own firms in the unincorporated sector of the economy.

To this one could add that in many LDCs a significant part of the corporate sector is made up of subsidiaries of multinationals. Even if their retention behaviour were to aim at maximizing utility of owning households, the households in question would be elsewhere. Also the profits generated by state enterprises can not be readily related to household consumption and saving decisions.

The profits of unincorporated household firms should not be simply added to the profits of large corporations, as is done for example in the LCH. The conditions under which production takes place and profits are earned differ vastly between small household firms and large corporations. The household firms are small; they rely on the exploitation of family labour; they have limited access to credit and they are price takers on both input and output markets. The large corporations have price setting powers and so can influence the size of their surplus. They also have easy access to domestic or foreign credit.

The conditions under which the corporations and the household firms earn their incomes are thus vastly different and it is likely that these differences also affect their saving behaviour. There are therefore good analytical and statistical reasons for separating the household from the corporate sector in the analysis of saving behaviour. To do this, the next section will start by looking at household savings.

3.3.2 Household savings

It is important to recognize that household savings estimates, as given in

National Accounts, rest on a weak statistical assumption. Household savings are estimated as the residual between household income and expenditure and are therefore sensitive to measurement errors in both. The National Accounts split income received by households into:

(a)   compensation of employees (wages)
(b)   income from farms
(c)   income from professions and other unincorporated enterprises
(d)   income from property (rent, interest, dividends).

Household savings are only available in aggregated form and cannot be broken down in this way. However, a fundamental characteristic of households in LDCs is the lesser degree of specialization; most households receive income from various sources (for example, from farm work and from wage labour) and make no distinction between the sources in their consumption and saving decisions. On the other hand, one would expect one type of income to be dominant in the case of most households and, on that basis, attempts have been made to identify the income sources of household savings.

Friend and Kravis (1957) provided early evidence, based on household survey data of the USA, that entrepreneurial households account for two-thirds to three-quarters of all household savings and use much of these savings (that is about half) to invest in their own enterprises.

Houthakker (1965) ran a regression on pooled National Accounts data for 28 rich and poor countries covering the period 1953–59 and concluded that the marginal propensity to save out of income from employment is lower than that out of other personal income.

Kelley and Williamson (1968) used household survey data on Indonesia to establish the same point. They ran the simple saving function $S_h/N = a + b\, Y_h/N$ for various socio-economic groups separately and found that the estimate for b, the marginal propensity to save, differs significantly. They found as estimate of b:

Farmers	0.107
Traders and craftsmen	0.426
Owners of businesses	0.308
Government employees	0.048
Other wage-earners	0.111

Cornia and Jerger (1982) drew on household survey data on ten countries to run, for each country, the regression

(15) $C_h = a + b\, YL + c\, YSE + d\, RI + e\, SS + f\, DU$

C_h = household consumption per capita
YL = wage and salary income per capita

104

YSE = income from self-employment per capita
RI = income from rent, interest and other capital earnings per capita
SS = pensions, social benefits and other transfers per capita
DU = dummy: 1 for rural households, 0 for urban households.

Concentrating on their results for the six LDCs in their study, it can be observed that the estimates of the coefficients differ considerably between countries. When one tries to find central tendencies, the following pattern emerges: the average value for b is 0.77, for c it is 0.49, for d it is 1.05, and for e it is 0.97. The coefficient of the dummy is always negative, suggesting a higher saving propensity for rural households. The range around these averages is very wide though, reflecting differences in economic conditions between the countries and probably also differences in coverage by and definitions in the surveys. The estimate for the coefficients d and e suffer particularly from wide ranges, which makes use of the averages given above questionable. But the results confirm quite convincingly the findings of Houthakker and Kelley and Williamson, that the propensity to save out of wage and salary income is smaller than that out of self-employment income; the value of c is smaller than that of b in five of the six LDCs covered. In fact, the value estimated for b is quite low; it suggests an average MPS for the six countries of 0.23, which is higher than the estimates suggested for wage-earners by Houthakker and Kelley and Williamson. The MPS of the self-employed is also higher than that suggested in other studies. The estimate of the MPS out of rental income, which even suggests dissaving, could be explained from a LCH perspective; it could also be explained by tendencies towards conspicuous consumption by the landlord class (Lewis 1954). In drawing conclusions from Cornia and Jerger's study it should be recalled that the figures presented above are averages calculated from six country regressions with wide differences between the countries, so they may be poor indicators of central tendencies.

One of the countries covered by Cornia and Jerger is Thailand. Using a 1973 sample of 1668 urban and rural households, they came to the following result:

(16) $C_h = 79.9 + 0.73$ YL $+ 0.34$ YSE $+ 1.80$ (RI+SS) -16.6 DU
       (7.5) (3.6)   (2.3)   (3.9)   (1.7)
$R^2 = 0.94$; D.W. $= 1.5$

These results fit the overall picture described previously and suggest that self-employed households have a considerably higher saving propensity than wage-earning households, and rural households a higher propensity than urban households.

As has already been observed, National Income accounts split household income into income received from employment, from self-employment (either on farms or in professions or other unincorporated enterprises) and from

105

property. This breakdown may be used to apply time series data to an equation like (15) or (16) above.

Running equation (15) on time-series data in nominal terms or logarithms of the variables would give problems of multicollinearity, because all the variables increase over time. To deal with that problem, equation (17) uses first differences of the logarithms (which is equivalent to growth rates) over the period 1961–86.

$$(17) \quad \Delta \ln S_h = -0.76 \ \Delta \ln YL + 0.68 \ \Delta \ln YP + 1.44 \ \Delta \ln YSE$$

$$ \quad \quad \quad (1.542) \quad \quad \quad (1.273) \quad \quad (3.064)$$
$$R^2 = 0.44; D.W. = 2.36$$

For the period 1969–86, it is possible to break down YSE into income received from self-employment on farms (YF), and income from self-employment in professions and other unincorporated enterprise (YNF).

$$(18) \quad \Delta \ln S_h = -0.60 \ \Delta \ln YL + 0.72 \ \Delta \ln YP + 0.89 \ \Delta \ln YF + 0.27 \ \Delta \ln YNF$$

$$ \quad \quad \quad (0.911) \quad \quad (0.956) \quad \quad (2.067) \quad \quad \quad (0.571)$$
$$R^2 = 0.40; D.W. = 2.40$$

The statistical results are not very satisfactory as most of the coefficients are not significantly different from zero and the R^2 is never high. Still, equations (17) and (18) strongly suggest that variations in household savings are determined mainly by variations in incomes from self-employed activities and, in particular, by variations in farm income. This finding confirms the evidence from household surveys discussed above and gives further support to the approach followed in this study in which household savings are interpreted as retained profits of household firms.

The negative coefficient for $\Delta \ln YL$, which is marginally significant in equation (17), is unexpected; there seems to be no reason why an increase in wage income should lead to a fall in household savings. An explanation will be suggested in section 3.3.3, where it will be shown that this finding further supports the interpretation that household savings are retained profits. As wages are a cost to the household firm, an increase in wages leads to a fall in profits.

In 1980, total household income was composed of 31 per cent wage income, 13 per cent property income, and 56 per cent self-employment income (20 per cent farm and 36 per cent non-farm); one could even suggest, therefore, that most of the household savings originate from self-employed households. In fact, data on household savings from the 1981 Socio-Economic Survey have been broken down by economic status of the household to show that about three quarters of total household savings came from self-employed households. Farmers and entrepreneurial households have the highest saving propensities (Siricharoengseng 1987).

106

The results of equations (17) and (18) may also be compared to the results of Cornia and Jerger (see equation (16)), which are based on household survey data. Given the different sources of data and the differences in the specification of the equations, the coefficients cannot be directly compared, but both results confirm the high saving propensity of self-employed households.

TDRI (1986) reported an alternative formulation for the period 1961–85:

$$(19) \quad \frac{S_h}{Y_h} = 0.84 - 0.26 \, \frac{YNA}{Y} - 0.51 \, \frac{YP}{Y_u} - 1.12 \frac{P14}{P} + 0.001 i_d$$

$$\quad\quad (2.7) \quad (1.9) \quad\quad\quad (3.2) \quad\quad (2.4) \quad\quad\quad (0.5)$$

$$\quad + 0.004 t_i + 0.0022 y_h$$

$$\quad\quad (0.4) \quad\quad (5.7)$$

$R^2 = 0.85$

S_h/Y_h = household savings over disposable income

YNA/Y = share of non-agricultural GDP in total GDP

YP/Y_u = household income from property over household income from unincorporated enterprises

P14/P = proportion of population below 14 years

i_d = deposit rate of interest and t_i = interest income tax

y_h = growth rate nominal household income

In an *ad hoc* manner, equation (19) combines a large number of quite different variables. In this place, our main interest is in the variables dealing with the sectoral origin of income. The findings of equations (17) and (18) are confirmed: the household savings ratio in equation (19) varies positively with the share of agriculture in GDP and with the share of unincorporated sector income in total household income.

Could these results be interpreted then as support for the post-Keynesian hypothesis, according to which savings are made out of entrepreneurial incomes? The answer is yes, but only in an indirect way. The main share of the income of households originates from self-employed activities and is therefore combined labour and property income. It is possible, of course, to separate artificially an imputed labour income share, as was done by, for example, Modigliani and Tarantelli (1975). But such a separation is really artificial and the households involved are unlikely to make such a distinction.

The main point is that self-employed households have different saving and investment opportunities and incentives. Clearly, a large number of self-employed households earn very low incomes that are hardly sufficient to cover subsistence needs, let alone to save. As was observed in Chapter 2 about three-quarters of all households in Thailand are self-employed. But incomes in the household sector are quite concentrated. Krongkaew gave estimates of the concentration in money income for all types of households in 1972: the 10 per cent with the highest incomes earned 48 per cent of all household money income; the top 20 per cent earned 64 per cent; and the top 40 per cent earned 83 per cent of all money incomes (Krongkaew 1980, p. 22). One could assume that the top of the income distribution is made up of mainly self-employed households. It is clear that even among these self-employed households, the saving potential is highly concentrated.

If the findings of so many household survey studies and of the above regressions are to be taken seriously, then the applicability of standard saving theories to LDCs must be questioned. These theories see the household as a consumption unit engaged in maximizing its utility. But household savings in LDCs typically originate from households that are simultaneously a production and consumption unit, and the factors pertaining to production may well be dominant in explaining saving behaviour. Of course, among the large number of self-employed households there are many that can hardly make ends meet (for example marginal farmers) and who save little, if at all. This may apply even more to the households that are largely dependent on wage income. The self-employed households that are somewhat better off will have slightly higher incomes from their family firm, which allow them to make some savings. They are likely to have strong incentives for saving, because the firm always faces an uncertain future and needs funds for investment and working capital; and their access to other sources of funds (for example, banks) may be limited, or such other sources may be expensive (for example, money-lenders). It may be appropriate, therefore, to look at the household saving behaviour from the perspective of the household as a production rather than a consumption unit.

3.3.3 A model for household savings

In this study the productive sector of the Thai economy is split into two segments: the corporate and the unincorporated sector. The unincorporated sector consists of small household firms, which use family labour and hire labour casually or on a limited scale. These firms operate on highly competitive markets and are price takers. In Chapter 2 it was shown that these firms are found mainly in the agricultural, trade and services sectors.

If household savings originate predominantly from self-employed households, these savings could be interpreted as retained profits from unincorporated enterprises, and the household savings ratio could be interpreted as the profit share of the unincorporated sector.

(20) $S_h = PR_u$ and

(21) $S_h/Y_u = PR_u/Y_u$

PR_u = the operating surplus of the unincorporated sector
Y_u = GDP of the unincorporated sector (as defined in Chapter 2).

108

The operating surplus is the difference between the proceeds of sales and the cost of inputs. The prices of the outputs of unincorporated firms are determined on competitive markets. Their inputs consist of labour, intermediate inputs obtained from the corporate sector and the cost of credit.

$$(22) \quad PR_u = p_u Q_u - (w L_u + p_c INT_u + i_u CR_u)$$

p_u, w, p_c, i_u = price of output of the unincorporated sector, the wage rate, the price of input obtained from the corporate sector, and the cost of credit to the unincorporated sector, respectively.

Q_u, L_u, INT_u, and CR_u = total volume of output, and the volumes of input of labour, intermediate inputs and credit used in production. The total wage cost wL_u should be broadly interpreted not only as the payment for hired labour but also the imputed cost of family labour. This latter component may be assumed to be equal to the consumption needs of the household. It is assumed that the unincorporated sector obtains all its intermediate inputs from the corporate sector, so that the price level in the corporate sector can be used to indicate their cost. The appropriate interest rate may be that of the unregulated money market on which household firms may to a large extent depend.

Equation (22) may be turned into a profit share by dividing it by the GDP of the unincorporated sector. Dividing by $Y_u = p_u y_u$ gives:

$$(23) \quad \frac{PR_u}{p_u y_u} = \frac{p_u Q_u}{p_u y_u} - \frac{w L_u}{p_u y_u} - \frac{p_c INT_u}{p_u y_u} - \frac{i_u CR_u}{p_u y_u}$$

This equation makes the profit share of the unincorporated sector dependent on a set of (relative) prices and on a set of technological coefficients. These technological coefficients are likely to change over a period of 25 years, but it may be assumed that in the unincorporated sector the change is limited. In Thailand growth in the agricultural sector, the dominant part of the unincorporated sector, has been due to the extension of acreage rather than to gains in productivity. In sectors like trade and services there may also be limited scope for technological progress. Hence it may be acceptable to assume that the technological coefficients in equation (23) have remained largely unchanged over time, so that the fluctuations in the profit share depend mainly on the changes in output and input prices. This relationship may be tested using the following equation:

$$(24) \quad S_h/Y_u = a_1 - a_2\, w - a_3\, p_c - a_4\, i_u + a_5\, p_u$$

The profit share in (24) is approximated by expressing total household savings as a proportion of GDP of the unincorporated sector (as defined in Chapter 2). The resulting profit share Sh/Yu is shown in Chart 3.1. Equation (24) cannot be directly estimated: there are no systematic and complete time series data on wages in Thailand from which a wage cost index could be derived. To form an indirect indicator of wage pressures, an index WP has been calculated by

109

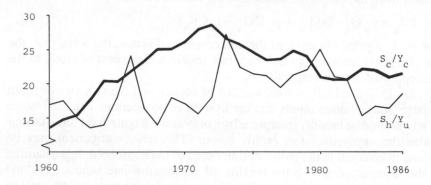

Chart 3.1   Profit shares (percentages)

taking deviations of the wage share in National Income from its trend value. Positive values for that index indicate a relatively high level of employment and/or wages, and probably both as these two may be connected.

The variable i_u is the cost of credit for the unincorporated sector. One would expect this sector to be dependent to a significant degree on the unregulated money market. No systematic data are available on the lending cost on that market. As an alternative, i_u has been replaced by i_l, the effective lending cost on the official money market. This would be justified if i_u and i_l are related in the sense that the lending cost on the unregulated market would follow the lending cost at the official market, albeit with a significant mark-up. The prices p_u and p_c are given by the rate of change in the GDP deflators for the two sectors.

Equation (24) in this adjusted form has been used for regression analysis over the period 1963–86. The result is:

(25) $S_h/Y_u = 9.92 - 1.10\, WP - 0.15\, p_c + 0.70\, i_l + 0.32\, p_u$

        (3.615) (3.085)   (1.117)   (2.655) (3.988)

$R^2 = 0.75$; D.W. = 2.09

The results show a strong positive relationship between output prices, as reflected by the GDP deflator p_u, and the savings ratio. Among the input costs only the wage pressure index is statistically significant, with the expected sign. Garnjarerndee (1981) also drew attention to the negative relationship between household savings and the wage share. He calculated the average household

110

savings ratio (household savings as a percentage of GNP) for four periods, 1961/66, 1967/71, 1972/76 and 1977/80, and compared these to the average of the wage share (total wage and salary income as percentage of GDP). In the periods when the household savings ratio was high, the wage share was relatively low. In the other periods, when the savings ratio was low, the wage share was relatively high. Garnjarerndee explained this by the fact that wage-earners are likely to have a higher propensity to consume than other income-earners. The analysis above and the regression results contained in equation (25) suggest that these trends may also be explained by the cost element in wages in the unincorporated enterprises that cannot so easily pass on wage and cost-of-living increases into their prices.

The coefficient of p_c, the cost of inputs from the corporate sector, has the right sign but is not significant. This may mean that the unincorporated sector does not use many inputs, but there is a statistical problem in that there is a correlation between the two price deflators, p_u and p_c. The interest cost variable has the wrong sign and is significant. This is difficult to explain from our perspective. It also runs counter to other findings (see for example equation (19) above) which often fail to find a significant effect for the interest rate. One needs to remember that the interest rate on which data are available is an inadequate indicator or real credit cost and changes only infrequently. Omit-

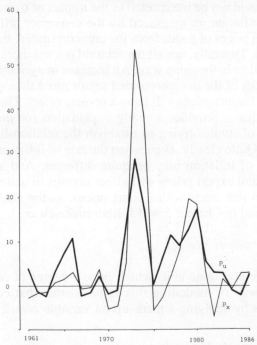

Chart 3.2   Export prices and GDP deflator unincorporated sector (annual rates of change %)

111

ting the input price and the interest rate variables from the equation does not change the values of the other coefficients very much, nor does it improve the overall fit of the regression.

The result, that household savings are strongly dependent on output prices, has important consequences. In the case of Thailand, the dominant output prices are those in the agricultural sector, and as most agricultural products are also exported, world market prices are a major factor in determining domestic prices. In Chart 3.2 the pattern of change in the deflator of the unincorporated sector (p_u) is plotted next to the changes in export prices (p_x), and the similarity is striking.

Knudsen and Parnes (1975) have used a permanent income hypothesis framework, in the context of an analysis of export instability in LDCs, to suggest that instability in export earnings can easily have the effect of increasing domestic savings. Equation (25) provides only provisional support for the Knudsen and Parnes hypothesis as other categories of savings, such as government or corporate savings, may also be sensitive to changes in export prices. Therefore, the effect on aggregate savings cannot be determined yet, but it will be clear that fluctuations in export prices can have a major impact on a significant component of aggregate savings.[11]

The large and significant impact of p_u on savings, as indicated in the regression results, should not be interpreted as the impact of overall inflation on savings. Overall inflation, as measured by the consumer price index, is made up of changes in prices of goods from the unincorporated, the corporate and the public sectors. Typically, not all the sectoral price indices move over time at the same speed or in the same way. An increase in agricultural export prices affects the prices of the unincorporated sector more than those of the corporate sector. The import prices will have a reverse effect. The advantage of equation (25) is that it provides a ready explanation for the poor and contradictory results of studies trying to establish the relationship between inflation and saving. Quite clearly, even when the rate of inflation is exactly the same, the nature of inflation may be quite different. And an inflation starting with agricultural export prices will affect savings in quite a different way than an inflation that starts with import prices, as the analysis in the subsequent sections and in Chapter 5 will further make clear.

3.3.4 A model for corporate savings

Corporations are large economic units which have a degree of price-setting market power. One way of modelling this is to assume that corporations determine their prices by applying a mark-up on variable cost. *Ex ante*, the price is set as:

$$(26) \quad p_c = C / \hat{Q}_c + (1+z)\{wl_c + p_m m + i_l cr_c\}$$

in which

112

p_c = unit price of output of the corporate sector
C^c = total fixed cost
$\hat{Q}_c$ = expected output
z = mark-up rate
w = wage rate
p_m = price of imported inputs
i_1 = loan rate of interest
$\hat{}$: a cap over a variable refers to a desired or expected value and l_c, m, and cr_c are the volumes of labour, imported inputs and bank credit per unit of output.

On this basis, expected profits ($\hat{PR}_c$) are:

(27) $\hat{PR}_c = p_c \hat{Q}_c - C - \{wl_c + p_m m + i_1 cr_c\} \hat{Q}_c$

or:

(27a) $\hat{PR}_c = z\{wl_c + p_m m + i_1 cr_c\} \hat{Q}_c$

The expected value added of the corporate sector is defined as:

(28) $p_c \hat{y}_c = p_c \hat{Q}_c - C - p_m m \hat{Q}_c - i_1 cr_c \hat{Q}_c$

and the expected profit share $\hat{PS}$ is:

(29) $\hat{PS}_c = \dfrac{\hat{PR}_c}{p_c \hat{y}_c} = \dfrac{z(wl_c + p_m m + i_1 cr_c)}{p_c - C/\hat{Q}_c - p_m m - i_1 cr_c}$

The main determinant of the profit share is, of course, the level at which the mark-up, z, is fixed. The corporations decide on their prices by taking into account the long-run goals of the firm and its market conditions. In line with Eichner (1973, 1985) and Wood (1975) it is assumed here that the aim of the corporation is to maximize growth of sales. The mark-up is set so that it will generate the savings that can finance the investments necessary to generate that growth. However, in setting the mark-up the corporations face a number of constraints, of which three are particularly relevant:

(a) The possible growth of sales is constrained by the overall growth of aggregate demand in the economy. In a fast-growing economy like Thailand's this may not have been a big constraint in most years, but the slowdown in growth in recent years has been considerable.

(b) More importantly, the level of the mark-up is constrained by the degree of competition. Too high profit levels may reduce sales or may invite entry of competitors. In LDCs domestic markets are often protected against foreign competition by tariffs, and the small size of the market and other government regulations may reduce the degree of competition even further. This was no doubt the case in Thailand in the 1960s, but gradually a more open economic policy has been pursued, and significant parts of the corporate sector are becoming more and more oriented towards export

113

markets. So, the average degree of monopoly may have fallen, even though it is impossible to find a good indicator of the degree of monopoly that could be used in empirical testing.

(c) The need to generate own finance is also dependent on the availability and cost of external finance. If domestic and foreign credit is readily available and cheap, there will be less need to generate own finance. One could argue that firms have a long-term view about the financing structure they prefer. It has been observed that corporations in LDCs tend to have a high debt–equity ratio: for example, medium- and large-scale firms in Thailand have debt–equity ratios (defined as total liabilities divided by net worth) ranging from 3:1 to 4:1 (World Bank 1983b, p. 31). A number of reasons have been suggested for this high indebtedness, such as: (a) narrow equity markets which make it difficult to raise share capital; (b) the tendency of foreign capital to come as debt rather than equity capital; (c) corporate savings which, at early stages of development and at times of rapid growth, are inadequate with respect to investment needs; and (d) the narrow share market, which may also make equity capital relatively expensive. As the narrow market makes it unlikely that one can make capital gains on shares, dividend payments have to be high to make up (see World Bank 1983b; Sundararajan 1985).

It could be added that the subsidy implied in loan rates that are kept low administratively makes debt-financing attractive. Usually, one would argue that, even under such conditions, corporations would prefer own financing because it would maximize their control over the firm. But such arguments may be less relevant in countries where there may be close personal links between the owners and managers of large corporations and those of financial institutions. As observed in Chapters 1 and 2, large corporations are often organized in groups, and the largest ones are those related to banks.

Once the level of the mark-up has been decided, it is likely that the corporations will stick to it for a while; they will only reconsider it at discrete intervals. Even so, it could be that the actual profit share will differ from the expected one. There are two possible reasons for this.

The first is a change in input prices. Looking at equation (29), it is clear that if increases in w, p_m or i_l are immediately and fully transmitted into output prices, the profit share will change. An increase in w will lead to a fall in the profit share, and increases in p_m and i_l to a rise. It is possible that such cost increases are only gradually transmitted into prices, in which case the profit share may fall following increases in the import cost or credit cost. There is no detailed information on the short-term pricing behaviour of Thai corporations, but clearly, price reactions will differ between firms: for example, firms operating on the protected home market may feel more secure in passing on cost rises than firms operating on competitive export markets. The result of this

114

diversity may be that the effect of cost increases on the profit share are difficult to discern. Attempts to include indicators of wage cost and of imported input prices in the regressions later in this section always failed to lead to significant results. The role of the cost of credit is more complex, as will be discussed below.

A second reason why planned and actual profit share may diverge from each other is unforeseen variation in capacity utilization. The forecast profit share in equation (29) is based on an expected level of output or capacity utilization. If actual capacity utilization is greater than anticipated, the fixed cost will be spread over a larger output, so that profits increase and the actual profit share will exceed the expected level. One might suppose that this factor would affect firms rather homogeneously: if aggregate demand increases, demand for most corporations will increase and their capacity utilization will go up. The effect of this on the profit share will depend, of course, on the relative size of fixed cost, which will differ from firm to firm, but the direction of the impact on the profit share will be unambiguous.

On the basis of these arguments, the following equation may be suggested for the desired level of the profit share:

$$(30) \quad \frac{\hat{S}_c}{\hat{Y}_c} = a_0 \frac{\hat{I}_c}{\hat{Y}_c} - a_1 \frac{CR_c}{\hat{Y}_c} - a_2 \frac{F_c}{\hat{Y}_c} + a_3 (i_1 - p_c)$$

CR_c = an indicator of availability of domestic credit

F_c = inflow of foreign capital to the corporate sector

$(i_1 - p_c)$ = real loan rate

$\hat{S}, \hat{I}, \hat{Y}$ = desired or expected levels of nominal savings, investment and value added of the corporate sector, respectively.

One would expect that in the long run firms would have more or less fixed ideas about the minimum proportion of their investments that they want to finance out of own capital sources; that is the meaning of the first term on the right-hand side of equation (30), $a_0 > 0$.

The variables CR_c and F_c are indicators of the availability of domestic credit and foreign capital. Domestic credit availability may be subject to monetary policy. The availability of foreign credit in Thailand may have increased over time, with the growing internationalization of capital markets and the growing creditworthiness of Thai corporations. If domestic credit and foreign capital are easily available, corporations will be under less pressure to generate their own investment funds. Thus the expected signs for a_1 and a_2 is negative. If the cost of credit, that is the real loan rate, is high, on the other hand, firms will have an incentive to save more so as to reduce their dependence on external finance: thus $a_3 > 0$. It could be that when the real loan rate is high, investments are discouraged, so that the savings will also fall.

The size and significance of the coefficients a_1, a_2 and a_3 may also provide an indirect indicator of the market power of the corporations. The mark-up and profit share will only fluctuate with the availability and cost of external finance if the firms have the power to change the mark-up rate.

In equation (30) the desired level of savings is an unobservable variable. As argued above, the actual level of the profit share may differ from the desired one, mainly because of variations in the level of capacity utilization. Direct observations on capacity utilization on a time-series basis are not available. As an indirect indicator, the lagged growth rate of corporate GDP will be used. This is based on the argument that if last year's growth of output was fast, this will be reflected in more profits being available in the current year.

(31) $\quad S_c / Y_c = \hat{S}_c / \hat{Y}_c + b_1 \, g_{c(t-1)}$

If actual capacity utilization exceeds the expected level (that is if growth is relatively rapid), the actual profit share will be above the expected level: $b_1 > 0$.

Another unobservable variable in equation (30) is desired investment, whose level may be determined in the standard way by looking at incentives (the past profit share and lagged growth rate of demand) and at (opportunity) cost which is reflected by the real lending rate.

(32) $\quad \dfrac{\hat{I}_c}{\hat{Y}_c} = d_0 + d_1 \dfrac{S_{c(t-1)}}{Y_{c(t-1)}} + d_2 \, g_{c(t-1)} + d_3 \, (i_l - p_c)$

The constant in this equation may be interpreted as reflecting replacement investment. If it is assumed that desired investment can be realized, equations (30), (31) and (32) may be combined into:

(33) $\quad \dfrac{S_c}{Y_c} = d_0' + d_1' \dfrac{S_{c(t-1)}}{Y_{c(t-1)}} - a_1 \dfrac{CR_c}{Y_c} - a_2 \dfrac{F_c}{Y_c}$

$\qquad + d_2' \, g_{c(t-1)} + d_3' \, (i_l - p_c)$

The signs in equation (33) indicate the expected direction of the relationship between the dependent and the independent variables. Note that the sign of the interest rate is ambiguous, because a high interest rate may, on the one hand, encourage own savings to reduce dependence on external finance, but on the other hand, may on (opportunity) cost arguments reduce the desire to invest and therefore the willingness to save. The impact of the lagged growth rate is also the result of two processes – the capacity utilization effect and the investment inducement effect of past growth – but these two effects will influence the profit share in the same direction.

In the estimation of equation (33) the profit share is measured by dividing gross corporate savings by the GDP of the corporate sector (as defined in Chapter 2). Chart 3.1 depicts the movements of that profit share (S_c / Y_c) over time. CR_c is defined as the change over the year in 'Claims on Business and Household Sector' of monetary institutions (mainly commercial banks) and of

116

finance companies. Of course, some of these claims are on the unincorporated sector, but the great majority may be assumed to be loans to the corporate sector. F_c is taken from the balance-of-payments statistics and defined as 'Direct Investments' and 'Long-term Loans and Credits to Private Enterprise and Government Enterprises'. (i_l-p_c) is the effective loan rate that financial institutions charge, deflated by the GDP deflator of the corporate sector, and $g_{c(t-1)}$ is the growth rate of the real GDP of the corporate sector over last year. Running equation (33) on annual observations for the period 1964–86 leads to the following result:

$$(34) \quad \frac{S_c}{Y_c} = 1.82 + 0.87 \frac{S_{c(t-1)}}{Y_{c(t-1)}} + 0.10 g_{c(t-1)} + 0.11 (i_l - p_c)$$

$$\quad\quad\quad (0.593) \ (8.058) \quad\quad\quad (1.270) \quad\quad\quad (1.721)$$

$$-0.07 \frac{F_c}{Y_c} + 0.02 \frac{CR_c}{Y_c}$$

$$(0.769) \quad\quad (0.571)$$

$R^2 = 0.77$; Durbin h-statistic $= -0.08$

These results are in line with the expectations. The high value of the coefficient for the lagged savings ratio, which is highly significant, indicates the great stability of the savings ratio. This is what one would expect in a sector where corporations have price-setting power and where they set these prices in a longer-term perspective. The coefficient of the real lending rate is positive and significant; theoretically this coefficient is ambiguous, as discussed above, but apparently the effect that dominates is the attempt to increase own savings when the cost of external finance is high. One could also say that over the period under study, the real lending rate has not been high enough to discourage investment.

The conclusion of most studies on the Thai credit market, as observed in Chapter 2 was that the amount of credit extended by banks is determined by demand. The availability of credit would not be a problem then, although its cost could be, so it is not surprising that the coefficient of CR_c in equation (34) is not significant. A similar argument could be applied to the F_c variable.

The F_c flow is made up of 'Direct private investment' and 'Long-term Loans and Credits', with the latter taking the major share. It is quite obvious that subsidiaries of multinationals can substitute between own funds, domestic credit and foreign capital. However, larger, domestically-owned firms and state enterprises also have direct access to international capital markets, and may also make such substitutions. Over the years, capital inflows have become more endogenous and determined by domestic capital needs. The negative sign of the F_c variable is in keeping with the studies reviewed in Chapter 1 (section 1.3), where a negative relationship between capital inflows and domestic savings was postulated. The advantage of the present model is that

117

it gives a theoretical context for the explanation of this relationship. The coefficient of the F_c variable is not significantly different from zero. The capacity utilization index has the expected sign but is not significant.

The results of equation (34) give further support to and raise confidence in the interpretation of saving behaviour advocated in this study.

3.3.5 Some comments on government savings

The household savings and corporate savings analysed above make up the bulk of domestic savings. To complete the analysis it is useful to make a brief analysis of the determinants of government savings. The Thai National Accounts define 'Savings of General Government' as the difference between total current revenue and consumption expenditure of the government. Thus:

(35) $S_g = T - C_g$

S_g = savings of general government
T^g = government revenue
C_g = consumption expenditure of government.

One could express (35) also in terms of proportions of GDP. There is an observed tendency for total government expenditure (that is consumption and investment expenditure) as a proportion of GDP (G/Y) to rise over time (see Bird 1971; Enzewe 1973; Diamond 1977; Jansen 1982). This tendency is so general that it has even been named 'Wagner's Law' after an early author who wrote about it. This trend can also be observed in Thailand: the G/Y ratio increased from around 13 per cent in the early 1960s to about 17.5 per cent around 1970 and about 18 per cent in the early 1980s. The ratio of current expenditure to GDP (C_g/Y) showed the same trend: from 10 per cent to 12.5 per cent and then to 15 per cent for the years indicated.

The Revenue/GDP ratio (T/Y) has also been the subject of intensive study.[12] In Thailand the T/Y ratio has been very stable (or stagnant) over time, ignoring short-term fluctuations, of course. It was around 13 per cent in the early 1960s, and it was not until the 1980s that it did show some tendencies to creep up from that level. The tax buoyancy is very low in Thailand. The tax buoyancy elasticity with respect to income (which measures the total change in tax income – due to overall income growth and to discretionary tax measures – when aggregate income rises) was over the period 1972–82 only 1.07, one of the lowest rates in Asia. The elasticity of government expenditure with respect to income is considerably higher (UN ESCAP 1985, p. 160). The composition of tax revenue changed significantly over the period, however, with the shares of income and of sales taxes rising and the shares of import duties and export taxes falling.

These considerations give rise to the following very simple model of government saving:

(36) $$\frac{C_g}{Y} = a_0 + a_1 t$$

t = time trend.

The Current Government Expenditure/ GDP ratio is explained by a trend element in line with Wagner's Law.

(37) $$\frac{T}{Y} = b_0 - b_1 \frac{F_g}{Y} + b_2 i_b + b_3 p_m + b_4 p_x$$

F_g = capital inflow from abroad to the government
i_b^g = bond rate of interest
p_m and p_x = rate of increase of import and export prices respectively

The revenue ratio is determined by the willingness of government to raise taxes. This willingness is influenced by the availability of other sources of income. Discussions in Chapter 1 (section 1.3) focused attention on the potential negative effect of foreign capital inflows on government tax efforts. To measure this effect, F_g, the inflow of foreign capital received by the government is included in equation (37). If such external sources of income are more readily available, there will be less pressure to raise taxes; thus the expected sign for b_1 is negative. The cost of borrowing i_b, the nominal interest rate on government bonds, has the reverse effect: if the cost is high, the government will try to become less dependent on external funds. The rates of increase of import and export prices have been added, because short-term fluctuations in the T/Y ratio may be expected to be sensitive to fluctuations in prices of imports and exports, both important tax bases. The expected signs are positive.

Inserting equations (36) and (37) into equation (35) gives:

(38) $$\frac{S_g}{Y} = (b_0 - a_0) - b_1 \frac{F_g}{Y} + b_2 i_b + b_3 p_m + b_4 p_x - a_1 t$$

Data for the period 1961-86 were used in testing this equation. The results are good:

(39) $\quad S_g/Y = 6.36 + 0.28\ F_g/Y - 0.33\ i_b + 0.04\ P_m - 0.03\ P_x - 0.13\ t$

$\qquad\qquad$ (9.139) (1.034) $\quad$ (3.055) (2.838) $\quad$ (0.220) (4.640)

$R^2 = 0.83$; D.W. = 1.68

The significant coefficients have the expected signs, with one exception, the interest rate. But that exception may be explained from the fact that in equation (38) the interest rate is introduced as a cost element which, when it is high, will stimulate the government to save more. But governments may be less concerned about the interest cost than private business, so that the effect suggested by (38) is absent or weak. At the same time, however, the interest cost is an important element in current government expenditure (at present about 25 per cent), and an increase in interest rates therefore has a direct effect on expenditure and thus a negative effect on government savings. In light of the discussion later in Chapter 5, it is useful to observe that government savings are sensitive to movements in international prices, as the coefficient of the import price variable is significant.

The coefficient of the capital inflow variable unexpectedly has a positive sign, but is statistically insignificant. Chapter 4 will show in greater detail that the Thai government never borrowed very much abroad, so that a negative impact could not have been anticipated.

The trend variable is negative and significant, showing a tendency towards a decline in government savings. Chapter 5 will return to this point later.

3.4   Conclusion

Summarizing the discussion of alternative theories of saving behaviour in section 3.2, one could say, for the purposes of this study, that they fall short in two ways. Firstly, they explain saving too much from a consumption perspective. Secondly, the theories tend to argue at too aggregated levels. The shortcomings may help, though, to explain the rather unimpressive results obtained in the empirical testing of these theories.

The Permanent Income Hypothesis explains fluctuations in the savings ratio by the slow adjustment of consumption to variations in income, and the Life-cycle Hypothesis explains saving by the desire to even out the level of consumption over a lifetime. The reality in LDCs is that economic units that are consumption units only (mainly wage-earning households), generally earn too little to save at all. The richer households that do save are generally self-employed in a family enterprise and so are a production unit as well as a consumption unit. It may be argued then that most private savings in LDCs originate from production units: family firms in the household sector and larger firms in the corporate sector. The possibilities and incentives of such units to save cannot be analysed completely from a consumption perspective only.

The classical saving hypothesis of the post-Keynesian models seems more relevant. It is assumed that savings are made by entrepreneurs out of profits and that wages are consumed. This breakdown is too simplistic though. Household firms earn labour and profit income, and their saving behaviour is determined not so much by the nature of the income as by the uncertainties of production, the opportunities for saving and the need for investment funds. These uncertainties, opportunities and needs will differ sharply among firms in the household sector and even more between household firms and large corpora-

120

tions. For this reason it is not very useful to analyse aggregate savings from an income distribution perspective, that is looking only at total profits and wages.

To deal with that problem, section 3.3 breaks down aggregate savings into savings of (i) the household sector or unincorporated business sector, (ii) the corporate sector, and (iii) government. The analysis of the household sector accepted the finding of numerous surveys that entrepreneurial households are responsible for most savings. An attempt was made to explain household savings by the production conditions of family firms. It was assumed that their production takes place under conditions of uncertainty and that they operate on competitive markets. The main determinants of household savings were found to be the price of output (largely determined by world-market export prices) and the cost of production (mainly wage cost, but this may include the cost of living of the household).

The analysis of corporate savings started from the assumption that these firms operate in a more certain environment and that they have a degree of power to set their price level and their profit mark-up. The factors entering into their decisions were analysed and it was found that corporate savings are quite stable, though sensitive to fluctuations in the cost of alternative sources of investment finance.

The brief analysis of government savings suggested that the interest rate has a negative influence. It was also concluded that there is a falling trend over time in the ratio of government savings, which were also found to be sensitive to international price movements.

It may be concluded that the saving behaviour of each of the three sectors looked at in section 3.3 is determined by quite different factors, which confirms the need for a disaggregated analysis. The breakdown applied here is still rough and dictated by data availability. With more detailed data, one could test whether further sectoral breakdown would be necessary, for example, into agricultural and non-agricultural household firms, between small and large corporations, or into corporations producing for the domestic market or for export.

The analysis in Chapter 4 will show that it is necessary, in the context of the present study, to point out the differences in production conditions and saving behaviour, together with differences in investment behaviour, because they are crucial to the explanation of the rapid growth in financial intermediation observed in Chapter 2. The household firms, with their fluctuating incomes and savings and uncertain production and investment opportunities, become the major suppliers of funds to financial institutions. The corporations with their more certain production conditions emerge as the major clients of the financial system. Chapter 4 will elaborate on these points.

Differences in saving behaviour and the intersectoral flows of funds through financial institutions also have implications for short-term macroeconomic stability. In Chapter 5 the results of this chapter will be applied in the analysis of the stability and stabilization patterns in Thailand.

Notes

1. This summary may not do justice to the complex growth models and theories that argue the importance of investment in human capital or of cultural factors. It could be argued that standard growth models overemphasize the role played by investment and therefore by savings.

    Chenery (1983) argued that experience shows structural change (for example, shifts of resources out of agriculture or growth of exports) to be quite significant in explaining differences in growth rates between countries. This suggests that not only the level of investment, but also its allocation over sectors is extremely important, a topic to which Chapter 4 will return.

2. Keynes (1936) argued that objective and subjective factors determine the propensity to consume and may be used to explain differences between countries in the propensity, but that within a country the propensity will tend to be stable over time.

3. Thirlwall's results are close to those of Newlyn. At a per capita income of $90 Thirlwall's equation gives a S/Y ratio of 0.12, and at $3,000, 0.21.

4. Two examples may be given, one from Indonesia (Kelley and Williamson 1968) and one from Ecuador (Barreiros 1985). The data for rural households are given:

Age of household head	Indonesia: income per capita (Rupiah)	Ecuador: expenditure per capita ('000 sucres)
<29	1072	10.2
30–39	902	9.7
40–49	854	9.2
50–59	944	10.5
60–69	890	9.9

    (Note: the last age groups in the case of Ecuador are 60–65 and then 66 years and over, but for both the same per capita expenditure level is given.)

    The age patterns are quite similar: there is a decline up to the age of 40–49 and an increase in per capita income after that age, that levels off at very old age. The urban income levels in both surveys are higher than the rural ones, and the patterns are rather different. In the case of Indonesia, the urban per capita income of older age groups falls, while in Ecuador it rises.

5. The conditions under which these additions are permissible are rather severe. They include the condition that households in the same age group must have the same saving function; that there is no change in saving behaviour over the period under study; and no changes in the age structure of the population (Ando and Modigliani 1963). It is particularly unlikely that these conditions will be met in developing countries; in periods of rapid transition and with sharp income differences between households in the same age group these conditions are unlikely to be met.

6. Modigliani and Tarantelli (1975) admitted that it is an incomplete proxy, because it excludes important elements of wealth such as real estate and the equity capital of unincorporated enterprise. Furthermore, the share of financial wealth in total wealth may have changed with financial development.

7. This multicollinearity is not simply a statistical problem; it follows from the interpretation given to equation (12). If rA_{t-1} is interpreted as the long-term average return on property A_{t-1}, then with a relatively constant long-term rate of return, r, the variable rA_{t-1} will be proportional to A_{t-1}, so that both variables should not be included in the same regression.

8. Hammer (986b) suggested that saving and children are substitutes. With financial development and financial liberalization, financial assets may become more attractive so that one would prefer to cater for old age by financial savings rather than by having children. He claimed that his empirical findings supported the hypothesis.

9. Gupta's definition of the Financial Intermediation Ratio differs from Goldsmith (1969) quoted in Chapter 1. He defined it as the ratio between a set of financial assets (M3 plus the capital accounts of financial institutions plus the liabilities of life insurance companies) to GNP (Gupta 1984, p. 81).

10. In Gupta's (1984) definition expected inflation $p_t^e = bp_t + (1-b)p_{t-1}$ and unexpected inflation is $p^u = p_t - p_t^e$. Thus unexpected inflation measures the change in the inflation rate: $p^u = \{1-b\}(p_t - p_{t-1})$. Since the VE index measures the change in the inflation rate over a three-year period it is likely that p^u and VE are highly correlated.

11. This impact of export prices may be shown by re-running equation (25) but replacing p_u by p_x, the rate of change in export prices. The results are:

$$S_t/Y_u = 11.37 - 1.38 \text{ WP} - 0.08 \text{ } p_c + 0.65 \text{ } i_1 + 0.11 \text{ } p_x$$
$$\quad\quad (3.035) \text{ } (2.986) \text{ } (0.376) \text{ } (1.687) \text{ } (1.598)$$
$$R^2 = 0.60; \text{ D.W.} = 1.82$$

12. See Jansen (1982) for references to such studies.

4 Intersectoral flows of funds

4.1 Introduction

In the previous chapter, the saving behaviour of the various economic groups was analysed and estimated. This chapter establishes the link between saving and financial intermediation. In the absence of financial development, the saver and the investor are one and the same person; or if they are different, the links between them are direct: one person makes money or real resources directly available to the other. In the later phases of financial development, there is increasingly a separation between saver and investor, and intermediation between them occurs increasingly through financial institutions. Financial intermediation is the process whereby surplus units obtain deposits in financial institutions, which then channel these funds to deficit units.

A saving theory that sees savings as retained profits from either unincorporated or corporate enterprises may appear to offer little scope for financial intermediation, as one would expect that the saving units would have a strong preference to re-invest their funds in their own firms. How can this be reconciled with the observed very rapid increase in financial intermediation? A number of ways may be suggested.

(a) Within firms there may be a lack in synchronization between the acts of saving and investment. If profits flow in gradually and investments are discrete and bulky, significant temporary balances may be deposited with financial institutions.
(b) Financial institutions have other sources of funds besides deposits of

124

surplus units. Specifically, they can and do borrow from the central bank and from abroad.

(c) Some surplus units may prefer the acquisition of financial assets over re-investment, as expected returns are greater.

The processes of self-finance, direct finance and financial intermediation can be observed and analysed by studying Flow-of-Funds Accounts. These enable one to observe, in the household, the corporate and the public sectors:

(i) how much is saved;
(ii) how much is invested;
(iii) how the surplus (S > I) is allocated or the deficit (S < I) is financed;
(iv) what the role of financial institutions in this process is.

Section 4.2 of this chapter introduces the flow-of-funds analysis. In section 4.3 the Flow-of-Funds Accounts for Thailand are analysed and the main intersectoral flows identified. In section 4.4 a brief analysis of alternative, or non-financial, channels for intersectoral transfer of resources in Thailand is made to indicate the relative importance of the financial flows.[1] It is concluded that the main channel for intersectoral transfers is financial flows. Section 4.5 attempts to explain the financial trends and flows as identified in the analysis in section 4.3. In section 4.5.5 the nature of the Thai financial institutions is discussed; as these institutions channel an increasing share of the intersectoral flows of funds, it is necessary to understand how they take decisions on the allocation of resources. Section 4.6 assesses the effects of the intersectoral financial flows on the sectoral balances in the economy and on income distribution. In section 4.7 government policies influencing the flow of funds in the economy are discussed and, finally, section 4.8 gives a brief summary of this long chapter.

4.2 Flow-of-Funds Accounts as an analytical tool

The Flow-of-Funds Accounts can help in analysing how the savings of a sector are allocated to investment in that sector or made available, directly or through financial institutions, to other sectors.

Flow-of-Funds Accounts are integrated with National Accounts, and also draw on balance-of-payments statistics, monetary and financial data, on government accounts, incidental or regular surveys, and so on. Using these sources, they try to put together a complete picture of financial flows between the various sectors in the economy.

The Flow-of-Funds Accounts are based on institutional sectors rather than on the production sectors as in the National Accounts. The sectors usually defined in the Flow-of-Funds Accounts include domestic sectors, consisting of households and unincorporated enterprises (subscript: h), incorporated businesses (c), government (g), financial institutions (f) and also the external sector or rest of the world (w) (Bhatt 1971).

The Flow-of-Funds Accounts show that the income of a sector (Y_i) can be consumed (C_i), transferred to other sectors directly (T_i), invested in physical assets (I_i) or in net financial assets (NFA_i). The subscript 'i' denotes the various sectors. Obviously, for each sector:

$$(1) \qquad Y_i + T_i = C_i + I_i + NFA_i$$

in which $Y_i + T_i$ is total disposable income. The precise definition of the current transfers depends on data collection and coverage: it may include tax payments and government subsidies, but might begin with post-tax incomes. Transfers then consist mainly of grants, remittances, interest payments, etc. Negative transfers can occur and negative net financial assets are acquired when the sector incurs financial liabilities to finance its deficit. Note that NFA in equation (1), and in the subsequent discussion in this chapter, refers to changes in the variable over the year. Financial statistics generally present the value of the stock of financial assets and liabilities at the beginning or end of a period. Flow-of-funds analysis deals with flows within a period or changes in stock values between the beginning and the end of a period. To simplify the presentation, the difference operator is not used in this chapter and NFA should be interpreted as a flow over the year.

Taking into account the rest of the world, one could write for the four sectors and for the entire economy:

$$(2) \qquad \text{h:} \quad Y_h + T_h - C_h - I_h \qquad\qquad\qquad = NFA_h$$

$$(3) \qquad \text{c:} \quad Y_c + T_c \qquad - I_c \qquad\qquad\qquad = NFA_c$$

$$(4) \qquad \text{g:} \quad Y_g + T_g - C_g - I_g \qquad\qquad\qquad = NFA_g$$

$$(5) \qquad \text{w:} \qquad\quad + T_w \qquad\qquad -X + IMP \qquad = NFA_w$$

$$(6) \qquad\quad Y \quad 0 \quad -C \; -I \quad -X + IMP = \qquad\qquad 0$$

in which X and IMP are respectively Exports and Imports of goods and services. Equation (5) defines the current account of the balance of payments. Adding up the four sectoral equations gives the familiar macroeconomic equation (6).

The Flow-of-Funds Accounts enable a more detailed analysis of the composition of the financial flows identified in equations (2)–(5). To do this the National Accounts data underlying the above equations are combined with financial data. The financial data give a breakdown of changes in NFA into its components: for example, on the asset side, changes in deposits, shares and bonds; and, on the liability side, changes in long-term and short-term loans, equity capital and foreign borrowing. The next step is to trace these financial flows from their sector of origin to their sector of destination.

In LDCs, one would typically expect NFA_h and NFA_w to be positive and NFA_c and NFA_g to be negative: that is, the household sector and the rest of the world are surplus sectors while the corporate sector and the government are deficit sectors (Bhatt 1971). This implies that in LDCs those who save are not always identical to those who invest. This separation of saving and investment decisions is central to the Keynesian analysis of short-term macroeconomic disequilibrium, a topic to which Chapter 5 will be devoted. In this chapter the analysis focuses on the impact of financial intermediation on the sectoral structure of investment and growth.

The statistical problems in putting together Flow-of-Funds Accounts are enormous. The various sources of data may give quite different estimates of relevant aggregates or may use different definitions or sectoral breakdowns. Combining various sources of information, however, allows for checks for consistency which helps to improve the data. On the other hand, it can lead to the discovery of quite irreconcilable differences. These problems are reflected in statistical discrepancies, which can sometimes be very large. These discrepancies might hide real flows out of or into a sector which could not be further traced, but it could also reflect erroneous estimates.

It may be assumed that the household and the corporate sector are most affected by statistical problems because:

(a) In the government sector, and for financial institutions and the rest of the world, reasonably reliable data are available from budget, monetary and financial and balance-of-payments statistics. Of course, even here these different sources are not necessarily compatible and complete; note for example the failure of balance-of-payments statistics to record the capital flight that took place in a number of developing countries. For the household and corporate sector, however, one has at best some sample survey data or tax returns (Bank of England 1972).

(b) In the household sector, many units are simultaneously a consumption and production unit, which makes it difficult to arrive at good estimates of household income, saving and investment (Bain 1973).

(c) Within and between the household and corporate sectors direct financial transfers can take place which are difficult to trace, even by sample surveys. One important example is the unregulated money market: financial transactions at this market take place mainly within the household sector and are impossible to trace in a Flow-of-Funds framework.

4.3 The Flow-of-Funds Accounts of Thailand

4.3.1 Introduction

Table 4.1 reproduces, in a slightly condensed form, the complete Flow-of-

Table 4.1   Flow-of-Funds Account of Thailand, 1983

	HH	Corp.	Govt	SE	RoW	FI	Total
A. Non-financial account							
1. Current income	689657	65885	124516	13371	25370	5455	924254
2. Current expenditure	618636		120665		−47109		692192
3. Net income	71021	65885	3851	13371	72479	5455	232062
4. Net transfers	2907	2863	1720	−733	−6757		
5. Gross savings	73928	68748	5571	12638	65722	5455	232062
6. Capital consumption		66092		6068		1226	73386
7. Net savings	73928	2655	5571	6571	65722	4229	158676
8. Gr. capital formation	36871	108960	36973	27228		2240	212271
9. Stat. discrepancy		25454				−5663	19791
10. Surplus/deficit	37057	−65666	−31402	−14590	65722	8879	
B. Financial account							
I. Acquisition fin. assets							
1. Currency and deposits	86340	4634	4068	1579			96543
2. Govt. securities	6785			821		20605	27631
3. Share capital	21724	1075	4202			185	27311
4. Domestic loans						114309	114309
5. Foreign assets		37232	5787	5419	115962	1238	165638
6. Other assets	5175	5639	−1855	689		−78	9570
7. Total	120024	48589	12202	8517	115962	136259	441553
II. Fin. liabilities							
1. Currency and deposits						96482	96543
2. Govt. securities			26730				27631
3. Share capital		18861		4647		3802	27311
4. Domestic loans	51486	72377					122900
5. Foreign loans		63712	11809	20333	49676	20108	165638
6. Other liabilities			−3889	−1359		6778	1530
7. Total	51486	154950	34650	23621	49676	127170	441553
III. Financial Surplus/deficit (I–II)	68538	−106361	−22449	−15103	66286	9089	
C. Sector discrepancy (A.10 – B.III)	−31481	.40695	−8954	514	· −564	−210	

Source: NESDB 1986
Note:
columns might not add up to the 'total' because some small entries have been deleted.

Funds Accounts of Thailand for the year 1983. Such tables are available for each year from 1967 to 1983. Seven institutional sectors are distinguished: households and unincorporated enterprise (HH, subscript: h), corporate business sector (CORP, subscript: c), central government and local government (combined in GOVT, subscript: g), state enterprises (SE, subscript: s), financial institutions (FI, subscript: f) and the rest of the world (ROW, subscript: w).

The Thai National Accounts data on income and expenditure by sector provide the basis for the upper part of Table 4.1. The lower part shows how savings are held, classified by financial instrument. These data may also be used to trace the flow of funds between sectors and to reveal, for each one, the sources and uses of funds. The Flow-of-Funds Accounts of Thailand contain a special set of Tables in which the sources and uses of funds of financial institutions are given by sector of origin and of destination, so that the directions of financial intermediation can be traced.

The data base of the Flow-of-Funds Accounts of Thailand has a number of weak elements (see Garnjarerndee 1982). Data on financial institutions, central government and the rest of the world are reasonably reliable. Data on local government are not so complete and those on state enterprises not very reliable, especially not before 1972. Since there are severe data scarcities for the household and the corporate sectors, they are treated as residual. In deciding on the allocation of flows to either of the two, the type of flow and the relationship of one sector to another in the economy is taken into consideration. In these allocation decisions, the same method is used for each year and, therefore, at least over time, consistency is maintained. Even so, it must be stressed that the statistical basis for the two main sectors in the Flow-of-Funds Accounts is weak because (i) the total of the two sectors is derived as a residual from the National Accounts and from the accounts of other sectors, and (ii) the distribution of these residuals over the two sectors is based, to a considerable extent, on assumptions. In view of these weaknesses, the Flow-of-Funds Accounts are used in this chapter only to study main trends which might be relatively unaffected by these problems. Even then, in view of the weakness of the data base, it may be best to see the conclusions as tentative or as hypotheses to be confirmed by other independent evidence where possible.

Line A.1 in Table 4.1 gives the current income of the domestic sectors and adds up to the GDP at market prices. Line A.2 shows current consumption, A.4 transfers, A.5 gross savings and A.8 gross investment; the last two add up to Gross Domestic Savings and Gross Domestic Capital Formation respectively.

Ignoring statistical discrepancies, the financial surplus or deficit of each sector is:

(7) $Y_i + T_i - C_i - I_i = NFA_i$

or, since $Y + T - C = S$:

(8) $S_i - I_i = NFA_i$

129

The lower half of the Flow-of-Funds table shows how this financial surplus is allocated over various assets, or how the financial deficit is covered by various liabilities. Fortunately, this part of the table is not netted, so it clearly shows, for example, that the household sector, which is on the whole a surplus sector, also incurs financial liabilities (FL) on a significant scale. So, one could rewrite equation (8) as:

(9) $\quad S_i - I_i = FA_i - FL_i$

or:

(10) $\quad S_i + FL_i = I_i + FA_i$

The left-hand side of equation (10) shows the sources of funds, which are own savings and financial liabilities incurred, and the right-hand side the uses of funds, which are own investment and financial assets acquired. The financial assets and liabilities are further broken down by type of financial instrument, as shown in Table 4.1.

4.3.2 Main sectoral trends

This analysis of trends in the flow of funds of each of the sectors concentrates on main entries. As Table 4.1 shows, many entries in the 'Financial Account' (part B) of the Flow-of-Funds Accounts are empty or contain only small amounts, so by concentrating on the main items one gets a good impression of the overall picture.

Chart 4.1 traces the main elements for the household sector (or in full: Households, non-profit institutions and unincorporated enterprises), expressed as percentages of GDP. The main source of funds for the household sector is household savings (S_h); the pattern in these savings was described in Chapter 2 and analysed in Chapter 3. The analysis of Chapter 3 suggested that the main determinants of the household savings ratio are the output (export) prices and the production cost, as reflected in the wage pressure index.

The household sector's own investments (I_h) have been rather stable and have not been affected by the fluctuations in the savings ratio. The level of household investment is relatively low, so that the sector has a considerable saving surplus ($S_h - I_h$), and this has enabled households to accumulate financial assets. Households obtain shares of corporations and financial institutions (EQ_h), but the main financial assets obtained by households are time and savings deposits with commercial banks and promissory notes with finance companies (FA_{hf}). Over the years, the importance of promissory notes from finance companies has grown, but bank deposits still account for over three-quarters of all the assets held by households in financial institutions. In recent years, due to problems faced by some finance companies, this proportion may even have increased.

It is interesting to note that, increasingly, households obtain access to credit

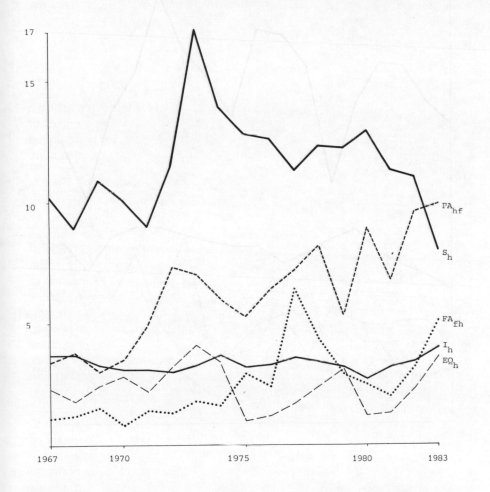

Chart 4.1   Household sector (main sources and uses of funds as % of GDP)

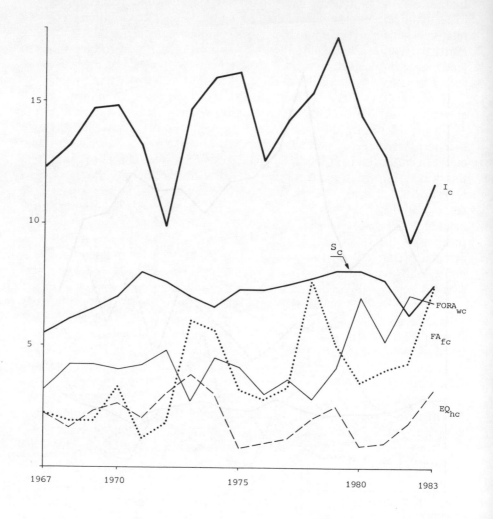

Chart 4.2   Corporate sector (main sources and uses of funds as % of GDP)

132

extended by financial institutions as shown by the 'Incurrence Financial Liabilities (FA_{fh})' in Chart 4.1. As will be seen later in this chapter, these bank loans to the household sector are not consumer loans; consumption credit is a relatively small part (less than 10 per cent) of total financial institution activity. Partly the increase in bank credit is due to government policy forcing banks to lend more to agriculture. Despite the increase in credit received, the household sector remains a net contributor of funds to the financial system.[2]

If, as argued in Chapter 3, household savings are profits of unincorporated enterprises, one would expect the rise in the household savings ratio in the 1970s to provide both the incentive and the funds to increase investment in the unincorporated sector, certainly if one also adds on greater access to bank credit (as reflected in higher financial liabilities) to the sources of funds. But this kind of increased investment is not visible. Nor did the household investment fall in the 1980s, when the household savings ratio started to decline. In discussing such trends, it is necessary to recall that the statistical basis of the Flow-of-Funds data is weak: the statistical discrepancy is large and positive in the 1970s and large but negative in the 1980s, so there is the possibility of relatively wide margins of error, particularly in the estimates of household savings and household investments. Despite these problems, section 4.4 below will attempt an explanation of these trends.

The main sources and uses of funds of the corporate sector (or, to give it its full name, incorporated private non-financial business) are given in Chart 4.2. It should be noted that the coverage of the corporate sector in the Flow-of-Funds Accounts differs from the definition of this sector used in Chapters 2 and 3. The analysis in the earlier chapters was based on National Accounts data which include in the corporate sector, state enterprises and financial institutions, both of which are separately presented in the Flow-of-Funds Accounts.

The main sources of funds of the corporations are their own savings (S_c), new equity capital acquired (EQ_{hc}) and loans from financial institutions (FA_{fc}) and from abroad ($FORA_{wc}$). They use these funds mainly to finance their investments (I_c).

As argued in Chapter 3, savings in the corporate sector are, to a large extent, determined by the price-setting behaviour of the corporations. This argument finds support in the pattern of the corporate savings ratio shown in Chart 4.2. It is relatively stable over the years, as one would expect from a price-setting sector. When taken together with the acquisition of share capital, the total of the sector's own capital sources (that is corporate savings and new share capital) as a proportion of GDP follows a pattern not dissimilar to that of corporate investment. The fluctuations in corporate investments are somewhat sharper and the gaps between investment requirements and own capital sources are filled with credit obtained in about equal proportions from domestic financial institutions and from abroad. There is a slight tendency over the years for the share of investment financed by credit to increase (see Chart 4.3). The main sources and uses of funds of the state enterprises are

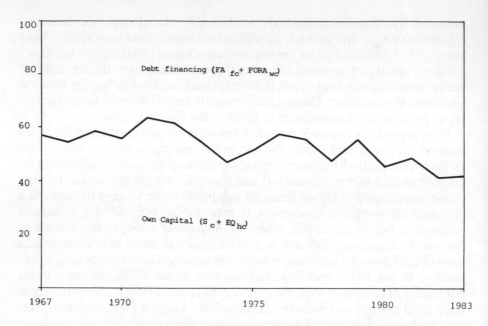

Chart 4.3   Corporate sector (main sources of funds as % of total sources)

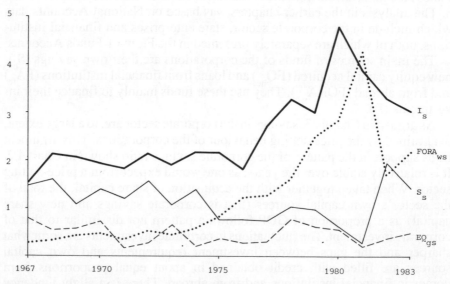

Chart 4.4   State enterprises (main sources and uses of funds as % of GDP)

presented as a percentage of GDP in Chart 4.4. The increase in the investment activities of the state enterprises (I_s) since the mid-1970s is striking. Charts 4.4

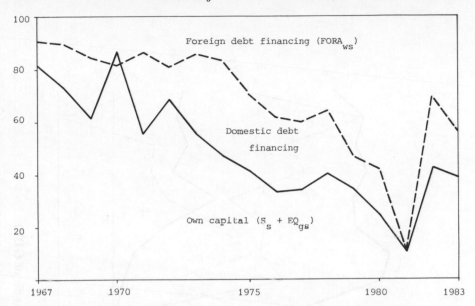

Chart 4.5   State enterprises (main sources of funds as % of total sources)

and 4.5 show that the degree of self-financing of these investments, out of their own savings (S_s) or out of newly acquired share capital (EQ_{gs}), has fallen dramatically, causing the savings deficit of the state enterprise sector to widen. The widening of this gap is due both to an increase in the investment ratio and a fall in the savings ratio.

State enterprises do not generally depend on domestic financial institutions for much of their financing. Even in 1980, an exceptional year in terms of state enterprise borrowing, they obtained only Baht 5.5 billion from financial institutions (compared to 23.7 billion, for example, obtained by the private corporate sector). The main source of investment finance of the state enterprises since the mid-1970s has been loans from abroad ($FORA_{ws}$). It appears that the availability of such loans has enabled state enterprises to increase their investment activities, and it may have reduced their need to generate profits and savings.

In Charts 4.6 and 4.7, the data on central and local government have been combined. The local government items are generally small in size and stable over time, which means that the fluctuations and trends are caused by the operations of the central government. Expressed as a percentage of GDP, government investment (I_g) has been relatively stable, except during the

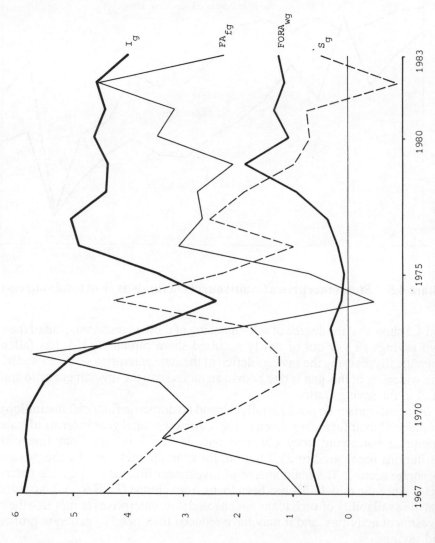

Chart 4.6   Government (main sources and uses of funds as % of GDP)

136

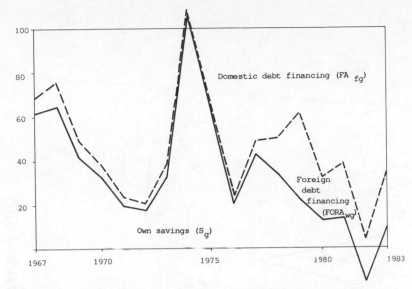

Chart 4.7   Government (main sources of funds as % of total sources)

policy-induced dip in the period 1972–75 which coincided with a peak in the government savings ratio (see Chart 4.6).

The degree of self-financing of government investments with government savings (S_g) has been declining over time to such an extent that it almost disappeared in the 1980s (see Chart 4.7). The deficit was financed mainly by domestic sources, in particular domestic financial institutions (FA_{fg}). In the absence of an active security market, most government securities are held by financial institutions. Up to 1977 the contribution of foreign capital ($FORA_{wg}$) to the financing of government investments was rather stable, but since then it increased and started to fluctuate in directions clearly opposite to those in domestic financing. It would appear that substitution takes place between domestic and international sources of finance.

Chart 4.8 shows the increasing role of financial intermediation. The financial sector has three main sources of funds. Its own capital (OC_f) consists of retained profits and newly acquired share capital. The main share of its funds comes from the deposits received from the private sector (FA_{hf}). The deposits shown in Chart 4.8 include the holdings of promissory notes from finance companies. Total deposits or financial savings as a percentage of GDP fluctuated from year to year but clearly showed an upward trend. A third source of funds for financial institutions is the international financial market. Chart 4.8 shows net borrowing abroad by financial institutions, that is the balance between the credits obtained and the foreign assets acquired ($NFORA_f$). There is negative net borrowing, or outflow of funds through financial institutions,

137

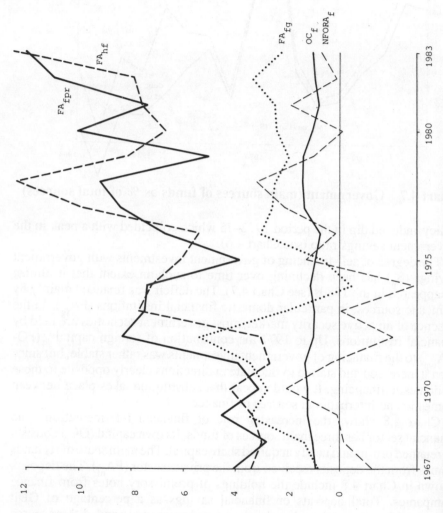

FA_{fpr}

FA_{hf}

FA_{fg}

OC_f

$NFORA_f$

12

10

8

6

4

2

0

1967   1970   1975   1980   1983

Chart 4.8   Financial institutions (main sources and uses of funds as % of GDP)

in many years. More recently, the financial sector obtained more funds abroad on average than it acquired foreign assets, but on the whole the international capital market is not a major source of funds for Thai financial institutions.

The financial institutions use their funds to extend credit to the public (FA_{fg}) and private sectors (FA_{fpr}). Loans to the government mainly take the form of purchase of government securities. Loans and advances to the private sector in particular have grown rapidly.

This analysis of the Thai Flow-of-Funds Accounts above may be summarized by the following points:

(a) Household savings as a percentage of GDP increased somewhat in the 1970s and have declined in the 1980s.
(b) The household sector has increasingly obtained credit from financial institutions.
(c) The household sector has allocated available funds to:
    (i) its own investments which were very stable over the years.
    (ii) acquisition of share capital which fluctuated but showed no clear trend.
    (iii) acquisition of financial assets in financial institutions, mainly in the form of time and savings deposits and promissory notes. This category has clearly increased over the years.
(d) The household sector has had a large savings surplus, that is, it has saved more than it has used for its own investments. On average, the surplus was somewhat larger in the 1970s than in the 1960s, but it has declined in the 1980s; household savings have fallen sharply, and household investment has increased somewhat.
(e) As a proportion of GDP gross corporate savings have been far more stable than the household savings ratio, as one would expect given the pricing behaviour and market conditions in these sectors (as analysed in Chapter 3). The funds that corporations obtained from increasing share capital have fluctuated with the investment activities.
(f) Corporate savings and increases in share capital have been insufficient to finance all investments. The deficit has tended to increase somewhat and has been financed by foreign and domestic borrowing.
(g) The savings of state enterprises as a percentage of GDP have fallen till a recovery started in 1981. The investments of state enterprises, on the other hand, have increased sharply from 1976.
(h) The deficit of the state enterprise sector has increased and has been financed by share capital obtained from the government and a strongly increasing dependence on foreign borrowing. State enterprises have obtained a relatively small amount of funds from domestic financial institutions.
(i) Government savings have fallen sharply and government investments have been relatively stable.

139

(j)   The deficit has been financed mainly by borrowing from domestic financial institutions and additionally, since the mid-1970s, from foreign sources.

(k)   Financial institutions have obtained most of their funds in the form of deposits and promissory notes. They have obtained funds from abroad to a lesser degree.

(l)   Their main uses of funds have been the extension of credit to the public and private sectors.

4.3.3 Intersectoral flows of funds

The data presented in the previous section indicate, for each institutional sector, the main sources and uses of funds. The account of each sector is constructed on the National Accounts principle of double-entry bookkeeping so that accounts must balance per sector. Now, however, the focus is on flows *between* sectors. To form an impression of the intersectoral flows of funds, one would need to identify, for each flow, the sector of origin (that is where the flow came from) and the sector of destination (that is the sector receiving the particular flow). Charts 4.1–4.8 showed the sector of destination, but not the sector of origin. The Flow-of-Funds Accounts of Thailand provide detailed tables to show from which sectors the financial institutions obtain their funds and to which sectors these institutions direct their flows, so that the intersectoral flows that occur through financial intermediation can be readily traced. Financial flows outside financial institutions can generally be traced indirectly by comparing the asset and liability side of the various sectoral accounts: for example the value of share capital obtained by the household sector as an asset tends to be similar to the amount of share capital obtained, as a liability, by the corporate sector and financial institutions. This justifies the conclusion that share capital constitutes a financial flow between the household sector, which is the sector of origin, and the corporate sector as destination. Of course, in theory, the government may acquire some private shares, foreign investors may engage in portfolio investment and banks may acquire shares of private corporations. In practice, though, such flows are quite small compared to the amount of shares acquired by the household sector and in the subsequent analysis such small flows are ignored. Similarly, the share capital obtained by state enterprises is balanced by an increase in share holdings of the government. On the basis of such findings one can work out the intersectoral flows of funds with institutional sectors of origin and destination for the major flows.

Ignoring small entries and statistical discrepancies, the main intersectoral flows may be written in a stylized way as follows. Note that in this presentation the first subscript denotes the sector of origin and the second the sector of destination. The difference operator has been deleted in this presentation although it should be clear that in the cases of Financial Assets, Equity Shares and Foreign Debt and Assets, one is dealing with changes over the year in the level of these categories. Financial Liabilities and Foreign Debt are introduced as Financial Assets of the sector of origin.

$$(11) \quad S_h + FA_{fh} \qquad\qquad = I_h + EQ_{hc} + FA_{hf} + EQ_{hf}$$

$$(12) \quad S_c + EQ_{hc} + FORA_{wc} + FA_{fc} = I_c + FORA_{cw} + FA_{cf}$$

$$(13) \quad S_s + EQ_{gs} + FORA_{ws} \qquad = I_s$$

$$(14) \quad S_g + FA_{fg} + FORA_{wg} \qquad = I_g + EQ_{gs}$$

$$(15) \quad S_f + EQ_{hf} + FA_{hf} + FA_{cf} + FORA_{wf} = I_f + FA_{fh} +$$
$$FA_{fc} + FA_{fg} + FORA_{fw}$$

Adding equations (11)–(15) gives:

$$(16) \quad (S_h + S_c + S_s + S_g + S_f) + (FORA_{wc} + FORA_{ws} + FORA_{wg} +$$
$$FORA_{wf}) = (I_h + I_c + I_s + I_g + I_{fh}) + (FORA_{cw} + FORA_{fw})$$

or:

$$(17) \quad I - S = S_w$$

which is the familiar accumulation balance.

Equation (11) indicates that the household sector obtains its funds from its own savings (S_h) or from credit extended by financial institutions (FA_{fh}) and uses these funds to finance its own investments (I_h), to obtain shares of corporations (EQ_{hc}) or banks (EQ_{hf})and to acquire financial assets with financial institutions (FA_{hf}). All the sectoral equations may be interpreted in that way. In adding up the equations, some entries cancel out others: for example, the shares obtained by households are the same as the shares issued by corporations. Similarly, the financial liabilities incurred by certain sectors are equal to the financial assets obtained by other sectors. What remains are the flows of investments and savings, including net foreign savings.

The equations above are presented in a matrix form in Table 4.2. A table like this, showing the sectors of origin and destination for the major flows, could be prepared for each year for which Flow-of-Funds Accounts are available and annual data used for detailed analysis. In this chapter, though, the focus is on the longer-term trends. To gain an impression of the major directions of intersectoral flows and of the trends over time, three-year averages have been calculated for three periods within the time covered by available Flow-of-Funds Accounts: 1967–69, 1974–76 and 1981–83.

In Table 4.3 the sources of funds for each sector are expressed as percentages of the total of funds obtained from all sources. The table shows, for example, that in the first period, 1967–69, state enterprises derived 50 per cent

Table 4.2   Intersectoral flow-of-funds matrix

Expenditures/ Sector of destination	Receipts/Sector of origin							
	HH	Corp.	SE	Govt	FI	RoW	Other sources	Total sources
Household sector (HH)	S_h				FA_{fh}			
Corporate sector (Corp.)	EQ_{hc}	S_c			FA_{fc}	FOR_{wc}		
State enterprise (SE)			S_s	EQ_{gs}		FOR_{ws}		
Central and local governments (Govt)				S_g	FA_{fg}	FOR_{wg}		
Financial institutions (FI)	EQ_{hf} FA_{hf}	FA_{cf}			S_f	FOR_{wf}		
Rest of the world (ROW)		FOR_{cw}			FOR_{fw}	S_w		
Investment	I_h	I_c	I_s	I_g	I_f			
Other uses								
Total uses								

Note:
For further clarification see equation (11) – (17) and related text.

of their funds from their own savings, 25 per cent from share capital provided by the government and 10.7 per cent from foreign loans. Table 4.4 shows the allocation of the total funds obtained from all the sources over the various uses: for instance, in the first period, the household sector used 21.3 per cent of its funds to purchase corporate shares, 38.3 per cent to acquire deposits with financial institutions and a similar percentage to finance its own investments.

Table 4.3 Intersectoral flow-of-funds: sources of funds
(as % of total value of funds from all sources of the sector)

	HH	Corp.	SE	Govt.	FI	RoW	Other sources	Total sources
Household sector (HH)	90.0				11.8		-1.8	100
	84.5				14.8		0.7	100
	71.6				24.1		4.3	100
Corporate sector (Corp.)	14.1	42.3			14.1	27.5	2.1	100
	9.5	42.0			23.1	23.1	2.4	100
	9.5	34.1			24.6	30.3	1.4	100
State enterprises (SE)			50.0	25.0		10.7	14.3	100
			31.3	9.4		28.1	31.3	100
			23.5	5.9		52.9	17.6	100
Central and local governments (Govt)				48.1	22.2	7.4	22.2	100
				52.1	22.9	2.1	22.9	100
				1.3	42.9	16.9	39.0	100
Financial institutions (FI)	69.2	5.8			15.4	1.9	7.7	100
	74.7	6.0			7.2	9.6	2.4	100
	69.6	4.3			3.6	5.8	16.7	100

Note:
The figures given are three-year averages for the periods 1967–69, 1974–76 and 1981–83.
They are presented as: A: 1967–69
B: 1974–76
C: 1981–83

Table 4.4   Intersectoral flow-of-funds: uses of funds
(as % of total value of all uses of funds by the sector)

	HH	Corp.	SE	Govt.	FI
Household sector (HH)					21.7
					24.7
					26.4
Corporate sector (Corp.)	21.3				33.3
	13.8				41.9
	12.7				40.3
State enterprises (SE)				9.2	
				6.8	
				4.9	
Central and local governments (Govt)					30.0
					11.8
					25.6
Financial institutions (FI)	38.3	1.9			
	53.4	2.8			
	61.1	3.8			
Rest of the world (RoW)		8.8			10.0
		9.1			14.0
		25.6			0.0
Investment	38.3	84.3	70.4	77.6	5.0
	29.3	84.7	69.0	81.8	5.4
	22.3	70.6	65.4	70.5	3.1
Other uses	2.1	5.0	29.6	13.2	0.0
	3.4	3.4	31.0	11.4	2.1
	3.8	0.0	34.6	24.6	4.7
Total uses	100.0	100.0	100.0	100.0	100.0

Note:
The figures given are three-year averages for the periods 1967–69, 1974–76 and 1981–83.
They are presented as: A: 1967–69
                                        B: 1974–76
                                        C: 1981–83

Table 4.5 Intersectoral flow-of-funds matrix: main intersectoral flows (as % of GDP)

Expenditures / Sector of destination	Receipts/Sector of origin						Other sources	Total sources	Stat. discr.
	HH	Corp.	SE	Govt	FI	RoW			
Household sector (HH)	9.9 13.1 10.1				1.3 2.3 3.4		-0.2 0.1 0.6	11.0 15.5 14.1	1.6 3.9 -1.6
Corporate sector (Corp.)	2.0 1.6 2.0	6.0 7.1 7.2			2.0 3.9 5.2	3.9 3.9 6.4	0.3 0.4 0.3	14.2 16.9 21.1	-1.7 0.7 5.1
State enterprises (SE)			1.4 1.0 1.2	0.7 0.3 0.3		0.3 0.9 2.7	0.4 1.0 0.9	2.8 3.2 5.1	0.1 0.3 -0.1
Central and local governments (Govt)		0.3 0.5 0.6		3.9 2.5 0.1	1.8 1.1 3.3	0.6 0.1 1.3	1.8 1.1 3.0	8.1 4.8 7.7	0.5 0.4 1.6
Financial institutions (FI)	3.6 6.2 9.6				0.8 0.6 0.5	0.1 0.8 0.8	0.4 0.2 2.3	5.2 8.3 13.8	-0.8 -1.0 0.9
Rest of the world (RoW)		1.4 1.6 4.1			0.6 1.3 0.0	2.2 2.5 5.7	1.1 0.2 1.7	5.3 5.6 11.5	0.0 -0.2 -0.1
Investment	3.6 3.4 3.5	13.4 14.9 11.3	1.9 2.0 3.4	5.9 3.6 4.3	0.3 0.5 0.4				
Other uses	0.2 0.4 0.6	0.8 0.6 0.0	0.8 0.9 1.8	1.0 0.5 1.5	0.0 0.2 0.6	0.4 0.1 0.4			
Total uses	9.4 11.6 15.7	15.9 17.6 16.0	2.7 2.9 5.2	7.6 4.4 6.1	6.0 9.3 12.9	5.3 5.8 11.6			

Note:
The figures given are three-year averages for the periods 1967–69 (top figure in each box), 1974–76 (middle figure) and 1981–83 (bottom figure).

To give a better impression of the relative size of the intersectoral flows involved Table 4.5 expresses the flows as percentages of (a three-year average of) GDP.

It should be realized that flow-of-funds structures, unlike, for example, input–output structures, may show large fluctuations from year to year. The financial flows are changes, sometimes quite large, in stocks of assets or liabilities. These fluctuations can be caused either by general economic conditions, which might influence, for example, the level of household savings, or by fiscal policies, which might affect the level of government savings, or by the private sector investment cycle. The analysis of the main sources and uses of funds of each of the sectors in section 4.3.2 above has given many examples of such short-term fluctuations (see Charts 4.1 through 4.8). The use of three-year averages does not always adequately correct for such short-term fluctuations, so care should be taken when extrapolating long-term trends from Tables 4.3 to 4.5. The tables can be used, though, to identify the orders of magnitude of the intersectoral flows and, when taken together with the more detailed analysis of sectoral patterns of the previous section, they may also help to identify some major trends over time.

Looking at Tables 4.3 to 4.5 from the perspective of financial development, there can be little doubt that the role of financial institutions, as measured by the ratio of their total uses, or that of their total sources, to GDP, has increased significantly. This was made possible by an increase in the flow of household savings to financial institutions, mainly in the form of time and savings deposits. Financial institutions also slightly increased their borrowing from abroad. These additional resources of the financial system were allocated to:

(a) The household sector: credit extended to this sector as a percentage of total sources of the sector and as a percentage of GDP increased substantially, although not as much as the deposits received from households.
(b) The corporate sector: the net deficit position of the corporate sector with respect to the financial institutions increased.
(c) The government sector: the net deficit position of the government increased in recent years.

The conclusion is that, in terms of net flows, it was mainly the corporate sector that benefited from the increased resources available to the financial system.

In terms of the various modes of financing mentioned in Chapter 1, there has been a shift from self-finance and direct finance to indirect finance. The proportion of corporate investment financed by own capital (own savings and new share capital) fell somewhat (see Chart 4.3) and the extent of own-capital-financing of state enterprises fell sharply (Chart 4.5).

At the same time, as Table 4.5 shows, indirect finance became more important, as the share of household funds allocated to financial institutions increased sharply, and these institutions became a more important source of funds for the unincorporated and corporate sectors.

The shift to indirect finance and financial intermediation also occurred within the household sector. The proportion of total household funds obtained through bank loans increased sharply at the same time that households increased their assets with financial institutions. This increased use of indirect finance within the household sector can also be caused by a shift of resources from the unregulated money market to official financial intermediation. Analysis later in this Chapter (see section 4.5.2) will suggest that the relative role of the unregulated money market has significantly fallen.

Another major change over the period 1967–83 was the increasing role of international finance as reflected in the funds received from the rest of the world. Most of these resources were channelled directly to private corporations and state enterprises; a lesser share went to the government and to the financial system. The integration of Thailand in the international financial system was facilitated by the absence of tight controls on international capital flows and by the stability of the Baht, which reduced exchange rate risk in international transactions.

4.4   The structure of economic growth and intersectoral transfers

The process of economic development entails structural change: some sectors expand rapidly, some grow slowly and some may even decline. Within sectors, important changes may occur in the organization of production, technology, and so on.

As discussed in Chapter 1, growth and structural change require an increase in investment resources and a channelling of these to the 'new' sectors. In the literature reviewed in Chapter 1, a number of channels for such intersectoral flows was identified. Part of the flow of resources may be forced, for example, by changes in relative prices or by tax measures. Another part might be voluntary, like the flow of funds through private financial institutions.

In the previous section the magnitudes of the intersectoral flows through the financial institutions were established. The rest of the chapter will deal with three remaining questions.

The first concerns the relationship between the intersectoral flows through financial institutions, and those through other channels. Do other channels, such as relative price changes or taxation, add to the financial outflow from the unincorporated sector, or do they compensate for it?

The second question concerns the determinants of intersectoral flows. Forced flows are clearly the outcome of market forces or government policy. But the voluntary flows through the financial system result from choices made by economic units and it should be possible to discover the determinants of these choices. In the context of this study, the second question is very important. If household savings are interpreted as profits of unincorporated enterprises, one would expect the household firms to use these funds to finance their own investments and not to deposit them in banks to such a great extent.

Finally, one would want to know the consequences of these intersectoral flows of funds. In Chapter 1 the concern was expressed that the outflow of resources from agriculture would lead, on the supply and demand side, to sectoral imbalances and economic instability. The question of what has happened to the sectoral balances in Thailand should therefore be raised, and that question could be extended by asking about the consequences of the intersectoral flows for employment and income distribution.

The former will be discussed in this section; the latter will be addressed subsequently.

As already observed in Chapter 1, intersectoral flows are often discussed in development theory as flows between agriculture and industry. Although the focus in this study is on the corporate versus the unincorporated sector, available data and studies often force the discussion to be framed in terms of agricultural and non-agricultural sectors of the economy. To a considerable extent, the agricultural and the unincorporated sectors overlap; agriculture is an important part of the unincorporated sector (as defined in Chapter 2) and other parts of the unincorporated sector, for example, rural trade and services, fully depend on the production and demand generated by agriculture. Whilst the available evidence forces the subsequent analysis to concentrate on the agricultural sector, the more general focus of this study on the various forms of organization of production, should always be borne in mind.

As discussed in Chapter 1, the central feature of the process of economic development is not only the mobilization of resources for investment and growth, but also the changing balance between the productive sectors of the economy (see, for example, Nurkse 1953; Lewis 1954; Mellor 1973; Kalecki 1976; Mundle 1985). In this process the 'new' sectors depend, for their investment resources, partly on the surplus generated by the 'old' sectors. In the literature 'old' and 'new' is often simplified to an agriculture–industry dichotomy. The agricultural sector should generate a surplus that can 'finance' industrialization. In this context 'financing' is understood as the transfer of real resources. The real resources that can be obtained from the agricultural sector include labour and the supply of agricultural products for industrial use (raw materials), for feeding the industrial workforce or for exports. The conditions under which these transfers take place are biased in favour of industry so that (a part of) the agricultural surplus is shifted to industry. This bias is generally brought about through government intervention; tax or price policies keep agricultural prices low so that the industrial inputs and the food for the industrial workers will be relatively cheap. An overvaluation of the currency can be used to undermine the earnings from agricultural exports and to subsidize the import-dependent industrial sector. The resulting low agricultural incomes and the supply of cheap food will contain the level of industrial wages that further increases the profitability of the industrial sector. The fiscal system can directly channel funds between the sectors when export taxes (or marketing boards) collect funds from exporting agriculture. These are then used to finance industrial expansion.

In the studies on the intersectoral transfers of resources the emphasis is on those channels that can 'force' transfers, for example, the tax system and the internal terms of trade. In many countries there is also a voluntary transfer through the financial institutions. Rich rural, agricultural households make deposits with financial institutions, which use these funds to extend credit to urban, industrial undertakings.

Over the last two-and-a-half decades Thailand has experienced a process of rapid economic growth and industrialization. A remarkable aspect of Thai development has been the strong performance of the agricultural sector, whose growth rate has been comparatively high. It is generally asserted that a substantial surplus has been extracted from this sector (see Ajanant, Chunanuntathum and Meenaphant 1986; Siamwalla and Setboonsarng 1987).

The main channels for resource transfer, apart from financial flows, are the fiscal system (taxes on and expenditure for agriculture), agricultural pricing policies, and the overall macroeconomic policies relating to external trade (tariffs and the exchange rate).

There has been no extensive taxation of the agricultural sector in Thailand, even the much-discussed rice export tax generated only a minor proportion of total tax revenues. Of course, the agricultural sector receives government expenditures (mainly for infrastructure and irrigation) and subsidized agricultural credit. Government expenditure in favour of agriculture, including the construction of roads, exceeds the revenues obtained from the sector. The net transfer *to* the agricultural sector through the fiscal system has been substantial and increasing over the last 20 years (Siamwalla and Setboonsarng 1987). In the early 1980s this net transfer was equivalent to around 11 per cent of agricultural GDP.

The principle mechanism for resource transfer out of the agricultural sector has been the rice premium and the rice export tax. The premium and the tax are imposed on exported rice. In addition, quantitative restrictions are occasion ally set for volumes of exports (Holtsberg 1980).

These policies are used not so much to stabilize the domestic price of rice as to influence the quantity of rice exported (and therefore the quantity left available for the domestic market), thus keeping the price of domestic rice relatively low (Ingram 1971; Usher 1978; Van de Meer 1981). Because Thailand cannot determine the world market price of rice, and domestic rice trading and processing is relatively competitive, the major effect of the rice export tax policies is for its domestic farm price to be reduced (Ingram 1971). The effect is to discourage technological progress in rice production because the cost of inputs, like fertilizers, and investments cannot be recuperated. This has contributed to the diversification of agricultural production to other crops such as maize, cassava and sugar, and as a result, Thailand has lost part of its share in world rice trade (Bertrand 1980).

The importance of the rice export tax for the intersectoral transfer of resources lies in its impact on domestic food prices: domestic crop prices in Thailand follow world market prices; the main effect of the taxation of the (small) proportion of the rice crop that is exported is to reduce the domestic wholesale and retail price of the entire crop. The burden is therefore on the rice producers. The resulting loss of income of rice farmers for 1975 was estimated at Baht 9.5 billion (Ajanant, Chunanuntathum and Meenaphant 1986) and for 1981 at Baht 13 billion (World Bank 1983a).

On top of this explicit export tax comes the implicit tax imposed by the overvaluation of the domestic currency. It is generally accepted that Thailand maintained an overvalued exchange rate in an attempt to support the import-dependent sectors of the economy. Ajanant et al. estimated that in 1975/76 the Baht was overvalued by 6.7 per cent (Ajanant, Chunanuntathum and Meena-phant 1986); by 1981 this overvaluation was even greater. As domestic agricultural prices closely follow world market prices the entire agricultural sector feels the impact of this overvaluation.

Siamwalla and Setboonsarng widen the coverage and method by including the impact of tax and price policies on various crops, not just rice, and by adding the impact of tariff and exchange rate policies on agricultural prices and income. Their calculations show a substantial transfer from agriculture to the rest of the economy. In the second half of the 1970s that transfer may have been equivalent to around 23 per cent of agricultural GDP. In the early 1980s that proportion declined to around 15 per cent as agricultural pricing policies and general external trade policies were gradually liberalized and the exchange rate overvaluation reduced (Siamwalla and Setboonsarng 1987). This change in policies did not benefit the agricultural sector much as it came at a time when international commodity prices were very low and declining. In fact, the world rice price has fallen considerably in recent years so that, as a result, Thai rice production has declined since 1985. The abolition of the rice export taxes in 1986 came largely in reaction to these adverse trends.

The transfers from agriculture would seem to benefit the urban consumers of agricultural products. All families in Thailand are rice consumers, but do they all benefit from the lower rice prices? The World Bank study observed:

It is also often argued that the benefits of the income transfers implicit in the system of rice taxation accrue to low-income wage earners. However, the real incomes of unskilled workers are mainly determined by the supply price of labor from alternative employment. The returns in rice production greatly affect this supply price. Given the extent of labor mobility which has been documented, the effect of the lower domestic prices for rice must be to reduce wage rates throughout the economy. This factor price effect of the rice taxation has important implications for the distributional results. If wage rates were reduced so as to keep the real wage rate constant with lower rice prices, this mechanism would transfer the benefits of reduced rice prices from low-income workers to their employers or to the consumers of the services or the products they produce. However, the real wage rate is likely to be decreased which implies even larger transfers from the rural economy and corresponding transfers from low-income unskilled labourers in general to high-income groups. The heavy taxation of the primary occupation of the vast majority of low-income Thais is a major regressive feature of the present tax system. (World Bank 1983a, p. 183)

This quotation brings together a number of interesting aspects of the distributional effects. A reduction of rice taxation would increase returns on rice cultivation to farmers and the supply price of unskilled labour; it would therefore increase the incomes of low-income farmers and unskilled workers.

Trairatvorakul (1984) carefully estimated all the effects of a rice price increase that would result from reducing the rice premium, taking into account the supply response, the wage response and consumption effects. His conclusion was that the net gains in the rural sector would be received mainly by the richer farmers with large marketed surpluses. Poorer farmers market much less of their production and may even be dependent on rice purchases. On balance, the lower income groups of the rural population would benefit, but not as much as the richer farmers. The net losses to the urban sector, in absolute terms, would be more or less the same for all income groups, but of course, relative to the income levels, much more severe for the lower income groups. So there would be a transfer from the urban poor to the rural rich, with a slight positive effect on overall poverty incidence because rural poverty falls a bit more than urban poverty rises.

On balance, a substantial net outflow of real resources from the agricultural sector can be observed through the fiscal system, pricing policies and trade policies. Besides these flows 'forced' through government intervention, there has been a substantial 'voluntary' flow of funds through financial institutions.

The Flow-of-Funds Accounts show that the 'household sector' is a net supplier of funds to the financial institutions as they deposit more than they receive in credit. The financial institutions use these funds to extend net credit to the corporate sector and the government. In about 1975 the net transfer of funds through the financial institutions was equivalent to about Baht 7 billion per year and increased to approximately Baht 35 billion around 1982. Of course, the 'household sector' is not equivalent to the agricultural sector, and the 'corporate sector' is not equivalent to the industrial sector, but in Thailand the overlap between these two breakdowns is very substantial.

Rough estimates suggest that the net outflow of resources from the agricultural sector as a result of the manipulation of relative prices, the benefits of government spending and the flows through financial institutions was equivalent to around 21 per cent of agricultural GDP in the late 1970s and early 1980s. The composition of these flows changed radically: the positive transfer through the fiscal system increased, the resource loss due to price and trade policies declined and the flows through financial institutions increased. Around 1975 the voluntary flows through the financial system accounted for about 40 per cent of total net transfer; by 1981 that proportion had increased to more than three quarters.

In assessing the overall situation with respect to the intersectoral resources transfers, it must be stressed that the statistical basis for the above estimates are weak. For instance, the calculation of the impact of the rice tax and of the shadow exchange rate is based on many assumptions some of which may be questionable. The Flow-of-Funds Accounts also suffer from many statistical problems, but it seems reasonable to conclude that the available evidence shows a substantial surplus appropriated through various mechanisms from the agricultural sector. It should be noted that the above estimates do not include the impact of the international terms of trade on agricultural real incomes. As observed, in Thailand domestic agricultural prices follow the fluctuations of world market prices, whereas industrial prices are much more rigid. Since the high level of international commodity prices in 1973 the agriculture–industry terms of trade have continuously declined.

4.5 Determinants of intersectoral financial flows

4.5.1 The household sector

In this section the determinants of the main financial intersectoral flows will be analysed in greater detail. The household sector deserves such attention, as it is the main sector with a savings surplus and the main supplier of funds to the financial institutions. These facts mean that in a study of financial development in Thailand the understanding of the behaviour of the household sector is crucial.

The Flow-of-Funds data presented in the previous section have shown that the main source of funds of the household sector is its own savings, although over the years credit obtained from financial institutions has become increasingly important. The main uses of funds are to finance its own investment, to provide equity capital to the corporate sector and to acquire financial assets with financial institutions.

The portfolio approach briefly discussed in Chapter 1 (section 1.4.1) suggests that rational households would determine their optimal portfolio of assets and liabilities on the basis of the returns, risks, and transaction costs (or liquidity) of the various assets. But is it realistic to assume that households are, or can be, so rational? Three points can be made:

(a) If, as is argued in Chapter 3, most household savings originate from self-employed households, one would expect such households to have a strong preference for re-investing these savings in their own businesses. This desire may dominate considerations of alternative rates of returns. Another part of household investment, particularly among urban households, is residential investment, which in many cases is more the satisfaction of a basic need than the result of careful evaluation of investment alternatives.

(b) Many households have limited access to, or information on, alternative uses for their savings. The acquisition of share capital, for example, in the absence of a large and active stock market, is limited to those with personal links to owners or managers of the corporations. The Stock Exchange of Thailand (SET) has been growing but is still relatively small. Similarly, the acquisition of deposits is dependent on the spread of financial institutions.

(c) Against these first two points that put the ability of households to compose optimal portfolios in doubt, should be placed the ample evidence that Thai farmers are sensitive to incentives. Numerous studies have found that the intensity of planting and the cropping patterns are sensitive to the level of agricultural prices and to relative price variations (see, for example, Pongtanakorn et al. 1987). It should also be noted that most of the household savings are in fact concentrated in the hands of a relatively small number of households. These may be engaged in production (for example, rich farmers or rice millers) or in commerce (traders or shopkeepers) and have the access and information required for rational allocation decisions. It is quite likely that most of the increase in credit received by the household sector from financial institutions and observed in the Flow-of-Funds Accounts has been received by this type of households, which could also be the main supplier of funds at the unregulated money markets (see section 4.5.2).

On balance, there seems to be no reason to doubt that the trends in the composition of the households' asset and liability portfolios are the outcome of rational decisions. Unless the rapid expansion of the share of households funds allocated to financial assets with financial institutions – which is in net terms even greater than their own investment – can be satisfactorily explained, the whole interpretation of household savings as retained profits of unincorporated enterprises will be in doubt. The retained profits of the corporate sector are entirely used to finance their own investments and one would expect this also to be the case in the unincorporated sector. Why is it not so?

To give a satisfactory answer to that question is not easy in the face of scarce evidence. Most of the evidence and information that is available is on the agricultural sector. As already observed, agriculture constitutes a substantial part of the unincorporated sector, and the incomes of other parts of the sector directly and indirectly depend on agriculture. The rural non-agricultural sectors of processing, trade and services tend to depend on the output of the agricultural sector or the demand generated by agriculture. Most rural industries are small-scale operations directed at local demand. Larger-scale production is concentrated around Bangkok (World Bank 1982).

It could be suggested, of course, that the investments of the unincorporated sector have been underestimated. In the National Accounts household investments are reckoned to consist predominantly of the construction of residences, and a considerable part of the business investments of the household firms could in fact be included in the corporate investment figure. So there is certainly an underestimation of the investment of the unincorporated sector, if 'unincorporate' investment is identified with 'household' investment, as recorded in the Flow-of-Funds Accounts. In the Flow-of-Funds Accounts of Thailand, the household sector generally shows a large positive statistical discrepancy, which may hide some unrecorded investment activity.

The extent of underestimation of investments by unincorporated firms may be quite limited though. All available indicators suggest very low levels of investment in agriculture in Thailand. Sinsup (1976) concluded from a sample of 1045 farmers in 20 provinces that, on average, their investments were low and mostly (around 80 per cent) in land and buildings. Close to half of these investments were 'financed' from own labour, the rest from own financial savings and credit. Panayotou (1985) observed that Thai agriculture uses relatively little capital, that its yields are amongst the lowest in the world, and have not increased much over recent years. Even though higher yielding varieties and better techniques are available, they are simply not applied.

Wong provided comparative data for agriculture in the ASEAN countries (Malaysia, Philippines, Indonesia and Thailand), and observed that in Thailand the proportion of the population active in agriculture is the highest and the Gini-coefficient for land distribution is the lowest (which implies that land is relatively equally distributed). Thailand also has the largest proportion of land operated by its owner, but paddy yields are the lowest and have shown the slowest growth over time, and the proportion of the area under high-yielding varieties and under irrigation is the smallest (Wong 1979). Douglass (1984) added some comparative data showing that in Thailand, fertilizer use and the share of agriculture in the loan portfolios of financial institutions (in 1974) was lower than in other Asian countries.

A more recent study, comparing paddy yields for 1979–81 of 12 Asian countries, concluded that in Thailand the yield per hectare is lowest and the growth of that yield over the period 1961–63 to 1979–81 slowest. Thailand was second lowest in the use of fertilizer and lowest in the share of area planted with modern varieties. On the other hand, Thailand had experienced the fastest (but one) growth of acreage (Osotsapa 1987).

These data clearly confirm the low level of investment in agriculture. Despite these modest investments agricultural growth has been rapid, as noted in Chapter 2. This may be explained by the nature of agricultural growth in Thailand, which has resulted from the expansion of area and the diversification of crops rather than from increases in productivity (World Bank 1982). The fact that new land was available meant that output could grow rapidly without much financial investment; that a comparatively large part of the population remained active in agriculture; and that the concentration in land ownership is still limited.

These observations might suggest that the level of investment was indeed low, but they do not explain the low level of investment. More investment in agriculture might have increased yields and therefore output and income even more. Why were these investments not undertaken when the sector apparently had the funds available to finance them?

In addressing that question, it has to be realized that investment opportunities in Thailand are concentrated: not all farmers and all regions have the same opportunities; farm households are highly diversified.[3]

Douglass (1984) provided a rough breakdown of agricultural classes in the Central Plain of Thailand. About 30 per cent of the households are landlords and commercial farmers, and another 40 per cent middle farmers who have enough land to be self-sufficient, but who are not wealthy enough to risk innovation. The remaining 30 per cent consists of marginal farmers and landless labourers. Phongpaichit (1982) studied three villages in different regions. In the economically most advanced Central Region village the top 10 per cent of households controlled 40 per cent of the village income.

This suggests that investment opportunities are highly concentrated even within villages. Richer agricultural households tend to have larger holdings and so have invested more in land. But they are not necessarily more dynamic and more productive farmers. Village studies suggest that rich households in the village often obtain a significant part of their income from non-farm activities such as renting out of land, rice milling, money-lending or official functions (see Visser 1978; Potter 1976).

Visser, who studied a village in the Central Region, observed that there were few differences between rich and poor farmers in terms of the extent to which they grew second crops, grew upland crops or used improved farming techniques (Visser 1978, p. 320). This suggests that even those who could invest in agriculture did not do so.

It should be noted that what are called here 'rich' farmers are not enormously rich households. They are rich when compared with the rural poor, but not to the urban rich. The main share of the agricultural surplus may be in the hands of a very few people, such as very rich farmers or landlords (for example in Central Region), traders (for example rice exporters), or processors (for example, owners of sugar factories). Many of these, like absentee landlords and export traders who live in the city, may be on the border between the rural and urban sectors. This may explain to some degree why only one-third of all financial savings are deposited with the rural branches of the financial institutions, even though all financial savings in the Flow-of-Funds Accounts come from households and the vast majority of households are living in rural areas. It may be recalled that the business 'groups' in Thailand, as briefly described in Chapter 2 (see also section 4.5.5 below), have their origin in regional merchant families, who were formerly engaged in agricultural trade that moved to Bangkok and then diversified to other activities. These groups may still function as an important channel for intersectoral flows of funds, as the trading activities of families in the group may generate surpluses that are deposited with the group's bank and channelled for use elsewhere. But obviously the question of why these groups do not wish to invest more in agriculture still needs to be answered.

The portfolio framework introduced in Chapter 1 might be helpful in trying to understand why those who control the surplus in the unincorporated sector have decided to invest more in financial assets than in physical assets within the sector.

Section 4.3.2 showed that households allocate their funds to three main uses: their own investment, corporate shares, and financial savings in financial institutions. The portfolio approach suggests that the allocation of wealth over alternative assets depends on the rates of return on these assets, on the uncertainty of these returns and on the transaction cost related to the asset.[4]

Rates of return and their uncertainty The main assets acquired by the household sector are physical capital goods, shares of corporations and deposits with banks.[5] The related rates of return are, respectively, the rate of return on capital in the unincorporated sector, the rate of return on equity capital and the deposit rate of interest. One would expect that in a perfect capital market there would be a relationship between the rates of return on different assets: at the margin, and allowing for differences in risk and transaction cost, rates of return should be equalized. Capital markets are obviously not perfect, but on the other hand, most savings are probably concentrated in the hands of the relatively few people who have an opportunity to make their own investments, have access to alternative assets, and who will be sensitive to differences and changes in relative rates of return.

Little information is available on the various rates of return. Some indirect indication may be obtained from the profit shares (that is retained profits as a percentage of sectoral value added) of the two sectors. These shares were used in Chapter 3 and were presented in Chart 3.1. The profit share of the unincorporated sector tends to be lower than that of the corporate sector. The factor shares of the two sectors are also likely to differ, with the corporate sector having a higher capital/labour ratio. Thus the higher profit share of the corporate sector does not necessarily indicate that the rate of profit is higher. If it is true, as suggested in Chapter 3, that the corporate sector has some degree of oligopoly or monopoly, one would expect its rate of profit to be higher than that of the more competitive unincorporated sector.

In 1977 the median rate of return on equity capital for the 95 largest manufacturing corporations was around 15 per cent. The spread was quite wide, though, with 22 companies reporting losses and 38 companies reporting returns in excess of 30 per cent (Vongvipanond 1980, p. 134). These figures are based on companies' reports and are not necessarily very reliable. The Security Exchange of Thailand (SET) reported a price/earning ratio of just below 10 per cent for the period 1975-81 for shares traded at the SET (SET 1982, p. 28). And TDRI (1986) reported a study on the rate of return of 67 selected stocks at the SET over a ten-year period. The average rate of return was around 16 per cent, the standard deviation was quite high, indicating a high risk. The risk of share holding lies not only in the uncertainty of dividend but also in the volatility of the entire market. The possibility of capital gains attracts many people to the stock market, but there may also be capital losses. After a speculative boom the SET trading collapsed in 1979. Since then many investors have preferred the more certain returns on bank deposits.

In a very interesting article, Usher had calculated, for an earlier period, a number of interest rates and rates of return, including two real rates of return on agricultural investments. The first was the rate of return on stockholding rice over the year, which was estimated at about 10 per cent but subject to risks due to fluctuations in the international price of rice. The second rate of return was calculated by comparing the rent paid on land to land prices. A small number of observations resulted in an average rate of return of around 8 per cent, but with variations between regions.[6] Usher compared these rates to the earning/price ratio of shares (12.5 per cent) and the commercial bank loan rate (between 10 and 15 per cent) (Usher 1967).

Given such rates of return, it is not surprising that agricultural investments remained low. More recently, it was observed that 'In the Upper North farmers underutilize their land because of low and unreliable returns' (Van de Meer 1981, p. 172). It is not known to what extent this observation applies to other regions in Thailand. It has been argued that the returns on investment in the unincorporated sector are so low that investment is only possible if they can rely on the exploitation of family labour. The scope for household investment is thus limited by the size of the household. New technologies in agriculture are not always labour saving; often more labour inputs are required, and returns may not be high and certain enough to justify the extensive use of hired labour.

Chart 3.1 very clearly shows that, whereas the profit share of the corporate sector was very stable over the years, that of the unincorporated businesses fluctuated quite strongly from year to year. This suggests that the returns on unincorporated enterprise may not only be lower but also far more uncertain than those of corporations. This applies very directly to the agricultural sector, where uncertain weather conditions, pests, and so on create an environment of uncertainty which makes the use of cash inputs (for example fertilizer) highly risky (World Bank 1982). In the case of export crops fluctuations in world market prices which are directly reflected in farm gate prices add further to the uncertainties.

Other factors in the agricultural sector contribute to this uncertainty. Forty-five per cent of all farm holdings have no legal title to their land (World Bank 1982, p. 30). These farmers are not tenants, but their farms are on unregistered forest land, etc. Since these farmers may run the risk of eviction, their incentive to invest is limited. The absence of a land title also means that they have no access to (cheap) official market credit. Feder (1986) concluded that in two North-eastern provinces, farmers with titles to their land used more variable inputs and had higher yields.[7]

In Chapter 1 it was suggested that the incentives to innovation in agriculture depend on the social relations of production. If the producer owns the land, he will reap the benefits of the investments made. Under land tenancy, he has to share such returns with the land owner so that the incentive to invest will be less. It may be relevant in this context that the region with superior investment opportunities in agriculture (the Central Region) is also the region where the incidence of land tenancy is highest, which might therefore reduce actual investments undertaken.

The rate of return on deposits is determined by the ceiling imposed by the Bank of Thailand. This ceiling changes only rarely, so its uncertainty is limited. The main element of uncertainty is the rate of inflation, which together with the fixed nominal deposit rate, determines the real deposit rate. The role of inflation is quite important: not only can the return on deposits turn negative when the rate of inflation exceeds the nominal deposit rate, but the real value of the outstanding deposits also declines. The value of physical assets and of shares may generally be expected to increase with the rate of inflation. Under conditions of inflation the corporate sector, with its price setting powers, is able to maintain its profits by adjusting its output prices. The demand pressures accompanying inflation may even increase the degree of capacity utilization and so increase the profit margin. The unincorporated sector does not have such price adjustment powers and may suffer more from inflation, unless of course that inflation originates with their output prices, for example, in response to an increase in world market prices for export commodities.

Inflation would therefore affect the returns of the corporate sector the least and those on financial assets the most. In evaluating the impact of inflation, on portfolio decisions, one has to consider expected inflation, as these expectations would induce the portfolio holder to make adjustments. In the monetary literature there are two theories on how inflationary expectations are formed. According to the 'adaptive expectations' hypothesis, people would learn, more or less rapidly, from past experience. In the 'rational expectations' hypothesis people 'know' what inflation will be by studying the relevant variables (such as the announced budget deficit that needs financing).[8] In Chapter 2 it was observed that the rate of inflation in Thailand has, on average, been relatively low and largely determined by the movements in world market prices. Given the low average rate of inflation, inflationary expectations may be low in general, and given the uncertain fluctuations due to world market prices, they might also have a short time perspective. The sensitivity of portfolio decisions to inflation might, therefore, be relatively low in Thailand.

The average *ex post* real deposit rate on time deposits was over 5 per cent in the 1960s, minus 2 per cent in the 1970s and close to 10 per cent in the 1980s. Given these rates, the patterns in the Flow-of-Funds Accounts of the household sector in Chart 4.1 (which show a rapid increase in the holdings of financial assets with financial institutions in the 1960s and, on average, a slower growth in the 1970s) are not surprising. The analysis in Chapter 2 (see section 2.3) suggests that the increase in financial savings is even larger, because within the financial assets there was a shift from the transaction-related narrow money balances (currency and demand deposits) towards the saving-related broad ones (time and saving deposits). The turnover rate on narrow money balances increased sharply as money was more efficiently used. The savings made in this way were apparently used to expand financial savings. These trends confirm the theoretical expectation formulated in Chapter 1 that, from an efficient portfolio perspective, there will be a tendency to minimize M1-balances (section 1.4.1).

The declining currency ratio observed in Chapter 2 may also be interpreted as a decline in the importance of the unregulated money market, as most transactions there use cash. The next section will make a more detailed analysis of the unregulated money market in Thailand and will show that, firstly, the rates of return on that market are not excessively dear if the high risks and transaction costs are taken into account; and, secondly, the limited evidence available indeed suggests that the relative size of the unregulated money market has declined over the years. An explanation may be that with the spread of official financial institutions, the transaction costs on the official credit market relative to those of the unregulated market have fallen, so that funds were shifted towards official financial institutions.

In conclusion, the average rate of return on equity capital is quite high, between 10 and 15 per cent on average, but there is a wide spread around that average. The returns on investments in the unincorporated sector are lower and subject to greater risks. It may be assumed that the real rates of return as calculated by Usher still have some relevance since technology and yields have not changed much. This would put the average rate of return on investments in agriculture between 5 and 10 per cent. The real return on deposits has fluctuated with inflation, and was around 5 per cent in the 1960s, negative during most of the 1970s and very high in recent years.

Inflation not only lowers returns on financial savings but also makes them more uncertain. If inflation moved relative prices against the unincorporated sector's investments, it would affect those returns, but would leave the returns of the corporate sector unaffected.

On the basis of these considerations, it is easy to understand why households that have a choice between investing in shares of corporations or in agriculture would prefer shares. The trend away from share capital, observed in Chart 4.1, could only be explained if, over the period, the level or uncertainty of the returns on shares changed. Chart 3.1 showed that the level of the corporate profit share has indeed fallen since the early 1970s. If it is assumed that the factor intensity in the corporate sector has not changed, it may be concluded that this fall in the profit share is due to a fall in the rate of profit. The fall in that profit rate could be explained by a fall in the degree of monopoly due to the increasing size of the domestic market, by the decline in tariff protection and by the increasing production for competitive export markets.

The growth in the holdings of financial assets by households appears to have been sensitive to the level of the real deposit rate, but it cannot be fully explained by the relative level of these returns. An important factor may have been the increased availability of the assets as a result of financial development which reduced transaction cost.

Transaction cost   Besides the rates of return and their uncertainty, liquidity or transaction cost is the third criterion in portfolio decisions. Investments in unincorporated enterprises or corporate shares are highly illiquid. Once the investment is made, it is quite difficult to dispose of the asset. Most corporations are not listed on the SET, where shares can be traded. Anyway, the SET is relatively small and inactive so that it may be difficult even to get rid of listed shares. Selling physical assets might be even more difficult and costly. It could be argued that this illiquidity does not really matter, since the household investing in its own firm or in shares of the corporation owned by its family will not have the intention to sell such assets at any time. But, on the other hand, this illiquidity, together with the uncertainty of the returns on such investments, may be a powerful argument for households to diversify into liquid financial assets.

In addition, the transaction cost of financial assets has significantly decreased due to the rapid expansion of financial institutions. Chapter 2 (section 2.3) described the rapid growth in the number of bank branches, which meant, for example, the travel time involved in depositing or withdrawing money in a savings account has been reduced. This factor makes financial assets more attractive.

Are the arguments listed above indeed capable of explaining the trends in the asset portfolios of households? The attempt to test them statistically concentrates on the financial asset holding by households, since this is the item that changed the most over the years. Households will want to hold more financial assets, or financial savings (FS) if:

(a) the rate of return on FS increases;
(b) the rate of return on alternative assets (that is physical investment or shares) falls;
(c) the transaction costs of the various assets change.

In a time-series analysis, it may be assumed that the degree of risk related to each of the assets does not change much. The transaction costs of physical investment and of share capital have also changed little, whereas the transaction cost of financial assets has changed with the growth of financial institutions.

On the basis of these arguments, the following equation is proposed:

(18) $FS/Y_u = a_0 + a_1 (i_d - p_{t-1}) - a_2 \, r + a_3 \, FD$

FS = financial savings
r = rate of return on physical investment in the unincorporated sector or on equity shares of corporations
FD = indicator of financial development.

In testing this equation use has been made of monetary and National Accounts statistics rather than of Flow-of-Funds data, as the former sets of data would allow testing over a longer period.

FS are defined as the annual change in the holdings of time and savings deposits with banks and of promissory notes of finance companies. Of course, not all these FS, so defined, are held by the household sector, but the bulk (80 to 90 per cent) is. The definition may also not capture all the financial savings made by households; a few other forms may exist, but these (for example, life insurance) are relatively unimportant in Thailand. The FS have been expressed as a percentage of the GDP of the unincorporated sector.

The real returns on financial assets are reflected by $(i_d - p_{t-1})$, the nominal ceiling deposit rate deflated by the consumer price index, lagged one year. As argued above, the expected return is important, so expected inflation should be used to deflate the nominal deposit rate. In the regression a simple lag structure of expected inflation is used, in which last year's actual inflation rate is taken as this year's expected inflation. Alternative formulations to derive the expected real deposit rate using, for instance, rational expectations or more complex lag structures were attempted, but they failed to improve the estimation results. The expected sign of this variable is positive.

The rate of return r on physical investment and on shares is unknown. Some incidental data are available and were mentioned above, but no consistent time series can be constructed. The regression therefore uses an alternative indicator, the growth rate of real GDP lagged one year. The idea behind this variable is that, if economic growth last year was quite good, then through some accelerator mechanism there will be a strong desire for directly productive investment in the unincorporated and the corporate sectors.[9] In that case, less funds will be used for FS, so the expected sign is negative.

The transaction cost variable FD is represented by the natural logarithm of the number of branch offices of financial institutions and is expected to have a positive impact.

The results of the regression for the period 1963-86 are as follows:

(19) $\quad FS/Y_u = -48.25 - 0.01(i_d - P_{t-1}) - 0.41g_{t-1} + 8.21FD$

$$\quad\quad (4.700) \quad (0.116) \quad\quad (1.664) \quad\quad (6.407)$$

$R^2 = 0.75$ and D.W. $= 1.61$

The coefficient of the real deposit rate is small and not significantly different from zero. The other coefficients are significant and have the expected sign. Equation (19) strongly supports the hypothesis that the substantial increase in financial savings is related to the rapid expansion of the financial system. In the short run, there is also a significant substitution between real investment and financial savings which is reflected in the growth variable.

A number of other studies have attempted to explain the rapid growth of financial savings in Thailand. Gupta separated total savings into financial savings (FS) and real savings (RS). He defined FS marginally wider than was done in equation (19) above and defined RS = S − FS as residue. His results were:

(20) $\quad FS = -41.095 + 0.002\, Y^p + 0.007\, Y^t - 0.68\, p^e - 0.42\, p^u\, +$

$$\quad\quad (1.55) \quad (0.02) \quad\quad (0.02) \quad\quad (2.57) \quad (3.10)$$

$$\quad\quad +4.04\, i_d + 0.75\, FIR$$
$$\quad\quad (1.05) \quad\quad (1.05)$$

$R^2 = 0.80 \quad$ D.W. $= 1.511$

And for real savings:

(21) $\quad RS = 100.714 + 0.40\, Y^p + 0.24\, Y^t + 0.74\, p^e + 0.34\, p^u\, -$

$$\quad\quad (6.46) \quad (8.14) \quad\quad (2.20) \quad\quad (4.80) \quad (4.22)$$

$$\quad\quad -11.60\, i_d - 2.38\, FIR$$
$$\quad\quad (4.89) \quad\quad (5.69)$$

$R^2 = 0.985;$ D.W. $= 2.13$
Y^p and Y^t = permanent and transitory income, respectively
p^e and p^u = expected and unexpected rates of inflation
FIR = Financial Intermediation Ratio (see equation (10) and note 9 of Chapter 3) (Gupta 1984, p. 124).

Gupta concluded that there was considerable substitution between financial and real savings because the coefficients of the rate of expected and unexpected inflation, the nominal rate of interest and the financial development indicator carry different signs in the two equations. As observed in Chapter 3, Gupta's equations probably suffer from multicollinearity between the income variables and the FIR. It is remarkable to find that the nominal interest rate has no significant impact on financial savings but does have a significant negative effect on real savings.

Go ran a regression using an equation more similar to equation (19):

(22) $\Delta M2/Y = 0.126 + 0.0027(i_d - p) + 0.0001\, y -$

    (1.27) (7.45)   (3.93)

    $- 0.0035g - 0.4363\, F/Y$

    (3.54) (3.38)

$R^2 = 0.81$; D.W. = 1.57

or:

(23) $\Delta M2/Y = 0.0059 + 0.0023(i_d - p) - 0.0039\, g -$

    (0.27) (5.24)   (3.06)

    $- 0.2166\, F/Y + 0.1508\, B/N$

    (1.43)   (1.62)

$R^2 = 0.68$; D.W. = 1.57
$\Delta M2/Y$ = growth of M2/GDP
y and g = the level and the growth rate of real GDP
B/N = the number of bank branch offices per 10,000 population (see equation (11) of Chapter 3).
F/Y = capital inflow from abroad/GDP   (Go 1984, p. 121).

These results confirm the negative impact of the growth rate (note that Go used the current growth rate rather than the lagged growth rate used in equation (19)). But contrary to equation (19), a significant positive impact of the real deposit rate is found. It is difficult to understand why Go included foreign savings as a variable; no explanation is given and the significant negative impact of the variable is difficult to interpret. Two equations are presented because y and B/N could not be included together given their high correlation. Their statistical significance means that there is a trend value in the financial savings ratio; this could be due to growing income levels or to the expanding financial system or both. Kuramochi (1987) ran a regression of the M2/GDP ratio (rather than the ΔM2/GDP ratio of equation (22)) for the period 1962–85 and also found a significant negative impact of the real growth rate and a significant positive impact of the real deposit rate and the financial intermediation indicator (the latter defined as the share of private investment financed from external sources).

The most interesting results were obtained by Kirakul, Sriphayak and Ploydanai (1984, hereafter KSP 1984). They used Flow-of-Funds data on the household sector over the period 1967–82 to explain household savings embodied in real or physical assets (I_h), acquisition of financial assets by households (FA_h) and the incurrence of financial liabilities by households (FL_h). The following results were obtained:

(24) $\quad \ln I_h = -2.4197 + 1.01776\ln Y_h - 0.4964\ln i_d + 0.00506 p^e$

$$\qquad\qquad (5.81) \qquad (20.99) \qquad\quad (2.13) \qquad\quad (1.18)$$
$R^2 = 0.989$; D.W. = 2.03

(25) $\quad \ln FA_h = -7.0159 + 1.3894 \ln Y_h + 0.02413\ (i_d - p^e)$

$$\qquad\qquad (6.51) \qquad (15.74) \qquad\qquad (2.36)$$
$R^2 = 0.961$; D.W. = 0.76

(26) $\quad \ln FL_h = -3.9399 + 2.22289 \ln I_h - 2.8278 \ln i_l$

$$\qquad\qquad (0.9) \quad (9.93) \qquad\qquad (1.42)$$
$R^2 = 0.942$; D.W. = 2.94

In which:
I_h, FA_h, and FL_h = as defined above
Y_h = nominal disposable income of the household sector
P^e = expected inflation, formed with adaptive expectations
i_d = weighted average of nominal deposit rates of commercial banks
i_l = maximum loan rate of commercial banks
(KSP 1984).

The results show that the income elasticity of household investments is around one and that of household financial savings greater than one. The coefficients of i_d in equation (24) and real i_d in equation (25) indicate the substitution between real investments and financial savings. Equation (26) for FL suggests that one of the means through which that substitution takes place is the effect of the higher loan rate (an increase in the deposit rate is likely to be accompanied by an increase in the loan rate). The higher loan rate discourages household investment, and this may make the funds available to increase the financial savings. The substitution is thus between physical investment and deposits and not between consumption and savings.

These results seem to confirm the findings of equation (19) above that, firstly, there is a long-term upward trend effect in the financial savings of households. In equations (19) and (23), this was captured by the significant impact of the financial development variable; in equation (25) it was captured by the income elasticity.[10] Secondly, all regressions reported suggest a short-term substitution between physical investment and financial savings. This substitution is the outcome of several factors. First of all, there is the effect of the real deposit rate of interest. With rather fixed nominal deposits rates, this mechanism works mainly through changes in the rate of inflation. A second mechanism suggested is the cost of credit. As KSP (1984) showed, the level of the loan rate does affect the demand for credit by households. And as the earlier section already noted (see section 4.3.2), households do increasingly use credit to complement their own resources. The third effect, suggested in equation (19), is that substitution takes place in response to changes in the expected returns on physical investments.

In summary, the findings of Chart 4.1, showing that over the years, households have changed their asset portfolios by holding relatively less equity shares, a more or less constant proportion of own investments and an increasing share of financial assets, can be explained as follows.

(i) The unincorporated firms in the household sector may have a preference for own investment but are discouraged in part by factors such as the size of the household and available labour, and by available technologies, but most of all by the low and uncertain returns on such investments. As the level of these returns and their uncertainty may not have altered considerably over the years, it is hardly surprising that the investment ratio of the unincorporated sector has also changed little.

(ii) The rapid growth in the holdings of financial assets in financial institutions by the household sector can only be partly explained by the attractive returns on such assets. In the 1960s these returns were attractive and certain, but in the 1970s they were often negative in real terms. A main reason for the increased holdings of these financial assets, then, may be institutional. Rapid financial development has reduced the transaction cost of financial assets, which has led to an increase in the share of households' funds allocated to these, and has also enabled households to adjust their portfolios more readily to short-term changes in returns.

(iii) The fall in the use of funds to purchase shares could be explained by the fall in the rate of return on shares, resulting from the fall in the rate of profit of corporations due to increased competition in the corporate sector.

(iv) In explaining these patterns, it should be recognized that most of the surplus of the household sector is concentrated in the hands of a few: rich farmers, traders, rice millers, etc. Such persons may typically have diversified business interests and may be able to shift resources between them. They may also directly or indirectly be connected to some of the 'groups' that dominate the Thai corporate sector. The role of the groups in the Thai economy is a subject on which there is little hard information, but it could be suggested that corporations, for reasons of strategic flexibility or for fiscal reasons, may have preferred to finance the increase in their activities by credits from the group's bank rather than by increased issue of shares. The families related to the groups would then increase their bank deposits rather than their share holdings. It has been noted previously that this may also be one of the channels by which the agricultural surplus leaves the sector through financial institutions: through traders and middlemen related to the groups.

(v) Short-term substitution processes have become more important. The main factors determining the direction of these processes are the fluctuations in the rate of return on physical investment and the changes in the rate of inflation, which affects the rates of return on equity, real assets and financial assets in different ways.

4.5.2 A digression on the unregulated money market

Chart 4.1 shows the increased involvement, on both the asset and the liability side, of the household sector with the official financial system. This official system, though, is only one part of the entire money and credit market. As discussed in Chapter 1, the other segment, called in this study the unregulated money market, can be quite important in developing countries and is certainly very relevant to unincorporated enterprises. Over time, with the growth of the official financial system, this market might be replaced by official institutions. Part of the increase in the holding of assets and liabilities with financial institutions might therefore be due to a replacement.[11]

The unregulated market can be separated into an urban and a rural segment. There is almost no information available on the urban segment in Thailand. Rozental (1970) conducted a small urban survey suggesting that 40 per cent of the firms participated in it and obtained about 25 per cent of their funds from it. These were mainly small industrial and retail firms depending on money-lenders, rotating credit societies, and so on (Rozental 1970, Chapter 7). The Household Savings Survey conducted by the Bank of Thailand in 1980 concluded that households in municipal areas obtained 61 per cent of their total liabilities from official financial institutions and 39 per cent from informal sources (Kirakul 1986).[12]

The rural credit market in Thailand has been the subject of more research, although not as much as one would wish. The most detailed study is still that of Thisyamondol, Arromdee and Long (1965, hereafter TAL 1965), covering a sample of 742 farmers over the entire country in 1962/63. A more recent study, but a less comprehensive one, is Onchan, Chalamwong and Aungsumalin (1974, hereafter OCA 1974) covering a sample of 90 farm households in Chainat Province in Central Thailand. Phongpaichit (1982) is a study based on a sample of 488 households in three villages in the Central, Northern and North-eastern regions of the country in 1981. This study did not specifically focus on credit markets but collected some useful information. Even more recent but again less complete is Feder, Onchan and Raparla (1986, hereafter FOR 1986), dealing with a sample taken in three provinces in the year 1984.

The Bank of Thailand also conducted a Household Saving Survey in 1980 among urban and rural households throughout the country (see Kirakul 1986). From these studies the following stylized facts may be derived.

(a) Most farm households are indebted. The actual percentages of such farmers were found to be: 68 per cent by TAL (1965); 72 per cent (OCA 1974); and about 60 per cent (FOR 1986).

(b) There appear to have been shifts in the origin of credit received by farm households. Breaking down the total value of credit by its origin shows:

	TAL (1965) (%)	OCA (1974) (%)	Phongpaichit (1982) (%)
Relatives and neighbours	47	49	46
Commercial lenders	46	29	13
Official financial institutions	5	23	41
Total value of loans	100	100	100

TAL (1965) and Phongpaichit (1982) cover villages in various regions of the country, OCA (1974) only a province in the Central Region. Commercial lenders include landlords, local stores, crop buyers and money-lenders. The various studies are not comparable in terms of coverage and location,[13] but the trend over time suggested by the three sources listed above is confirmed by other data as well. The 1980 survey of the Bank of Thailand observed that rural households obtained 58 per cent of their total credit from official financial institutions (Kirakul 1986). Panayotou reported on a 1979/80 survey of 795 farmers: most farmers were indebted (only one-third were not) and about half of them had access to official institutional credit. Only 18 per cent of the sample farmers were exclusively dependent on unregulated market sources (Panayotou 1985). The enormous increase in the role of official financial institutions, among which the BAAC is dominant, is confirmed by monetary statistics on the sectoral allocation of credit (see later). This pattern of change also applies to the non-agricultural sector. Onchan (1985) presented data on the sources of funds of non-farm enterprises. In 1965 such firms depended more on the unregulated money market than on the official financial institutions. By 1978 both the smaller and the larger non-farm enterprises depended mainly on official sources of credit. The role of commercial lenders remains very important. In Thailand the role of the professional money-lender is comparatively small, the commercial lenders are predominantly traders, rice millers, etc. Quite often these commercial lenders are, in their turn, borrowers themselves from the banks. The role of landlords as commercial lenders may not be as widespread in Thailand as in some other LDCs, as land tenancy is not dominant. Hence it is likely that the interlocking of the credit market is more with the commodity markets than with factor markets.

(c) The relative size of the unregulated money market is difficult to assess. TAL (1965) used their estimate of the average indebtedness of the households in their sample to calculate a total rural indebtedness in Thailand of Baht 9 billion, of which 95 per cent came from the unregulated market. The size of the urban unregulated money market in that year is unknown. In 1963 total credit extended by official financial institutions to the urban and rural private sector also amounted to around Baht 9 billion, so that the unregulated and the official market segments were more or less of the same size. Wai (1977) gave an estimate, relating to 1970, of rural/agricultural indebtedness as being equivalent to 30 per cent of the claims of the banking system on the private sector. Sources and methods of calculation are not mentioned. Go (1984, p. 68) reported an estimate for the end of 1980 of a total agricultural credit of Baht 47 billion, of which Baht 25 billion was from official financial institutions and the rest from the unregulated market. The Household Savings Survey of the Bank of Thailand reported a total indebtedness of rural and urban households at the informal market of Baht 47 billion in 1980, equivalent to about 17 per cent of the credit extended by official financial institutions to the entire private sector. Taken at their face value these estimates indicate that the unregulated money market, when corrected for inflation, is hardly growing. Relating the estimates of outstanding rural/agricultural non-official credit to total agricultural GDP gives a proportion falling from 36 per cent in 1963 to 29 per cent in 1970 and 14 per cent in 1980. All these figures and proportions are based on very rough estimates, but the trend seems to be clear: the unregulated money market is relatively stagnant and a rapidly expanding official credit market is taking care of a growing share of credit.

(d) All studies agree that the demand for credit on the unregulated market is predominantly short run, say for less than a year and often even for less than half a year, and also seasonal in nature. In the first half of the year, farmers have just harvested and use the proceeds to repay debts and accumulate cash balances. In the second half of the year, the planting and growing season, credit is needed to finance inputs and family consumption. To a significant extent the seasonal cash flow pattern of traders and millers is precisely the reverse of that of farmers (TAL 1965). Most credit is used for productive purposes, for working capital if that term is widely interpreted as covering, next to the cost of purchased productive inputs, also the living expenses of the household when they work on the farm. These consumption needs arise out of the seasonality of the production process. It is observed in various studies that most loans are made available in cash; only a small proportion is in kind.

(e)   The interest rates charged on the loans show a great variation, depending on the type of lender and on other factors such as duration and size of loan, TAL (1965) observed an average interest rate of 2.4 per cent per month on the unregulated market compared to 0.8 per cent on the official market. OCA (1974) gave an average of 1.75 per cent per month, and FOR (1986) suggested an annual rate of 48 per cent compared to 15 per cent at the official market. Panayotou (1985) reported an average interest rate of 24 per cent. Vongpradhip (1986) quoted interest rates charged in various informal money market activities (such as personal and business rotating credit societies, trade credit and cheque discounts). The various interest rates tend to circulate around 30 per cent, with the exception of the personal rotating credit societies, where the rates are higher. Taken together, these studies suggest an average rate of interest of between 20 and 30 per cent per year. Of course, some loans, such as consumer loans or loans for households in distress, may carry much higher rates (see Usher 1967). These rates are considerable but probably not excessive given the economic arguments that were discussed in Chapter 1 (section 1.4.1). Most observations on the market conditions in Thailand's rural areas suggest that the degree of monopoly of traders is limited (Long 1968; Rozenthal 1970; Ingram 1971). If agricultural trade is not monopolistic, there would seem to be little scope for traders to be so when extending credit.[14]   The diversity of the sources of credit, which all studies show, also suggests that monopoly power is limited.

(f)   It is likely that there is significant complementarity and overlap between the unregulated and the official credit market segments. It has already been observed that suppliers of non-official credit may themselves be borrowers from banks and may simply pass the money on to their borrowers, who tend to be farmers without access to these banks themselves. Small and medium-sized firms that do have some access to bank credit could borrow simultaneously on the unregulated market when in need of short-term funds or a quick disbursal. One popular credit activity in Thailand is the 'pia-huey' or rotating credit society; it is described by Rozenthal (1970) as a predominantly urban phenomenon, but Go (1984) suggested that it is also quite common in rural areas. Many people active in these societies can simultaneously hold deposits with or have credit from banks and other financial institutions. It would appear, then, that the official and the unregulated money markets are partly competitive and partly complementary. There are quite a number of channels which link the unregulated and the official credit markets and along which substitution between the two credit market segments can take place in response to changes in relative rates of return.

These studies on the unregulated money market lead to a number of clear conclusions. First of all, while the market may have grown in absolute terms, after correcting for inflation, not much of the growth remains and, when expressed in relative terms, for example, in relation to the size of the official credit market or to the agricultural production, the importance has been declining. This is what one would expect, of course. With economic and financial development, the official financial institutions take over from the unregulated market. At the same time, one would not expect the unregulated market to disappear altogether. Banks remain closed to certain groups, to certain sectors and to certain activities.

A second conclusion is that there have been significant shifts in the asset and liability portfolios of the rural part of the unincorporated sector. On the liability side, firms have shifted from the unregulated market to the official financial institutions, and there has been a related shift in their assets towards deposits with these institutions. The causality between the two trends runs both ways: the increase in deposits allows rural bank branches to extend more rural credit, while firms will hold deposits with the banks to have easy access to credit. The increased role of the official financial system in extending agricultural credit is also the result of government policy which, since 1975, has forced banks to increase their agricultural lending (see Chapter 2, section 2.4).

It is likely that the majority of rural deposits comes from a relatively small number of households; that is richer farmers, traders, millers, and so on, who may also be active as suppliers of funds on the unregulated credit market. Why should such people shift their resources to banks rather than increase their own credit activities? A main reason may be that the demand for non-official credit has fallen with the growing role of official lenders.

In the context of the present chapter, dealing with intersectoral flows, the role of the unregulated money market may appear not to be very important, as it channels few intersectoral flows. To a large extent, both supply and demand originate in the household sector. The sources are mainly relatives and neighbours, traders and rich farmers who extend credit to poorer farmers. In fact, the unregulated market may have functioned as a channel of funds from the official money market to the unincorporated sector, for instance, when traders used the credit obtained from banks to extend loans. The transfer of activities from the unregulated to the official financial market has intersectoral implications though. The households have increased their deposits with banks more than their loans from banks, so that the net resources available to the financial institutions have increased. These resources have been used to extend credit to the non-household sectors. The rural branches of commercial banks, as observed in Chapter 2, channel funds from the the rural areas to the cities because their deposits exceed their loans. So the shift from the unregulated to the official financial system might also affect the size and direction of the intersectoral flow of funds, although it is impossible to assess to what extent.

4.5.3 The corporate sector

In the previous sections, the household sector was analysed in considerable detail because of its importance as the main domestic surplus sector in the Flow-of-Funds Accounts. In this and the next section, some brief comments will be made on the behaviour of the corporate and the public sectors.

The model proposed in Chapter 3 asserts that corporations decide on their desired level of investment and subsequently determine optimal patterns of financing them. Their portfolio behaviour, in the context of an analysis of the financial system, is therefore concentrated on choosing an optimal liability portfolio. All sources of finance have their particular cost and uncertainty. Retaining profits may be the easiest and most attractive way of financing investment. Most gross profits are retained in the corporations; it was estimated that over the 1962–78 period, retained profits and depreciation allowances were equal to about 80 per cent of total gross profits (Vongvipanond 1980). Retained profits might be increased by raising the output price, but that could hinder the growth of sales and benefit competitors. If the corporation issues new shares, this will subsequently raise required dividend payments, and could weaken the control over the corporation. Bank and foreign loans will carry interest charges.

Of course, individual corporations differ in the extent to which they can make use of these different sources, but for the corporate sector as a whole the following picture emerges.

As Chart 4.3 shows, there has been, over the years, a tendency for the contribution of 'own capital' (that is retained profits and new share capital) to fall, but on the whole this source still accounts for about half of the total resources and finances over 60 per cent of corporate investment. Vongvipanond (1980) provided some data on a small sample of firms registered at the SET which suggest a higher proportion of self-financing of investment. According to these data, external funds are only used to finance a small part of fixed investment and all of working capital needs. The contribution of own capital may have fallen because the increased competition that corporations face has put the gross profits under pressure. It has also been observed that issuing new shares is a relatively costly way of financing a corporation. New shareholders expect a dividend that is at least higher than the deposit rate of interest; to pay such dividends, firms require quite substantial pre-tax profits (World Bank 1983b, p. 36). So it should not be surprising that the dependence on external funds has increased, particularly considering that the supply of these funds has been readily available. The dependence on external funds leads to a relatively high debt–equity ratio: the median value of this ratio for the 95 largest manufacturing firms in 1977 was 2.75 : 1 (Vongvipanond 1980); and Chapter 3 (section 3.3.4) reported an even higher ratio for medium-sized and large firms.

It may be suggested, then, that the availability of own savings is largely determined by long-term market conditions. The relative market power of the corporation (degree of monopoly) might have decreased somewhat in recent years, but on the whole corporate savings are rather stable. Given the relative stability of the corporate savings ratio, the fluctuations in the level of investment are reflected in variations in external funding. The two main sources of external funds for the corporate sector are loans from domestic banks and loans from abroad. As Chart 4.2 and Table 4.3 show, the dependence of corporations on foreign finance has always been quite high. This may have been largely related to international trade financing and to the activities of multinational corporations in Thailand. But in recent years, with the rapid development of international financial markets, large domestic corporations have also obtained direct access to international markets for credit.

Chart 4.2 and Table 4.3 also show that the contribution of domestic banks to the financing of the corporate sector has significantly increased with the increase in funds available to these banks. And Chart 4.2 further shows that since the 1970s, when large corporations started to get access to international credit markets, the contributions of domestic financial institutions and of foreign capital markets have often changed in directions that offset each other, strongly suggesting that there is substitution between the two in response to changes in the relative interest cost or the availability of domestic credit. There is a tendency for the share of foreign loans in total external sources (that is foreign loans and domestic credit) to fluctuate with the interest rate differential between international and domestic financial markets, so that the share of foreign loans rises when these loans are relatively cheap.[15]

4.5.4 The public sector

The trends observed in the government and state enterprise sectors are discussed together because the movements in both sectors are difficult to explain from a portfolio perspective and are more likely to be due to political and institutional factors.

The number of state enterprises in Thailand is small compared to that in other Asian countries like Indonesia, South Korea or India. Their contribution to domestic capital formation, between one-third and one-fourth of the total, has been substantial, though, and has increased since the early 1970s (UN ESCAP 1985, p. 172). The main sectors where state enterprises are active are transport and communications and public utilities (Go 1984). These corporations contribute some of their profits to the government and they receive equity capital or grants from the government to finance their investment.

The investment activities in the state enterprise sector increased rapidly in the period covered by the Flow-of-Funds, as Chart 4.4 clearly shows. This is due not to an increase in the number of enterprises but to an increase in the activities of existing firms. The contribution of 'own capital' (that is, retained profits and new shares) to the financing of these investments fell, and the increasing gap was filled completely by foreign borrowing (see Chart 4.5).

Government savings as a proportion of GDP fell over the years for reasons analysed in Chapter 3. The government investment ratio also fell somewhat, but not enough to prevent an increase in the financing gap. This gap was filled by increased borrowing from domestic financial institutions, and the contribution of foreign loans also increased (see Charts 4.6 and 4.7).

The reduction in own financing by state enterprises and government is not the outcome of portfolio adjustment based on comparing the relative economic costs of the various sources of funds. It is rather the outcome of political processes that made it difficult to increase the tax burden or the prices charged by public enterprises. Many of the state enterprises (for example, public transport and public utilities companies) are in energy-intensive sectors. After the oil price increases in 1973 and 1979, the government preferred to subsidize such activities to soften the domestic inflationary impact of these external shocks. As a result, the profits of state enterprises fell.[16] The compensation for this decline in profits and the resources for the expanded investment activities of the state enterprises were obtained through borrowing abroad (Leeahtam 1985).

But the changes at the international financial markets are also important. Since the mid-1970s, lending to LDCs by international banks has increased enormously. These banks have a strong preference for public sector loans which can be guaranteed by the government. Thus government and state enterprises have preferential access to these markets. It could even be argued that their easier access to international finance has reduced saving efforts of government and state enterprises. The possible negative impact of foreign capital inflows on domestic saving efforts was discussed in Chapter 1 (section 1.3). In Chapter 3 where analysis was based on National Accounts data, the state enterprises were included in the corporate sector. Equation (34) in Chapter 3 showed that the foreign capital inflow had a negative, but statistically not significant, impact on the corporate savings ratio. It could be argued that this effect, to the extent that it exists, is due to the behaviour of the state enterprises. Equation (39) in Chapter 3 did not find a negative coefficient for the foreign capital variable in the government savings equation, although the positive coefficient was not statistically significant. This might not be so surprising as the Thai government finances most of its deficit from domestic sources.

4.5.5 Financial institutions

Financial institutions have only limited freedom of choice in the adjustment of their asset and liability portfolios. On the liability side, their main source of funds is time and savings deposits. Financial institutions have to accept all deposits that are offered to them at the imposed ceiling for the deposit rate of interest. Apparently, banking business has been quite profitable, for banks have very actively tried to increase their deposits. As the 'price' of deposits (that is the rate of interest) is fixed, competition for deposits through the price mechanism has been impossible, so that other means (for example, rapid expansion of branches and advertising and the offer of other bank services to clients) have been used to attract deposits.

As the studies reviewed in Chapter 2 concluded, commercial banks tend to follow the demand for credit. But, of course, there are limits to the extent to which banks can satisfy demands. The expansion of credit leads to an increase in outstanding demand deposits, so that banks have to increase their holdings of required reserves. To the extent that loans are being used to make cash withdrawals or foreign payments, the banks lose reserves. The amount of available reserves may therefore limit credit expansion. To be able to follow the demand for credit, banks must either have excess reserves, or be able to increase their funds by attracting more savings deposits, or be able to borrow extra reserves from the central bank or abroad.

It was observed in Chapter 2 that banks tend to hold excess reserves. This is one of their ways of dealing with the uncertainties surrounding the supply of and demand for funds. The other main way is borrowing from financial institutions abroad. The fluctuations in the net foreign liabilities of financial institutions are shown in Chart 4.8. The pattern of this variable is the outcome of a complex process. Since the large corporations have started to borrow directly abroad, a pattern is emerging in which corporations vary the foreign share of their borrowing requirement in response to interest rate differentials. If corporations borrow relatively more from abroad, they need less domestic credit and, therefore, financial institutions have less need for reserves. The result is that net borrowing abroad of banks often moves in the opposite direction from that of corporations.

There could also have been a substitution between public and private borrowing from banks. When the government became worried about its external debt after about 1981 it increased its borrowing at local markets. The private corporations, crowded out at the local capital markets, were forced to borrow more abroad (World Bank 1986).

Credit extended to the corporate sector has increased rapidly with the increase in funds available to the banks. Credit extended to the unincorporated sector has also increased significantly over the period under study. This might be due to a considerable degree to the gradual shift of funds from the unregulated credit market to official institutions. It has also been supported by government policies forcing banks to allocate a given share of their credits to the agricultural sector.

The credit extended by financial institutions to the government can be and is forced by such instruments as (i) the inclusion of bond holdings in the reserve requirement, and (ii) forcing banks to hold bonds as a precondition for permission to open new branches.

It was observed before that banks follow the demand for credit, but does that imply that all loan demands are satisfied? Obviously not: banks have to turn down some loan requests. In the literature reviewed in Chapter 1 (section 1.4.3), it is suggested that banks will judge loan requests rationally, on the basis of the expected returns and risks of the project to be financed with the loan. In so doing, banks would guarantee an efficient allocation of resources and financial development would contribute to economic growth. But whether banks really do follow that line of action has been questioned. What is the nature of financial institutions in Thailand?

As already discussed in Chapters 1 and 2, business in Thailand is rather concentrated. There are a number of conglomerates or 'groups', centred on one or a small number of families and generally active in many different lines of business. There can be no doubt that such groups are extremely important in Thailand: Krirkkiat Phipatseritham collected detailed information on them, and some of the main groups and the businesses they control are described in Phipatseritham and Yoshihara (1983). In that study also some characteristics of the Thai business groups are identified:

(a) Compared to the Japanese Zaibatsu, the groups in Thailand are still much less concentrated, probably due to the relatively recent start of the industrialization process in Thailand. Groups are not always dominated by one family but often centre around two or more families. Some corporations can also be the member of two groups (for instance, one group centred on a bank and the second a more industry-centred group) or they can form joint ventures with multinationals.

(b) All groups started their capital accumulation in trade, and all groups are dominated by families of Chinese origin. Historically, these families were engaged in the trade of rice, sugar or tin, or in the import trade. They diversified later into industrial activities.

(c) All groups are Bangkok based. Even those that originated in regional trade subsequently moved to Bangkok.

(d) All groups engage in political patronage or, in recent years, participate in political parties. Through these links they can obtain information, influence decisions and receive protection. The political links are particularly important for commercial banks.

Prasartset (1980) emphasized that the concentration of economic power in Thailand is increasing rapidly for three reasons. In the first place, as Thailand is a latecomer in the industrialization process and technologically dependent, there is a tendency towards large production units in a relatively small market. This can easily result in monopoly power. Secondly, there is a lack of countervailing power: trade unions are impotent and the government stimulates rather than controls the concentration of economic power. A third important reason is that the prominence of banking capital lifts the restrictions of self-finance, enabling some firms to grow very quickly indeed. Of course, this gives the banks great strength. Not surprisingly the most powerful and dynamic groups in Thailand are those centred around banks (see also Hewison 1981).

The picture that emerges is one of Thai banks controlled by a few families and located at the centre of a network of trading and industrial enterprises, many of which are characterized by significant monopoly power. Prasartset (1985) reported data on the asset holdings of the 65 largest business groups in Thailand in 1978–79. The 12 groups organized around banks consisted of 398 separate corporations, which owned 73 per cent of the assets of all 65 groups. The banks control the firms in their groups through interlocking directorships and through share holding (Prasartset 1985). In fact, the economic power of the group and its political connections can often help to increase protection for the group's firms and so further increase its monopoly powers. The market position of banks in particular is carefully protected. New banks are not allowed and foreign banks may not establish branches.[17]

It seems somewhat naive to assume that these banks would allocate their resources purely on grounds of economic efficiency. Many studies (see Chapter 2) have shown that medium- and small-scale firms have limited access to bank credit.

What can be said about the allocation of credit by financial institutions? Three tendencies can be identified: (i) a concentration on large firms and projects; (ii) a concentration on the corporate sector; and (iii) a concentration on the Bangkok area. On the first point, the concentration on large customers, data were already provided in Chapter 2 showing that large loans account for most of the credit given. Loans in excess of Baht 5 million together accounted for 58 per cent of all loans, and 20,000 clients held 70 per cent of all loans.[18]

Table 4.6 presents some information on the second point, the sectoral allocation of credit. The share of the agricultural sector has increased in the 1970s but is still low compared to the contribution of this sector to GDP. Using the definitions of the corporate and unincorporated sector as given in Chapter 2 is difficult here, as the monetary statistics on which Table 4.6 is based use a different breakdown. In addition, the unincorporate-corporate dichotomy is a breakdown of production, whereas it is clear from Table 4.6 that banks not only finance production but also trade and consumption. But however one tries to resolve these statistical difficulties, the outcome is always that the proportion of credit allocated to the unincorporated sector is smaller than the share of that sector in GDP would suggest. Comparing the monetary statistics in Table 4.6 with the Flow-of-Funds data does not lead to a change in the earlier conclusion that there is a net outflow of funds, through financial institutions from the unincorporated sector to the corporations. The sectoral allocation of credit from finance companies is even more directed towards the corporate sector (see, for example, Viksnins 1980; Go 1984).

Table 4.6   Sectoral breakdown of commercial bank credit
(% distribution)

	1970–74	1975–79	1980–84	1985	1986
Agriculture	2.1	4.8	6.8	7.4	7.3
Mining	1.1	0.7	0.7	0.6	0.6
Manufacturing	16.5	18.6	21.1	23.1	22.8
Construction	5.4	4.9	5.2	5.6	5.6
Real estate	5.2	3.3	3.0	3.7	3.8
Imports	18.7	13.3	9.3	6.5	5.9
Exports	10.0	12.0	9.3	8.5	9.1
Wholesale & retail trade	22.1	22.0	23.6	23.1	23.2
Public utilities	1.2	1.9	2.1	1.8	1.7
Banks & other fin. institutions	4.3	6.1	5.9	6.0	6.1
Services	5.3	4.1	4.5	5.1	5.2
Personal cons.	7.9	8.3	8.3	8.6	8.8
Others	0.1	–	–	–	–
Total	100.0	100.0	100.0	100.0	100.0

The regional concentration of economic activity in Thailand is high. It was already observed that all business groups are Bangkok-based, and the entire corporate sector has a strong tendency to concentrate around Bangkok. Commercial banks reflect that centralizing tendency and have contributed to it. Around 1965, 87 per cent of all commercial bank credit was extended in the Bangkok area, and around 1980 that proportion was still 75 per cent. The deposits collected by the banks in the Bangkok area were 73 and 62 per cent of the total for these two periods. Commercial banks, through their provincial branches, have thus helped to shift resources to the Bangkok region. Table 4.7 gives more detailed information on this flow. The credit/deposit ratio (CDR) in the provincial areas (that is, all areas except Bangkok) was low: up to the mid-1970s, less than half of rural deposits were re-lent locally. In 1977 the monetary authorities introduced a rule that bank branches had to re-lend locally 60 per cent of the deposits collected. Since then the provincial CDR has indeed increased, but it remains considerably lower than the CDR for Bangkok, so the flow of finance from the provinces to the city has continued. In Table 4.7 the provincial deposit surplus (that is deposits–credits) is also expressed as a percentage of the credit extended in Bangkok. The conclusion is that, on average, about one-fifth of the Bangkok credits was financed by transfers from the rural areas. Until the early 1970s, there appeared to be a tendency for this proportion to increase; in recent years government policy has helped to bring it down.

Table 4.7   Credit/deposit ratio of commercial banks (percentages)

	Provinces	Bangkok	Transfer*
1964	45	–	18
1965	41	107	21
1966	38	93	26
1967	42	95	23
1968	46	90	22
1969	47	100	21
1970	48	102	21
1971	47	96	22
1972	44	83	29
1973	47	99	30
1974	43	108	28
1975	49	111	27
1976	52	111	25
1977	64	110	19
1978	73	117	15
1979	77	131	11
1980	69	122	18
1981	73	129	–

$$*\text{Transfer} = \frac{\text{(deposits–credits at provincial branches)}}{\text{credit extended in Bangkok}}$$

The figures in Table 4.7 refer to the activities of commercial banks only, but bringing in the activities of other financial institutions would not change the overall trend, since commercial banks account for 80 per cent of all rural deposits and credit. The other financial institutions for deposits that have a rural presence are the Government Savings Bank, which also collects deposits in the rural areas and uses this money to finance the government deficit and, on the credit side, the BAAC, which channels funds it obtains from commercial banks to rural lenders. The finance companies are mainly an urban enterprise.

The preference of financial institutions for large loans, corporate clients and urban location can partly be explained by economic motives. Extending large loans in the city, near to the headquarters of the bank, reduces administration costs and increases control. Loans to corporations involve lower risks than those to smaller companies or to agriculture. These economic arguments, though, refer to the bank's operation cost and profitability, rather than to the economic benefits of projects to be financed; they do not indicate that from a social perspective, banks are 'efficient'. The preferences of the banks are also based on non-economic arguments such as personal contacts, group alliances, etc. This implies that it is premature to assume, as some studies reviewed in Chapter 1 did, that an increase in the role of the financial system in allocating resources will contribute to social efficiency.[19]

4.6 Financial intermediation, growth and distribution

4.6.1 Effects of intersectoral flows: sectoral balances

The main channel through which resources flow out of the agricultural sector appears to be the flows through financial institutions. These voluntary flows are the result of economic calculation of where such funds would earn the highest returns. One could therefore argue that these flows of funds help to shift resources to the more dynamic industrial sectors and thus stimulate the growth and diversification of the economy. As the profit share of the corporate sector is greater than that of the unincorporated sector, it might also help to increase the overall profit share of the economy and thereby increase the savings ratio.

But, as discussed in Chapter 1, sustained development requires an appropriate balance between the various sectors in the economy. In the development literature, the problem of sectoral balance is discussed mainly in terms of a balance between the agricultural and industrial sector. Economic development is only possible if a surplus can be generated and mobilized for investment. In the early stages of development agriculture is virtually the only sector where such a surplus is generated, so it is inevitable that part of this surplus will be mobilized for investment elsewhere in the economy. But the repercussions this has on the agricultural sector need to be analysed carefully on both the supply and the demand side.

In the context of these theoretical considerations, the case of Thailand is quite special in two respects: as a net exporter of food and as a land surplus economy. In the first instance, as Thailand is a major exporter of basic necessities, any increase in the domestic demand for these goods can be met by reducing exports. This could undermine growth because the exports are necessary to finance the imports of investment goods, but the result is that the internal terms of trade are not much affected by the increasing demand for food. The prices of agricultural goods are largely determined by world market prices, thus an increase in domestic demand will have no effect on prices. This explains the absence of domestic inflation in Thailand.

Stagnation in agriculture may obstruct economic development (see Chapter 1, section 1.2). Has the agricultural sector restrained industrial growth in Thailand by supply constraints (for example, the foreign exchange earning capacity) or by keeping domestic demand low? In Chapter 2 the sustained rapid growth of the agricultural sector was noted. Agricultural growth has a number of aspects:

179

(i)   Rice output grew, on average over the last 20 years, at an annual growth rate of around 3 per cent, so it could easily cope with population growth, whilst leaving a comfortable export surplus.

(ii) Most of this growth was due to acreage expansion. The acreage under rice increased from around 5.9 million hectares around 1960 to about 9.6 million hectares around 1980. The yield per hectare over these years increased only from around 1600 kg to 1800 kg.

(iii) The increase in the rice acreage was not at the expense of other crops: the areas under other major crops, such as rubber, maize, kenaf, cassava, sugarcane and coconut also increased. In fact, a major aspect of Thai agricultural growth has been the rapid diversification of crops.

(iv) Unfortunately, slow growth or stagnation in yields was also observed in other crops (World Bank 1982).

(v) Agricultural growth, then, was due to population growth, the availability of new land and the introduction of new crops, rather than to the intensification of production, so it is understandable that such rapid growth rates could be realised with so little financial investment. Of course, if more had been invested in agriculture, even higher growth rates might have been achieved. Lipton (1977) argued that investments in agriculture are more efficient than those elsewhere. As the incremental capital/output ratio (ICOR) in agriculture is smaller than that of other sectors, the investment of a given amount in agriculture leads to a greater increase in output than its investment in other sectors. The average ICOR of the agricultural sector in Thailand, over the period 1971–84, was 2.2, and that for the non-agricultural sectors was 3.9. But it is difficult to conclude from those figures that agriculture is more efficient. Most of the output growth in agriculture is due to growth of the labour force and to opening up of new land; little is due to investment outlays. Therefore, the overall growth of agriculture may have little to do with the investment projects undertaken in the sector and, for this reason, the ICOR says little about relative efficiency.[20]

(vi) On the supply side, the sectoral balance was not in danger, as agricultural output could grow without much physical investment. The rapid growth of output also ensured rapid growth in income and in the demand for new industrial goods, so that, also on the demand side, the balance was maintained.

Given these arguments, it cannot be concluded that the outflow of funds from agriculture was at the expense of growth in that sector, or that sectoral balances were endangered.

4.6.2 *Effects of intersectoral flows: income distribution*

Of Thailand's poor, 80 per cent live in rural areas and 75 per cent are farm-operating households. One could therefore expect that any strategy based on an outflow of resources from the agricultural sector could intensify poverty, but rapid agricultural growth has prevented this.

Studies on the income distribution show that between 1962/63 and 1975/76, the annual growth of per capita income was fastest in the poorest rural regions in the North and the North-east, so that the income gap between the regions and also between the urban and rural areas narrowed (Meesook 1979).

The incidence of poverty fell between 1962/63 and 1975/76 in all urban and rural areas of all regions in the country (Meesook 1979). Islam (1983) criticized Meesook's approach because it used the Consumer Price Index to deflate the incomes, rather than an index that was more specific to the poor's consumption basket. However, even when a more appropriate deflator was used, the incidence of poverty declined over the years mentioned. Between 1975 and 1981, this trend continued in all regions of the country, with the exception of the Central Region, where the percentage of poor people stagnated in the rural areas and increased in the urban ones (Krongkaew 1985).

This latter fact may be explained by the fact that the Central Region is the most advanced in agricultural development and, as a result, the stratification within agriculture has become more pronounced. Generally, it is found that between 1962/63 and 1981 the Gini-coefficient increased in both the rural and urban areas and in all regions. This suggests an increasing divergence between those who benefit from the new opportunities and those who do not (Meesook 1979; Krongkaew 1985).

The reduction of poverty was mainly the result of the expansion of agricultural land and the diversification of crops (Meesook 1979; Krongkaew 1985). Government policies contributed little, except through the provision of irrigation facilities and infrastructure (Krongkaew 1985). Although no data are available, it is likely that since 1981 poverty in the rural areas has increased with the decline in agricultural prices and income.

Studies of the incidence of government tax and expenditure show that tax incidence is slightly regressive over the income classes (Likitkijsomboon 1985), and that incidence of expenditure is progressive, in particular for the lowest income groups (World Bank 1978; Krongkaew 1980). Given the heroic assumptions on which such incidence studies are based one has to treat these conclusions with caution.

The overall conclusion could be that the rapid growth of agriculture based on extension has made it possible for the incidence of poverty to decline. The income distribution became somewhat more unequal, as often happens during periods of rapid growth. It appears that landlessness and unemployment are not yet major problems in Thailand, although no detailed data are available. The special nature of Thailand, as a land surplus country, has made it possible for agricultural production to increase along with rapid growth of the population. This has created new employment and income, eradicated poverty and, at the same time, created a demand for industrial commodities and a surplus of

181

investment resources that generated rapid growth in the other sectors of the economy.

4.7   Political factors and intersectoral flows

In most of this chapter, intersectoral flows through the financial system were analysed as the outcome of private sector decisions. But many of the parameters of these private decisions may be determined by policy interventions. In general, one would expect a government in a developing country to have political objectives with respect to the balance between sectors and to apply policy instruments to try to influence the sectoral allocation of resources. What has been the extent of intervention by the Thai government?

Some forms of intervention have already been identified in earlier Sections (see, for example, Chapter 2, section 2.4 and section 4.4 above). A first set of policies relates to relative prices. As observed earlier, the level of the relative prices has been influenced by government policy. The export tax and premiums on rice and rubber have had a depressing effect on the farm-gate prices of these commodities. At the same time, import tariffs protected the domestic market for industrial producers, so that they could charge higher prices. Thailand has maintained a relatively high exchange rate which also depresses domestic prices of (agricultural) export goods and subsidizes the import-dependent industrial sector. These policies have not helped to stimulate the profitability of investments in the unincorporated sector.

A second set of public policies are fiscal policies. It was observed above that the tax burden on the unincorporated sector is limited and less than the government expenditure directed to agriculture, so that, on balance, the fiscal effect should be positive. But there are distributional effects, as the rice tax affects all rice farmers but government expenditure benefits only those with access to government services (for example, an irrigation scheme).

The effects of these two sets of policies suggest an urban bias in public policy in Thailand. What are the political processes behind this policy bias?

The term 'urban bias' draws attention to Lipton's book. The standard breakdown of political groups in the literature on the urban bias is in four groups (Lipton 1977; Mitra 1977). On the urban side, there are the capitalists and the workers and on the rural side, the big farmers and the small (subsistence) farmers.

Lipton argued that a coalition between the two urban groups and the big farmers agrees to keep the food prices low by turning the terms of trade against agriculture. The big farmer, who suffers from this, is kept in the coalition by compensating measures, such as subsidies on inputs, cheap credit and benefits from public investment programmes. The poor farmer suffers from the low prices and has no access to these compensating benefits (Lipton 1977).

Mitra, using the same class breakdown, and like Lipton basing his study on the Indian experience, concluded that a coalition between urban capitalists and big farmers turns the terms of trade in favour of agriculture at the expense of poor farmers and urban workers (Mitra 1977).

It is remarkable that the same, Indian, experience can give rise to such different interpretations of the facts (movement of terms of trade) and of political forces (class alliances) (see Moore 1984). Yet both authors argued the same political process: class alliances operating on the state apparatus to ensure interventions that would influence intersectoral flows.

In Thailand the ruling coalition is dominated by the urban élite composed of political leaders (both military and civilian) and capitalist entrepreneurs who own and manage the corporate sector firms. Farmers and workers have no political power; farmers' organizations and trade unions are actively discouraged. Given this unequal power structure, it is perhaps surprising that the bias against agriculture has not been stronger. One reason may be that many of the capitalist groups have strong interests in the trade of agricultural products.

Feeny (1982) analysed agricultural development and agricultural policies in Thailand over the period 1880–1975. He concluded that before the Second World War, there was little public investment in agriculture because:

(a) investments in railroads were preferred as they increased bureaucratic and military control over the territory.
(b) the returns on investments in agriculture could not be captured by the élite. In more recent years, the public investments in agriculture have increased but they are still modest and do not compensate for the negative impact of other public policies (such as protection and rice taxation). This is not surprising given that the urban élite continues to dominate policy making (Feeny 1982).

Despite these political forces, increasing concern is being expressed about the prospects for agricultural growth in Thailand. This concern is based on three grounds.

First of all, the progress in agriculture has so far been based on an expanding acreage. But fertile and cultivatible land is quickly running out, so that future growth will have to come from productivity increases. Such growth may be more 'costly' in terms of investment resources and may require the channelling of more resources to the agricultural sector. If that is not undertaken, stagnation and increasing poverty will result (Ramangkura et al. 1981).

A second concern is that the employment opportunities created by the corporate sector are limited. It might be, as, for example, Akrasanee (1981) argued, that more export-oriented industrialization with less distorted factor prices might create more employment, but even then it may be impossible to deal with the rapid growth of the labour force. If that is so, the unincorporated sector will need to create more employment opportunities to avoid mass unemployment.[21]

A final concern is that, after poverty has been reduced over the last decades, the remaining core of poverty might be more difficult to eliminate. In addition to this the incidence of poverty could easily increase in the future, as the opening of new lands becomes more difficult.

Based on such concerns, the government has attempted to stem the flow of funds out of the agricultural sector. It is interesting to note that the main emphasis in this attempt has been on financial policies that aim to redirect the intersectoral financial flows. Government policies dealing with relative prices and the fiscal policies have hardly been involved in these new sectoral policies. The relevant financial policies are:

(i)   The establishment of the BAAC.
(ii) The obligation since 1977 by rural branches of commercial banks to re-lend 60 per cent of their deposits locally.
(iii) The mandatory allocation since 1975 by commercial banks of a proportion of their credit to agriculture; this started with 5 per cent in 1975, but has gradually increased to 20 per cent. If banks cannot meet these quota, they may hold equivalent deposits with the BAAC. This is the course followed by most commercial banks.
(iv) Special rediscount facilities for agricultural loans since 1967.

The data in Table 4.6 on the sectoral allocation of credit and in Table 4.7 on the provincial credit/deposit ratios suggest that these policies had some results, although one must bear in mind that banks do have considerable flexibility and fungibility in labelling a loan provincial and agricultural. The data in Chart 4.1 and Table 4.3 also showed that the unincorporated sector has increasing access to official financial institutions.

The BAAC has been growing rapidly: its loans to the private sector increased from Baht 263 million in 1961 to Baht 23,105 million in 1986. The BAAC is an efficient organization reaching 40 per cent of all farm households (World Bank 1983b). Its growth is dependent on government support, as its own deposit collection is negligible. The mandatory agricultural loans of the commercial banks has helped the growth of the BAAC; many banks deposit their share with the BAAC. The rediscount facilities for agricultural loans are not used much because the margin between the discount rate and the rate banks may charge on such loans is too narrow (Panitchpakdi 1981; Go 1984).[22]

It is in general observed that banks find it difficult to satisfy the requirements of extending a mandatory share of their credit to agricultural loans and to provincial loans. Whether this is due to the absence of bankable rural projects or to the banks' inherent attitudes is difficult to assess. Most studies conclude that government policies have effectively increased the official credit extended to the agricultural sector, but they have also observed that the main beneficiaries have been large farmers, traders and millers (Panitchpakdi 1981; World Bank 1983b; Go 1984).

While these financial policies may thus have reduced the net outflow of funds from agriculture, they have not stopped it. This outflow of funds from agriculture to non-agriculture, or from the unincorporated to the corporate sector, has significantly contributed to the structural change in the Thai economy.

4.8   Conclusion

In this chapter the Flow-of-Funds Accounts of Thailand have been used to analyse the intersectoral financial flows. To finance economic development, a transfer of resources from the agriculture to industry is necessary. There are various mechanisms by which such a transfer can be arranged, such as the terms of trade, fiscal measures and financial institutions. It is suggested that in the case of Thailand, the financial system is in fact the main channel.

The Flow-of-Funds analysis clearly shows a rapid increase in financial intermediation. Financial flows, within the unincorporated sector and between the unincorporated and the corporate sectors, are increasingly channelled through financial institutions. There is also an increased integration with international financial markets, through which state enterprises and corporations particularly obtain additional funds.

The main factor behind the increase in domestic financial intermediation is the relative shift in the household portfolios from loans at the unregulated money market, own investments and equity shares to financial savings, mainly time deposits with commercial banks. Four factors may be held responsible for this shift.

The first is that own investments in agriculture, and probably investments in the unincorporated sector in general, have highly uncertain results. These risks and the high administration costs could also be a reason for the relative decline of the unregulated money market and its replacement by transactions with official financial institutions.

A second point worth mentioning is that returns on financial savings have been quite good in many years, but there have also been inflationary years in which returns were negative. An important factor indirectly contributing to the returns on financial savings is that the transaction costs have been reduced, due to the rapid expansion of the number of bank offices.

Thirdly, it has been observed that household savings are highly concentrated in the hands of a few rich households. These households could have links to business groups in the corporate sector and might use the banks to channel funds to these groups.

Finally, partly on their free will but mostly forced by government regulations, banks have started to lend more to the household sector. As a logical counterpart to this lending household deposits have gone up.

The effect of these intersectoral transfers on the development of the agricultural sector has not been negative, mainly because agricultural growth could continue with relatively little financial investment being required. This rapid agricultural growth also ensured a fall in the incidence of poverty. Despite these positive findings there has been a change of policies in recent years and measures have been introduced to try to force financial institutions to allocate more resources to the unincorporated sector.

Notes

1. In this context, financial flows are understood as flows through financial institutions. Non-financial flows – which may be in monetary form – are those flowing through other channels such as the government budget.
2. There is, of course, a direct relationship between financial assets and liabilities of households with the financial institutions. In general, a loan is given by opening a credit line to which the client can write cheques, so that a deposit (asset) and a loan (liability) are simultaneously created. It has also been suggested that the reverse is true, that is, that firms hold savings deposits with banks to ensure access to loans. In that way the deposits act as collateral or as a roundabout way for banks to increase the loan rate.
3. The Centre for World Food Studies (1980, p. 27) concluded that the savings ratio increases with farm size and that about half of total farm savings come from large farms. But about 90 per cent of all savings come from non-farm households. Unfortunately, the sources and method of estimation are not made very explicit and the results seem to rest on a number of strong assumptions.
4. The portfolio approach deals with portfolios of a given size. One could question again whether the rate of return on savings would influence the size of the portfolio, that is, whether it would increase savings. The discussion in Chapter 3 reached the conclusion that the relationship between aggregate savings and the rate of interest could not be established convincingly.
   Bhalla (1978) replaced the interest rate, as indicator of returns on savings, by an indicator of investment opportunities open to farmers, arguing that if farmers have good investment opportunities (that is if high returns can be earned on invested savings), they will save more. He found for a sample of Indian farmers, that rich farmers with good investment opportunities saved less, and poor farmers with such opportunities saved more. The reason for the difference is that rich farmers have access to cheap credit and have financed the investment from such loans, while they have increased their consumption in response to the wealth effect of the future higher income. Poor farmers, who could not borrow so easily, have increased their own savings. The balance effect on total savings is ambiguous.
5. In fact the portfolio choice is more complex than presented here. As discussed in section 4.3, households also incur financial liabilities which they use to finance consumption or to acquire assets. To be precise, one could say that in this Section we take the amount of total resources available, including credits, as given and study its allocation over various uses.
6. The figures given by Usher (1967) are based on a small sample and they vary considerably, between 2 and 25 per cent. Although Usher made some comments on regional variation the sample size seems too small to justify such statements.
7. The finding reported in the text for the two North-eastern province, was not repeated in Feder's study for the more commercially developed Central Region province. Feder argued that in this province even the untitled farmers can get credit from traders against the crop rather than on land collateral (Feder 1986). However, that argument is not fully convincing: the traders' credit is likely to be more expensive than the bank credit to which titled farmers would have access, so one would still expect a difference.

186

8. To say that people 'know' what the rate of inflation is going to be does not mean that they will never be wrong and that expectations are always fulfilled, but people will not be systematically wrong and will quickly learn from mistakes.

9. It could be suggested that in equation (18) the growth rate of the unincorporated sector should be used to explain desired investments in that sector, and the corporate sector's growth rate for the investments in the corporate sector. As the two growth rates are highly correlated it is impossible to include them both in the regression.

10. It should be noted that the overall savings ratio S_h/Y_u does not have a clear trend value, so that any trend in the financial savings ratio should be explained by a changing allocation of savings. The financial development variable gives an institutional reason for this change. An alternative structural reason might be the growth of the corporate sector. The income variable is only a distant indirect indicator of such structural processes. Hence the financial development variable is preferable.

11. Some studies have interpreted the statistical discrepancy of the household sector in the Flow-of-Funds Accounts as an indirect indicator of the size of unregulated credit market activities. Kirakul, Sriphayak and Ploydanai (1984) attempted to do this, but the analysis failed to arrive at good statistical results. This is not surprising, because firstly, the statistical discrepancy captures all errors and omissions, and, secondly, unregulated credit transactions largely take place within the household sector, with some units financing others. Such intrasectoral exchanges would not show in sector accounts.

12. Bavovada (1984, p. 61) argued, on the basis of Bank of Thailand surveys, that formal financial assets account for over 85 per cent of all financial assets (the latter including informal loans, rotating credit societies, and so on). In urban areas that proportion is even higher. This suggests a smaller size of the urban unregulated money market compared to the data quoted in the text.

13. FOR (1986) give a breakdown not by value but by numbers of loans. In their sample, 5 per cent of loans came from neighbours and relatives, 46 per cent from commercial lenders and 48 per cent from financial institutions.

14. The competitive nature of marketing in Thailand applies certainly to rice trade and probably to most other crops. Hewison (1986) argued, though, that sugar processing and trade has significant oligopolistic elements.

15. The interest rate differential, given a relatively fixed domestic loan rate, is mainly determined by fluctuations in the international interest rate. As the demand for foreign loans is also determined by other factors as well, such as the level of desired investment and domestic monetary policy, one would not expect the relationship between the demand for foreign loans and the interest rate differential to be perfect. But certainly for most years, the relationship can be observed.

16. The rise in state enterprises' profits in recent years is partly due to the conditionality imposed as part of the Structural Adjustment Loans that Thailand received from the World Bank. See *Far-Eastern Economic Review* (21 April 1983 and 19 January 1984).

17. The Commercial Banking Act 1979 tried to break the family control over banks by forcing them to divest their shares over more shareholders and to prevent an accumulation of shares in the hands of single individuals. Most banks have met these requirements, but whether that has changed actual control over the banks and their behaviour very much may be doubted.

18. The *Far-Eastern Economic Review* (27 March 1981) quoted Nukul Prachuabmoh, the Central Bank Governor, as the source of these figures. He added that they reflected increasing concentration over the years and requested banks to do something about it.

19. In dealing with the unincorporated sector, banks also tend towards richer and larger firms. Visser (1978) observed that the average income of farmers in his sample village with access to financial institutions was Baht 18,000 and that of those dependent on other sources of credit was Baht 11,000.

20. The level of the ICOR may also say little about the private profitability and attractiveness of investment. Private costs and returns may be different from national investments and output. In addition, the striking aspect of the agricultural ICOR is its instability: it fluctuates sharply from year to year. This may not upset the planner dealing with the medium term, but will deter the private investor.

21. NESDB (1985), for example, emphasizes that Thailand's 6th Plan should deal with the problem of the growing labour force and the limited growth of employment opportunities.

22. No detailed data are available on rediscounted agricultural bills, but some figure on export bills may be an interesting indicator of bank practice. Akrasanee and Ajanant (1982) observed that the amount of export bills rediscounted with the central bank amounted to one-third of total merchandise exports. In 1979, ten exporters accounted for 34 per cent of all bills rediscounted, and 76 exporters for 74 per cent.

5 Stability and stabilization

5.1 Introduction

The review of short-term stabilization models in Chapter 1 came to the conclusion that, if one interprets short-term imbalances as gaps between planned savings and investments, the chance for such gaps to develop will increase when, with financial development, there is an increasing separation between savers and investors. This raises the question of whether there are adjustment mechanisms to maintain equilibrium in the economy. An *ex ante* excess demand may lead to increases in real output, prices and interest rates that would bring actual savings and investments together *ex post*. The survey of theories and evidence in the earlier parts of this study concluded that these automatic adjustment mechanisms are not necessarily effective; in fact, they could even drive investment and savings further apart. An active stabilization policy will then be required; and according to most short-term macroeconomic models for developing countries the main instruments for such a policy are monetary policies.

Most short-term models emphasize the role of credit controls and interest rates. However, the effectiveness of these instruments has been deeply affected by the changes in the international financial conditions. The integration of domestic financial markets into the international financial system has seriously undermined the effectiveness of short-term monetary policy instruments. The results of Chapters 3 and 4 suggest new directions for the analysis of stability and stabilization patterns. This chapter argues that the findings on the disaggregated saving behaviour in Chapter 3, and those on investment behaviour in Chapter 4, have important implications for the analysis of short-

189

term disturbances in Thailand. The main conclusion of Chapter 3 was that the saving behaviour of the three main types of economic institutions – households, corporations and government – are determined by quite different factors and may react in quite different ways to a given external impulse. It is likely, then, that short-term disturbances affect the saving behaviour in the three sectors in different ways. It is also likely that different types of disturbance have different effects on the saving behaviour of each sector.

Chart 2.2 of Chapter 2 presented the savings ratios of the household sector, of corporations and of the government as a percentage of GDP over the years. It is clear that the savings ratios of the three sectors vary widely over the years and often move in opposite directions. Standard short-term macroeconomic models which only include an aggregate saving function fail to capture these differences and, therefore, cannot provide an adequate explanation of saving behaviour in the short run. In addition, because such models do not allow one to trace changes in aggregate savings to the sectors from which they originate, the models also fail to link the analysis of saving to the analysis of investment or of portfolio adjustment in a satisfactory way. An increase in household savings may lead to an increase in financial savings (that is, savings deposits with banks); an increase in corporate or government savings may do that much less. An approach that simply observes an increase in aggregate savings, without accounting for its origin, will find it difficult to trace adequately the portfolio implications and might also fail to establish the link between the changes in saving, in portfolio adjustments and in investment.

The analysis in Chapter 4 already suggested the limited effectiveness of monetary policy. Changes in monetary policy, such as credit controls or interest rates, result far more in portfolio adjustments or substitution between various assets and liabilities than in changes in the level of aggregate investment and savings. In the substitution processes in the corporate sector and in the financial system, international capital flows play an important role.

The differentiated saving behaviour and the importance of substitution processes imply that the effects of short-term disturbances and of stabilization policies will affect the balance between sectors in the economy as much as, or even more than, the overall macroeconomic aggregates.

To illustrate and substantiate these points further, this chapter analyses the past record of short-term[1] stability in Thailand (section 5.2) and traces the adjustment patterns following economic disturbance (section 5.3). Together, these two sections argue in favour of a more structuralist analysis of short-term dynamics in which the main sectors of the economy are separately introduced because their production conditions and short-term behaviour are quite different.

This chapter does not give a detailed analysis of short-term economic developments and policies in Thailand, nor will it argue for a particular type of short-term policy. Its only aim is to show the importance of an alternative approach to the analysis.

190

5.2   The record of stability

Measured by the two usual indicators of macroeconomic stability, the rate of inflation and the current account deficit, Thailand experienced a period of remarkable stability up to the mid-1970s. This stability is remarkable because over these years Thailand went through a process of rapid growth and structural change. Since the mid-1970s, this stability record has deteriorated, as could be expected given the greater instability of the entire world economy.

In Chart 5.1 the two instability indicators are brought together. The chart presents a rather unexpected picture. In the stabilization literature, both the inflation rate (p) and the current account deficit (CAD) are usually presented as expressions of excess demand. Excess demand will result, under conditions of free trade, in a greater domestic demand for traded goods – which pushes up the current account deficit – and has an increasing effect on prices of non-traded goods. But Chart 5.1 shows that quite often, the Thai rate of inflation and the current account deficit moved in opposite directions.[2] This was most dramatically the case in 1974, when inflation was at an all time high and the current account deficit was at a very low level, but it also occurred in other years. After 1975 and up to 1982, the rate of inflation and the current account deficit tended to move in similar directions, but in the most recent years the more differentiated pattern can again be observed.

As discussed in Chapter 2 (see Chart 2.3), inflation in Thailand largely follows international inflation. The price changes of import goods (mainly intermediate goods) work through in the cost pricing of the corporations. Most export goods are also domestically consumed and international prices directly affect domestic prices.

It is often argued that an inflationary impulse, for instance from export or import prices, could set off an inflationary process because a number of propagating mechanisms operate to translate the impulse into a sustained process of inflation. Propagating mechanisms include wage increases, fiscal reactions and inflationary expectations. But they are not very effective in Thailand where trade unions are rather powerless, and where international prices affect government revenue as much as government expenditure (see regression in Chapter 3), where inflationary expectations are short and quickly adjusted and where fiscal and monetary policies are cautious in most years.

In conclusion, it may be said that the movements in international prices are a major determinant of domestic inflation. Domestically created excess demand is more likely to affect the balance of payments than the price level. This finding does not mean that inflation is unimportant. As Chapter 3 noted, the changes in export and import prices are important determinants of domestic saving behaviour, particularly in the household and government sectors. And, as there are few changes in the ceilings on the deposit and loan rates of interest, changes in the rate of inflation are a major determinant of the real rate of interest and of the consequent changes in portfolios. Of course, international inflation

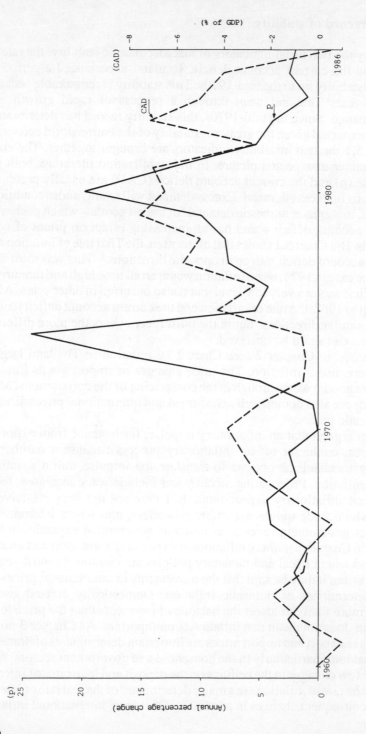

Chart 5.1 Indicators of macroeconomic stability

also has direct balance-of-payments effects. Inflation therefore remains an important phenomenon, but the findings above do suggest that conventional anti-inflationary policies are unlikely to be very successful in bringing down inflation that has originated abroad.

The other indicator of macroeconomic stability, the current account deficit, is directly linked to the saving and investment behaviour through the accumulation balance: $I - S = IMP - X$.

However, in order to study short-term adjustment processes it will be useful to break up savings and investments by main sectors, households, corporations and the public sector (made up of government and state enterprises).[3]

$$(1) \quad (I_h - S_h) + (I_c - S_c) + (I_{pu} - S_{pu}) = IMP - X$$

In Chart 5.2 the savings and investment ratios (as percentages of GDP) for the household sector, the corporations and the public sector are presented, based on the Flow-of-Funds Accounts of Thailand.

The public sector savings (S_{pu}) and investment (I_{pu}) ratios do not show much short-term variation, except for the policy-induced disturbances around 1974 and a similar shock (but in different direction) around 1980. On the whole the public sector shows a steadily growing deficit. For the study of short-term fluctuations the private sector is more apposite.

Chart 5.2 shows a very interesting contrast: the household sector has a very stable investment ratio (I_h), together with a strongly fluctuating savings ratio (S_h). The corporate sector has a more or less opposite pattern: the savings ratio (S_c), on average, increases at first and declines in later years, but does not show erratic year-to-year fluctuations; the investment ratio (I_c), however, fluctuates quite violently. The analysis of sectoral saving behaviour made in Chapter 3 can explain the contrast in the short-term behaviour of the savings ratios.

In the interpretation of Chart 5.2 it is necessary to remember once more the statistical problems underlying the analysis of saving and investment. Household savings are derived as a residue in National Accounts and Flow-of-Funds Accounts and household investments are estimated as mainly residential investments. A significant share of the investments of unincorporated household enterprises may therefore be included in corporate investment, but the analysis of Chapters 3 and 4, gives some more confidence in the interpretation followed here. In Chapter 3 the stability of corporate savings was accepted not just as a statistical (arti)fact, but was explained from the theory of the 'corporate' firm. And the fluctuations in household savings were explained from the movements in income and production cost of the household firm. In Chapter 4 it was elaborately argued that the unincorporated firms invest relatively little; the bulk of private investment is undertaken, therefore, by large corporations and the level and rise and fall of private investment reflect corporate investment behaviour.

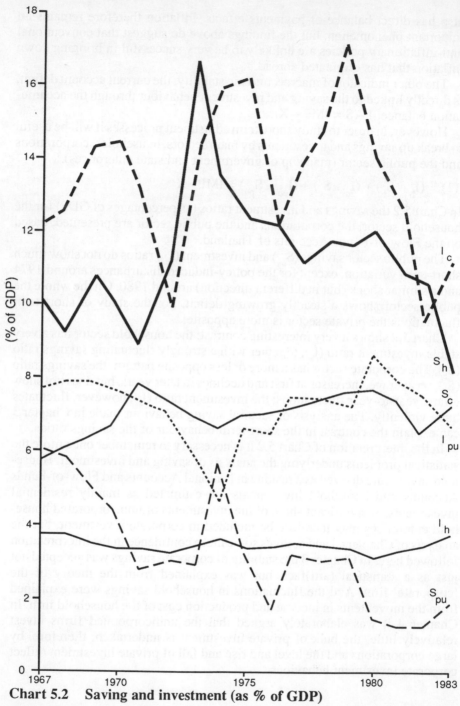

Chart 5.2   Saving and investment (as % of GDP)

5.2.1 *The nature of instability*

With movements in the household savings ratio, and its stable investment ratio, the saving surplus of the household sector fluctuates quite sharply over the years. The variations in the corporate investment ratio, together with the relatively stable corporate savings ratio, result, on the other hand, in fluctuations in the corporate deficit. These instabilities in the major component of domestic savings, household savings, and in the major component of domestic investment, corporate investment, could make the economy very unstable unless the movements in these two components were related in some way. Such a relationship could exist if both variables are determined by the same set of factors, for example, if the growth of income determines changes in savings and in desired investments, or if there are adjustment mechanisms that force savings and investments to come together. Can such relationships be established?

Are household savings and corporate investments determined by the same factors? In Chapter 3 it was found that the household savings ratio is dependent on the price of output of the unincorporated sector, which in turn is closely related to changes in export prices and in the production cost of the unincorporated sector as represented by the wage pressure index. In that chapter it was assumed that the level of desired investment of the corporate sector was determined by past profitability, demand conditions and opportunity cost (see equation (32) of Chapter 3):

$$(2) \quad \frac{\hat{I}}{Y_c} = d_0 + d_1 + d_1 \left(\frac{S_{c(t-1)}}{Y_{c(t-1)}} \right) + d_2 g_{c(t-1)} + d_3 (i_1 - p_c)$$

As it was assumed that the corporations can realize their desired investments, equation (2) can be directly estimated. To estimate this function, I_c has been replaced by total private investment (that is household and corporate investments) so that National Account data (for which a longer time series is available than for the Flow-of-Funds Accounts) can be used. As observed above, the level and the variations in private investment are mainly determined by corporate investment. Private investment is then expressed as a percentage of total GDP. In a similar way, g_c was replaced by the growth rate of total GDP as an indicator of demand conditions. As an indicator of credit cost the nominal effective lending rate minus the GDP deflator of the corporate sector was taken. Using data for the period 1963–86, the following results were obtained:

$$(3) \quad \left(\frac{I_{pr}}{Y} \right) = 7.61 + 0.29 \frac{S_{c(t-1)}}{Y_{c(t-1)}} + 0.21 g_{(t-1)} - 0.11(i_1 - p_c)$$

$$(3.374) \ (3.403) \qquad (1.923) \qquad (2.313)$$

$R^2 = 0.57$; D.W. = 1.03

The fluctuations in private investment are determined by fluctuations in the

195

lagged profit share, which, as Chart 5.2 shows, does not change much, and in the real loan rate, which fluctuates mainly with changes in the rate of inflation, and in the real growth rate. The relatively low level of explanation, $R^2 = 0.57$, is not surprising as other variables, particularly business expectations ('animal spirits'), may play a large role in the determination of desired investment.

It would appear, then, that household savings and private and corporate investments are determined by quite different factors, so that there is little a priori reason to expect that they will move together. Are there mechanisms operating to coordinate the movements in the two variables?

The financial repression school suggests that financial intermediation provides such adjustment. A higher level of savings, and of financial savings, allows financial institutions to extend more credit, so that more investment projects can be financed. This is based on the assumption that investment is finance constrained. Household savings then determine the amount of financial savings available, which in turn determines the amount of credit banks can extend to finance corporate investment (see, for example, Fry 1980). The analysis in Chapter 4 showed that most of the funds of financial institutions do indeed come from household savings and that a substantial part of their funds are used to provide credit to corporations. But could it be argued that the level of corporate investment is constrained by the availability of such bank credits?

In Chart 5.3 the fluctuations in the I_{pr}/Y ratio are compared to trends in the ratio of financial savings (FS, defined as changes in holdings of time and savings deposits and of promissory notes) to GDP, and to trends in the ratio of new credit extended to the private sector to GDP (DC_{pr}). If private investment were constrained by available credit, peaks in the investment ratio should coincide with peaks in the financial savings ratio. However, the chart clearly shows that that is not always the case: peaks in financial savings do not always bring peaks in investment (for instance 1972, 1982, 1983), nor are all investment peaks made possible by high financial savings (for instance, 1963, 1969, 1979). Why is this not the case? There are two reasons, both of which are based on the detailed analysis in Chapter 4 of the behaviour of corporations and financial institutions.

Firstly, by necessity, financial savings (as a major source of funds of financial institutions) and private sector credits (as their major use of funds) should move closely together, with the financial savings ratio on average exceeding the credit ratio since banks also have to hold reserves and extend credit to the public sector. But, as Chart 5.3 shows, credit expansion does not always follow available financial savings: for example, in the years 1972, 1980-82, 1984-86, banks seemed to have extended far less credit than seemed possible. These were all years in which private investment was relatively low, which may have diminished the demand for credit. This certainly means that the assumption of the financial repression school that the availability of credit is the main determinant of investment is invalid. This conclusion is further supported by the fact that attempts to include a variable indicating credit

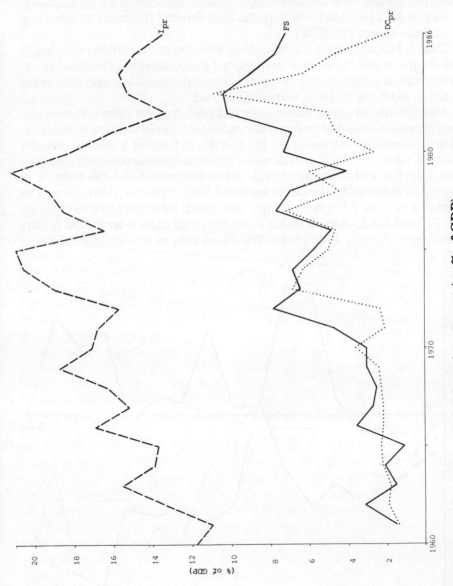

Chart 5.3 Financial savings and private investment (as % of GDP)

availability in equation (3) failed to contribute to the explanation of private investment.

In a few other years (1963–65, 1970, 1973, 1979, 1983), the expansion of credit seems to have exceeded available financial savings. In some of these years, private investment was very high, making the demand for credit strong. In such years banks tend to satisfy the high demand for credit by attracting funds from abroad (see Chart 4.8).

Chart 5.3 clearly shows that in the long term, the private credit ratio closely follows the trends in financial savings, but that relatively substantial short-term discrepancies can easily occur as banks can accumulate excess reserves or attract extra resources by borrowing abroad.

A second reason why financial intermediation does not force investment to keep pace with available financial savings is that corporations have access to alternative sources of finance. As the analysis in Chapter 4 showed (see, for example, Chart 4.2), there are variations in the amounts corporations obtain by issuing shares or borrowing abroad, the volumes of which often move in directions opposite to the credit received from financial institutions. The foreign debt acquired by the corporate sector was, for example, relatively high in 1980 and 1982, years in which domestic credit expansion for the private sector was relatively low. Thus corporations can, in financing their invest-

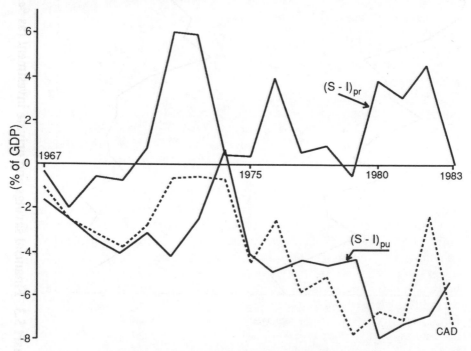

Chart 5.4   Macroeconomic balance (as % of GDP)

ments, substitute between various sources of funds; the level of their investments is not constrained by available domestic credit.

Adjustments between household savings and corporate investment are therefore unlikely to take place through domestic financial intermediation. If private investment is not kept within the limits set by available savings, it is likely that discrepancies between savings and investment will be reflected in the balance of payments, as equation (1) suggested.[4]

Chart 5.4 is based on Flow-of-Funds data which allow a separation of the private sector savings surplus into a surplus (or deficit) of the household sector and of the corporate sector: $(S - I)_{pr} = (S_h + S_c - I_h - I_c)$; and of the public sector savings surplus into that of the government and that of the state enterprises: $(S - I)_{pu} = (S_g + S_s - I_g - I_s)$.

In general, 1967–72 was a period in which the household savings ratio was relatively low and the current account deficit relatively high. After a peak in household savings in 1973/74 and the related low external deficit, 1974–80 were years in which the savings ratio was stable and high and the current account therefore fluctuated with the private investment ratio. Since 1980 the household savings ratio has fallen continuously, and the current account deficit has been high.

Chart 5.4 clearly shows two facts. First of all, the upward trend in the current account deficit that can be observed as an average over the longer term is associated with the systematic increase in the public sector savings deficit. Secondly, the short-term fluctuations in the current account deficit closely follow the variations in the private sector savings surplus. In quite a number of years, household savings and private investment moved in opposite directions, and these trends were reflected in changes in the current account. The only significant exceptions to these trends occurred in 1973 and 1974, when fiscal policy reduced the public sector deficit significantly, albeit only for a short while.

Chart 5.4 also indicates the specific nature of short-term adjustment in Thailand. The fluctuations in the major component of savings, household savings, and in the major component of investment, corporate investment, are, in the short term, unrelated and determined by quite different factors. The imbalances that arise out of this are covered by fluctuations in the net flow of foreign capital, either through the financial institutions or directly through the corporations. This is, in itself, a useful way of short-term management of the economy, as it brings stability without any undue reduction in the level of investment. If it can be assumed that in the medium term, variations in household savings and corporate investment will be cancelling out or balanced by indirect income and demand effects, then short-term adjustment through foreign capital flows is desirable. If longer-term imbalances arise, however, an accumulation of foreign debt could occur, which would affect the creditworthiness of the economy on international financial markets.

This section on the two indicators of macroeconomic instability, the rate of inflation and the current account deficit, may be summarized in four points:

(a) The two indicators often move in opposite directions. Domestic inflation is, to a large extent, caused by international price movements which sometimes improve the current account (if export prices rise) and sometimes do not (if import prices rise).

(b) Although the rate of inflation is not an indicator of domestic instability, it has important effects on short-term fluctuations in the economy: for example, changes in export prices have a direct effect on domestic savings. Changes in the rate of inflation are the major determinant of the level of the real rate of interest and, through that rate, of portfolio decisions of the household sector and of investment decisions of the corporate sector.

(c) The upward trend in the current account deficit over the years is related to the widening public sector deficit. The private sector has, on average, a savings surplus. This does not necessarily imply that public sector behaviour *causes* the current account deficit to widen. As discussed in Chapter 2, there are many trade-related reasons for the current account deficit to rise. The patterns in Chart 5.4 may then be interpreted as saying that many of these external shocks have been absorbed by a growing public sector deficit.

(d) The short-term fluctuations in domestic savings and domestic investments are due to a rise and fall in household savings and in corporate investments. The balance of these fluctuations is reflected in the current account of the balance of payments.

5.3   Short-term adjustment patterns

The previous section concluded that the main indicator of short-term stability in Thailand is the current account deficit. The changes in the rate of inflation do not reflect domestic instability; they are rather the domestic reflection of international instability. That does not mean that inflation is not important: it only means that it is not a policy problem. Given a regime of a fixed exchange rate and free trade and capital movements, the government should not have political objectives with respect to the rate of inflation. Instruments of short-term fiscal and monetary policy should be directed at controlling the current account.

Two conclusions were reached in the previous section with respect to the current account deficit. The first was that the long-term trend of deterioration in the current account deficit is reflected in the growing public sector savings deficit. Its causes were analysed in Chapters 3 and 4, where it was argued that there is a trend-like increase in the budget deficit of the government and a

200

decline in the degree of self-financing by the state enterprises. These factors are not analysed further in this chapter.

The second conclusion was that the year-to-year fluctuations in the current account deficit follow fluctuations in the private sector savings surplus, whose movements are fully determined by the household savings and the corporate investments; the other elements in the private sector, household investments and corporate savings, are relatively stable over time.

The analysis in Chapters 3 and 4, and the private investment function estimated earlier in this chapter, suggest that the short-term determinants of household savings and corporate investments are quite different, as decisions about household saving and corporate investment are made by economic units facing quite different production and market conditions. It was also observed that domestic financial intermediation does not force an equilibrium between savings and investments because corporations in Thailand are not strictly finance constrained.

These findings suggest that short-term macroeconomic models that do not explicitly include saving and investment functions — and even models that include them but make aggregate or sectoral savings a function of only aggregate or sectoral income — are unlikely to give an adequate picture of short-term disturbances and adjustment processes in the economy. To illustrate this further, this section provides a description and analysis of what happens in the Thai economy when an exogenous disturbance or shock affects one of the two main determinants of the private sector savings surplus: the household savings and the corporate investment. The two cases to be discussed are:[5]

(a) An increase in export prices affecting household savings. In Chapter 3 it was found that export prices have a direct effect on household savings. Fluctuations in export prices are exogenous to the Thai economy since they arise from world market conditions. How does the Thai economy react to such disturbances?

(b) A sudden increase in desired corporate investment. As argued in Chapters 3 and 4, corporations are able to realize desired investment either by increasing their own funds or increasing their borrowing or both. As equation (3) above showed, private investments are only partially 'explained' by past profits, demand pressures and credit cost; a significant part of the changes in investments remains unexplained, reflecting the impact of changes in business expectations and other exogenous factors. What happens as a result of the rise in investment in the rest of the economy?

These two cases are analysed in a descriptive way in order to show the importance of a disaggregated analysis of saving and investment behaviour. The particular aim of this analysis is to demonstrate that the breakdown of production, saving and investment into an unincorporated and a corporate sector is crucial for a proper understanding of short-term adjustment processes and of the role of financial intermediation in the short term. The findings of the analysis are compared with the outcomes that existing aggregated models suggest. The conclusion is that these aggregated models could lead to inappropriate policy conclusions. It is therefore desirable that a structuralist short-term model for the Thai economy be developed.

5.3.1 Increase of export prices

In existing models, the effects of a higher export price on the economy are felt through the increase in the income of the export producing sector. It is possible, of course, that in years in which the export price is high, total export earnings are not high because the higher price is caused by lower supplies. In Thailand, however, in years in which export prices were high (for example 1966/67, 1972/74, and 1979/80), the total exports/GDP ratio also tended to be high.[6]

In the monetary approach to the balance of payments models, an increase in export earnings leads to an increase in total income and therefore expenditures. This leads to an increase in the demand for imports and in the demand for money. The higher exports also bring in the foreign exchange to finance the higher imports and the foreign reserves to finance an expansion of the money supply. Thus after all the adjustments have taken place, income, imports and money balances are at the higher level that the increased exports allow (Polak 1957). If the interest rate is introduced into such models, the increased inflow of foreign exchange and the resulting increase in the money supply will lower the interest rate. At the same time, the higher income will increase the demand for money, which would have an increasing effect on the interest rate. The immediate impact of the increased money supply will influence a fall in the interest rate; this leads to a higher demand for money and for investments and a reduced capital inflow from abroad (Polak and Argy 1971).

By dividing nominal income changes into a real component and a price component, the adjustment mechanisms can be further explained. The increase in export prices directly affects domestic prices and real income, and therefore has an effect on the money demand. The real income effect and the relative price effect (that is the increase in domestic prices in relation to import prices) expand the demand for imports. Through these mechanisms the conventional monetary approach results are achieved (Khan and Knight 1981).

Meesook and Jivasakdiapimas (1981) used their small quarterly model to simulate the effects of a 10 per cent increase in the demand for Thai exports. They mainly emphasized the demand effects, as is done in the monetary approach models, and found that the export increase leads to a rise in income and expenditure which pushes up the price level. It also increases the money supply through the inflow of foreign reserves, and government revenue rises with exports and income. Hence there is a direct demand effect (through income and expenditure) and an indirect demand effect (through the money supply and government revenue). Of course, imports increase with income and due to a relative price effect. After a number of periods, the demand for money stabilizes and expenditure begins to level off, thus reducing inflationary pressures.

The interest rate effect is different in the financial repression models because these typically use broad money definitions in which financial savings (time and savings deposits) depend on the real rate of interest. In such models, inflation lowers the real deposit rate and thus lowers financial savings and this further contributes to macroeconomic instability. Shaw argued that an increase in export income will increase savings, but will also push investment and government expenditure beyond the levels sustainable in the longer term, when export prices may fall again. There will be an immediate inflationary effect when export prices rise, and the subsequent demand pressures will add to inflationary pressures. The acceleration of inflation will deepen the financial repression which will have a negative effect on savings and on the efficiency of investment (Shaw 1973, Chapter 8).

In the neo-structuralist literature, there is less attention for the effects of increases in export prices, but there is extensive analysis of the effects of a devaluation which, to some extent, could have similar effects. Taylor and Rosensweig (1984) designed a general equilibrium model of the Thai economy based on a disaggregated Social Accounting Matrix in which saving and investment behaviour is disaggregated by sector. They used the model to simulate the effects of a 10 per cent devaluation.[7] Using their optimistic assumption on the price elasticity of export supply, the outcome is that export income increases and real GDP increases. This leads to a rise in savings, in particular savings of households and of the government. The overall savings/GDP ratio rises. The growth of savings is also reflected in a higher level of bank deposits, so that the supply of loans increases and the real loan rate thus falls. This in turn stimulates private investment, but the increase in investment is less than that in savings, so that the current account deficit falls.

In short, the monetary approach models emphasize the income and expenditure effects on inflation and on the balance of payments. The financial repression models add the impact of inflation on financial repression and therefore on financial savings. Neo-structuralist models pay more attention to saving effects, caused either by increases in income, or by a redistribution of income through inflation to profit-earners. The analysis of saving behaviour in Chapter 3, and of portfolio choices in Chapter 4, gives rise to a somewhat different analysis of the adjustment path. To illustrate this, it may be useful to follow the events that occurred in Thailand after the increases in export prices in 1966 and in 1972.

The increase in inflation in 1966 – from less than 1 per cent in 1965 to 4 per cent in 1966 – could be interpreted as a typical case of excess demand inflation. In the Annual Report of the Bank of Thailand (BoT) for 1966, the acceleration in inflation was indeed attributed to a shortage of supply due to an excess export of rice, to capacity constraints (for example for cement) and to an inefficient import system (BoT, *Annual Economic Report 1966*, pp. 67–9). In 1966 there were strong expansionary pressures in the economy due to (i) a sharp increase in US government military spending in and aid to Thailand, and (ii) an expansionary fiscal policy. These factors resulted in a sharp increase in imports and in a trade deficit, but the current account showed a surplus due to a large inflow of dollars on the Services and Transfer Accounts.

In 1967 the same expansionary effects operated, but now led to a small current account deficit; the rate of inflation remained at the same level as in 1966. In 1968, however, the rate of inflation fell to below 2 per cent, despite the fact that US government military spending and domestic fiscal policy continued to exert expansionary pressures. It can be argued that the inflation of 1966 and 1967 was not caused by excess demand, although this might not appear to be the case. Three arguments may be listed:

(a) In the first place, in a country with relatively free trade, excess demand spills over into imports. Indeed, imports increased by 51 per cent in 1966, by 14 per cent in 1967 and by 12 per cent in 1968. Trade policy in this period was to liberalize imports rapidly: of the 79 commodities for which imports were controlled in 1965, only 25 remained by 1968 (BoT, *Annual Economic Report 1968*).

(b) The dollar inflow and the expansionary fiscal policy had an expansionary effect on the money supply. However, much of this expansion was absorbed firstly by the increased liquidity of commercial banks (their credit/deposit ratio fell from 0.89 in 1966 to 0.80 in 1968) and, secondly, by an increased private sector savings surplus: in all three years the growth in financial savings of the private sector was larger than the expansion of credit to the private sector. The high liquidity of the banks is difficult to combine with excess demand.

(c) Inflation in these years was mainly in food prices; the prices of non-food items in the consumer price index rose little. These trends can be explained by world market prices. The high world market price of rice affected domestic wholesale and retail prices. In addition, the high prices invited excess exports, bringing on domestic shortages which further pushed up prices. The policy response to these events was to control rice exports and to increase the rice premium and taxes, and thus increase domestic supply and reduce domestic prices.

It would appear then that little remains of the excess demand interpretation of inflation in those years. The attack on inflation was not through fiscal policy, which was expansionary, nor through monetary policy, which in any case would have been difficult, as banks were very liquid. Nevertheless, inflation came down in 1968.

Table 5.1   Short-term adjustment indicators

	X/Y	Y_a/Y	W/NI	S_h/Y	FS/Y	I_{pr}/Y	CDR
1960	18.0	39.8	27.8	11.3	–	11.8	–
1961	19.4	39.2	27.0	11.7	1.5	11.0	–
1962	17.1	37.1	27.5	9.9	3.1	13.3	91
1963	16.2	36.1	28.3	8.9	1.5	15.5	86
1964	18.7	33.5	28.9	8.9	2.1	13.9	88
1965	18.6	34.9	28.3	11.4	1.1	13.7	89
1966	19.4	36.5	27.0	15.6	3.5	16.9	82
1967	19.8	32.5	28.7	10.1	2.7	15.2	80
1968	18.2	31.5	29.8	8.6	2.5	16.3	80
1969	17.4	31.4	30.5	10.9	3.0	18.7	81
1970	16.6	28.3	24.3	10.2	3.0	17.2	86
1971	17.2	28.2	25.6	9.3	4.7	16.9	81
1972	19.9	30.3	24.6	10.9	7.8	15.7	73
1973	20.5	33.8	22.5	17.1	6.4	18.9	86
1974	23.0	31.4	23.0	13.6	6.8	20.5	89
1975	19.5	31.3	25.0	12.9	5.7	20.9	92
1976	21.4	31.0	26.1	12.5	4.8	16.4	89
1977	21.4	28.2	26.8	11.2	7.6	18.5	93
1978	21.9	27.5	28.8	12.2	6.9	19.2	100
1979	24.1	26.4	30.3	12.2	4.0	21.1	111
1980	25.1	25.4	30.7	12.8	7.2	18.1	101
1981	25.6	23.9	31.4	10.2	6.8	16.0	99
1982	25.0	22.3	34.6	10.9	10.0	13.2	93
1983	22.4	22.1	36.3	7.9	10.2	14.4	98
1984	24.5	19.3	37.0	8.3	8.9	14.9	95
1985	26.0	17.1	37.4	7.8	7.7	13.6	93
1986	28.2	16.7	37.5	8.8	6.7	13.1	86

The stabilization patterns operating in the Thai economy in this period may be observed in Table 5.1. The initial increase in export earnings (see X/Y in Table 5.1) pushes up incomes of farm households (Y_a/Y) and has a direct and strong effect on household savings (S_h/Y). At the same time, the increase in the world market price of the main export crop, rice, leads to a rise in the domestic price of this major wage good. This, together with rigid nominal wages, results in a fall of the real wage and in the wage share in National Income (W/NI). The analysis of household savings in Chapter 3 showed that these savings, being the surplus of the unincorporated sector, are very sensitive to output prices (or export prices) and to the wage cost. Both factors contributed to the sharp increase in the household savings ratio in 1966, and a significant part of these additional savings were channelled to deposits in financial institutions (FS/Y). The good demand conditions, and the real lending rate which fell with inflation, resulted in somewhat greater investment activity in the corporate sector (I_{pr}/Y), but not to such an extent that it exceeded available credit: the credit/deposit (CDR) ratio fell sharply.

The inflation of 1972–74 started in a similar way to that of 1966/67. International inflation had pushed up import prices since 1970, and this was followed by an explosion in export prices in 1973. On top of this came the oil price increase in late 1973.

Again, at first sight it seemed that the inflation was of the excess demand type. In 1972 and early 1973, fiscal and monetary policies were expansionary and capital inflows large, so growth of the money supply was high. But this growth was largely endogenous – the result of high export earnings and a rapid increase in financial savings – and was thus not inflationary in nature (Siamwalla 1978).

The indicators in Table 5.1 suggest that the stabilizing processes observed above worked again. The increase in export earnings was reflected in increased incomes of farm households, which saved a large part of this additional income, partly again in the form of financial savings. Again, part of these increased savings were absorbed by an increased liquidity of the banks: the credit/deposit ratio fell in 1972, also because private investment was relatively low.

The increase in food prices cut the real wage level: the real wages of unskilled workers in Bangkok fell between 1970 and 1974 (ARTEP 1982). The wage share in National Income decreased and remained very low over the entire period 1973–76. This further contributed to the increase in household savings. Under these conditions of strong demand and low real cost of credit, private investment increased rapidly after a poor year in 1972 and rose to very high levels in 1973, 1974 and 1975.

Initially, the policy response to the acceleration in inflation was similar to that in 1966/67: trade policy measures were applied. The rice premium was adjusted and export controls introduced to control domestic food prices, and later import duties were adjusted and subsidies extended (for example, on petrol) to soften the domestic impact of international inflation. In 1973, however, and even more strongly in 1974, there was a shift to a tight fiscal and monetary policy. It has been argued that the fiscal system of Thailand has some built-in stabilizers: as inflation accelerates real expenditure falls and *ad valorem* trade tax revenue increases (Siamwalla 1978). In 1974 there was an additional conscious attempt to increase tax rates and reduce expenditure by delaying projects, resulting even in a budget surplus in that year.

In retrospect, the contractionary fiscal policy, in addition to the active automatic adjustment caused by the high household savings, turned out to be excessive. Even the high level of private investment in 1974 did not exhaust the available domestic savings. Thus the fiscal policy resulted in under-spending and a very low growth rate in 1974, but this had no effect on the inflation rate because, despite the fiscal contraction, the rate of inflation was unprecedentedly high in 1974.

The lesson that should be learned from the above is that in an open economy like that of Thailand, domestic inflation is largely determined by international prices. The task of fiscal policy in such a system is to bring about a balance between domestic expenditure and available resources so as to ensure an external equilibrium. This was not a problem in 1973 and 1974 precisely because inflation had started with an increase in export prices; therefore, the contractionary policy was unnecessary.

In 1975, when, in reaction to this, a more expansionary fiscal policy was followed, it led to a wider current account gap as private investment had also caught up. However, this excess demand did not prevent the sharp fall in the rate of inflation. So while an export income increase could conceivably have set off a process leading to increased expenditure and inflationary pressures, this did not happen in Thailand for four reasons:

(i)   The initial shock benefited an income group with a high marginal propensity to save, the household sector. Government savings also increased slightly in 1967 and sharply in 1973 and 1974, but the increases in the latter years were also due to policy shifts.

(ii) The fall in the real wage as a result of the rise of food prices further increased the profitability of the unincorporated sector and had a further deflationary demand effect.

(iii) The higher income of the household sector, reflecting the increased profits of the unincorporated sector, hardly led to an increased level of investment in this sector. Apparently, the sector interpreted the sudden increase in income as a temporary phenomenon which did not justify new investment.

(iv) Hence most of the increase in household savings ended up in deposits with financial institutions, despite the fall in the real deposit rate. In 1973 and 1974, the real deposit rate was even negative, but this did not prevent a sharp increase in financial savings: the income effect prevailed over the substitution effect.

The trends observed in the savings ratio are in keeping with the conclusions arrived at by the neo-structuralist models, but the patterns behind the adjustment are less explicitly expressed in these models. In those models savings increase with the rise in real income or with the fall in real wages. In the above analysis, the direct effect of the export price on the profits of the unincorporated sector is emphasized. The fall in the real wage level raises the profits of the unincorporated firms and has only little, or no effect at all, on the profits of the corporations, since wage costs are only a small part of total costs and since the output prices of the corporate sector do not rise with export prices. It is remarkable that in 1972 and 1973, when the household savings ratio increased, the corporate savings ratio fell after a long period of continuous increase. The analysis in Chapter 3 suggests that the main reason for this fall is the negative real loan rate which made external funds very cheap. But it should be noted that the real loan rate turns negative because of the acceleration of inflation in those years. One could also suggest that corporate profits fell because the rapid and sudden increase in import prices was not immediately transmitted into increased output prices.

The analysis clearly shows that the other models underestimate the savings effect of an increase in export earnings and thus overemphasize the expansionary effects. This has resulted in an incorrect analysis of the causes of inflation and an incorrect policy choice: because inflation was believed to be caused by excess demand, demand policies were applied. In fact, inflation was determined by international prices, so that a contractionary policy, as applied in 1974, only led to a recession without having much effect on the rate of inflation.

5.3.2 Excess demand

This section analyses what happens if the macroeconomic disturbance initially affects the other of the two unstable variables, corporate investment.

A disturbance caused by planned investment exceeding planned savings was analysed by Leff and Sato (1980), who argued that the two mechanisms that could, *ex post,* bring investment and savings together are real income changes and price changes. As observed earlier, their analysis suggested that the effects of income and price changes on investment and saving are unlikely to be stabilizing.

In the literature on stabilization in LDCs, the typical case of excess demand that is usually analysed is that of an increase in government expenditure financed by money creation. Implicitly, many of these studies assume that domestic excess demand arising from private investment is unlikely because such investment is constrained by available domestic credit. Many of the results of the analysis of increases in government spending will also apply in the case of increased private investment, so it is useful to follow the simulations through.

In the monetary approach to the balance of payments models, an increase in government expenditure financed by monetary expansion increases income and thus leads to higher demand for money and for imports. The higher imports lead to a loss of foreign reserves and in turn a fall in the money supply. This process continues till, through the loss of reserves, the money supply, income level and import level are brought back to the level they had before the policy was initiated (Polak 1957). Introducing the interest rate would hasten this process, as the initial increase in the money supply caused by the monetary financing of government expenditure leads to a fall in the interest rate, which stimulates investment and may cause a capital outflow, making the outflow of foreign reserves even quicker (Polak and Argy 1971). To this, the financial repression models would add that the inflation caused by the excess demand lowers the real deposit rate, thereby affecting saving and the efficiency of investment.

All these effects may be found in the formal models of the Thai economy that have been used to simulate the effects of an increase in government expenditure. Chaipravat, Meesook and Garnjarerndee (1979) used the large Bank of Thailand model to simulate the effects of an increase in government consumption expenditure by 5 per cent, to be financed by borrowing from the Bank of Thailand.

The result is that real output and prices increase. Household savings, which are a function of income and the real deposit rate, increase because the effect of higher income dominates over the negative effect of the decline in the real deposit rate. As household savings rise, bank deposits increase. The real loan rate in this model is determined by the demand for and the supply of loans. The demand for loans increase with desired investment, which rises because of higher output levels; and the supply of loans grows with deposits. The net effect is that the real loan rate rises slightly but not enough to discourage the increased investment demand. The balance of payments worsens, as is foreseen, leading to an outflow of reserves and a decline in the money supply.

The model, then, confirms that the fiscal and monetary expansion will have a positive effect on real output in the short term, but that in the longer run, inflation and the balance of payments will redress these positive effects.

The neo-structuralist models introduce other adjustment patterns. They emphasize the role of the interest rate as (i) a cost element in the mark-up price equation, and (ii) a variable in the investment function. Given these conditions, a fiscal expansion financed by money creation would have an immediate positive effect on real income and, through a Keynesian saving function, on savings. What happens to the interest rate depends on the saving-investment interaction: if investment demand is very sensitive to income changes, the growth of real income may induce an increase in the desired level of investment in excess of the savings that the higher level of income has generated. In that case the interest rate will rise to balance savings and investment, and with higher interest cost, prices will rise. If the investment demand is not very sensitive to changes in income, desired investment may fall short of the level of savings and the interest rate may fall, affecting the rate of increase of corporate prices through the price equation. It is therefore possible, in the neo-structuralist models, that an expansionary fiscal policy would reduce the rate of inflation (Taylor 1981, 1983).

Taylor and Rosensweig (1984) use their model to simulate the effects of a 5 per cent increase in government current expenditure financed by central bank borrowing. The results show that real output and income increase together with prices. Household savings, which are a function of household income, increase; corporate savings do not change much. The increase in household savings leads to an increase in deposits and in the loan supply. With the increased demand and a slight increase in profits, private investment increases, but on balance the real loan rate falls, which further stimulates investment and induces corporations to borrow less abroad.

The increase in imports, as a result of higher demand and increased investment, and the reduction in foreign borrowing together lead to a loss of reserves which, in the end, is almost equal to the amount originally borrowed by the government from the central bank: an outcome remarkably similar to the outcome of the monetary approach models.

The same adjustment mechanisms that follow an increase in government spending financed by domestic credit expansion could also be expected when the disturbance starts with an increase in the desired level of corporate investment. Corporations can finance a sudden increase in desired investment by borrowing from the domestic financial institutions or from abroad. In both cases, domestic expenditure and the money supply are likely to increase simultaneously, as in the case of government expenditure financed by central bank borrowing. The effects that are expected in the various types of short-term models analysed above may be summarized as follows:

(a) Real income rises, and with it household income, household savings and financial savings.
(b) Prices rise. This will reduce the real deposit rate which may exert a downward effect on financial savings. It is generally expected that the income effect on financial savings will be greater than the interest rate effect, so that financial savings will rise.
(c) The increase in the financial savings supply and the increase in the rate of inflation may lead to a fall in the real loan rate.
(d) There will be several effects on the balance of payments:
  (i) exports will fall as the increase in domestic demand will reduce the volume of exports and inflation leads to an appreciation of the real exchange rate.
  (ii) imports will increase as domestic demand increases and the appreciation of the real exchange rate will lead to substitution.
  (iii) if the real lending rate falls, corporations will borrow less abroad.
  All three effects will lead to a deterioration of the balance of payments and a loss of reserves. This loss of reserves can, in turn, affect the loan supply and the real loan rate.
(e) The subsequent effects on investment are uncertain. They depend on (i) how sensitive investments are to the changes in income and (ii) what happens to the real loan rate and how sensitive investments are to the interest cost.

All the simulation models discussed above conclude that real output increases in the short term, as a result of the increase in expenditure, but that in the longer run these gains are unsustainable given the balance of payments consequences. From the perspective of the analysis of saving behaviour as shown in Chapter 3, all these models may be criticized for using rather simplistic assumptions with respect to the determinants of savings.

In Chapter 3 it was established that household savings are particularly sensitive to fluctuations in the output prices of the unincorporated sector, which, in turn, are largely determined by changes in export prices and to changes in the cost of production, which are reflected in the wage pressure index. The corporate savings ratio was found to be rather stable over time and to fluctuate mainly with the cost of credit.

The simulation models claim that the expansionary effects of the increase in investment expenditure are, at least to some extent, compensated by an increase in the savings of households and corporations; Taylor and Rosensweig (1984), for example, noted in their simulation that household savings increase by 1.7 per cent and household income by 1.4 per cent, so that the household savings ratio increases. But why should this be so? The increase in output as a result of the excess demand mainly affects the non-agricultural sector. In the simulation made by Chaipravat, Meesook and Garnjarerndee (1979), even the entire output increase takes place in the non-agricultural sector. This is to be expected, given the short-term inelasticity of supply in agriculture. It is also unlikely that agricultural prices will increase as a result of increased demand, firstly because the demand for agricultural commodities may be relatively income inelastic and, secondly, because agricultural prices are set by the world market. The incomes of households in the agricultural sector, which is the dominant part of the household sector, are therefore unlikely to increase as a result of an expansion of corporate investment. The increase in prices in other sectors of the economy could even increase the cost of living and push up wage levels, thereby reducing the surplus available to household firms, so there is good reason to argue that household savings will fall rather than increase. If they do, the expansionary effects of an increase in corporate investment will be stronger than is suggested by the simulations described above.

Do the savings of other sectors increase as a result of excess demand? It was observed in Chart 5.2 that the corporate savings ratio is quite stable over time: no sharp short-term fluctuations occur. Excess demand could have two possible effects on corporate savings. Firstly, the increase in real output will tend to increase the rate of capacity utilization. This could increase the profit share, although the regression in Chapter 3 did not lead to a significant coefficient for the capacity utilization variable. Secondly, the increase in desired corporate investment may induce corporations to retain more profits or increase their prices (that is, increase the mark-up rate) to generate more own savings to finance these investments. On the other hand, if inflation reduces the real lending rate, there could be a negative impact on the corporations' desire to save.

There is no empirical evidence to support the belief that changes in the real deposit rate affect total household savings, but it could be that the fall in the real deposit rate affects the households' portfolio choices and reduces the share of their savings that is placed in deposits. This may have an effect on the loan supply and the loan rate.

In Chapter 3 the post-Keynesian saving theory was discussed, which argues that an increase in the investment ratio would increase the savings ratio, through a redistribution of income to profit earners. The main mechanism to redistribute income is inflation. But Chapter 3 concluded, after a brief review of available studies, that a relationship between the aggregate savings ratio and the rate of inflation could not be convincingly established. This finding was confirmed by the reported attempts to fit an aggregate saving function for Thailand (see Chapter 3, section 3.2.6). In most of these attempts, the rate of inflation is introduced in combination with the nominal deposit rate, as the real deposit rate (i_d-p). However, as the nominal deposit rate changes only very seldom and then only by small margins, the real deposit rate in regressions in fact captures the impact of inflation. Some of the regressions on the aggregate saving function for Thailand reported in Chapter 3 showed a positive effect of inflation (see equation (11) in Chapter 3), others a negative (equation (13) in Chapter 3). The analysis above suggests at least two reasons why excess demand resulting from increased corporate investment does not lead to increased savings. Firstly, the effect of excess demand on inflation is probably overestimated. As argued at length earlier in this chapter, the main effect of domestic excess demand, given a regime of free trade, will be felt on the balance of payments rather than on the domestic prices.

Secondly, the post-Keynesian income redistribution also fails to occur because the underlying production relations are quite different from what is assumed. Production in the unincorporated sector takes place under competitive conditions with output prices, particularly of agricultural crops, being largely externally determined. Thus the profits of a main part of the productive sector of the economy cannot be increased through price rises. The corporate sector could increase prices, but will do so only if production costs increase. A dominant element of production inputs are imported raw materials, intermediate and capital goods, which makes the corporate sector prices very sensitive to the import price level. Corporations could also increase prices through a rise in the mark-up rate, but will do so only if the relative cost of external credit justifies it and if market conditions such as domestic and international competition permit it.

Testing these theoretical arguments on reality is quite difficult as the excess demand type of disturbances – that is sudden increases in government spending or in corporate investment – seldom occur in isolation. Generally there are other disturbances simultaneously to the economy.

In the absence of a complete model, incorporating all the elements suggested by the findings of this study, that could be used for simulations, all that

212

can be done is a rather crude test on the movements of some of the main variables in response to excess demand.

In the period analysed in this study, eight years may be singled out in which very sharp increases in domestic autonomous expenditure – either in government expenditure or in private investment or in both – were combined with a substantial increase in domestic credit or foreign borrowing, namely, 1967, 1970, 1971, 1973, 1974, 1976, 1979 and 1982. These were years, when there was excess demand.[8] What are the patterns that may be observed in those years?

In five of the years inflation accelerated. But it was only in 1967 and 1982 that this could not be explained by changes in international prices. The effects on real output are difficult to discern in this crude analysis, as the impact of other factors is ignored. The growth of real output in the unincorporated and in the corporate sectors was in some of the eight years above average and in some below.

More importantly, in six of the eight years the household savings/GDP ratio fell. In one other year the ratio remained unchanged. In the year in which the ratio increased, 1973, there were strong external factors (as analysed in section 5.3.1).

The corporate savings/GDP ratio increased in four years, declined in three and remained unchanged in one. But the changes in this ratio were always small. In general, the increase in corporate savings was not enough to offset the fall in household savings. The aggregate savings ratio fell in seven of the eight years and increased in one, 1973, in which the export price increase must have dominated over any demand effects.

The acceleration of inflation lowers the real deposit rate and so negatively influences financial savings. The regressions reported in Chapter 4 failed to establish convincingly a relationship between the financial savings ratio and the real deposit rate, and that finding is confirmed here. The financial savings/GDP ratio had an overall upward trend over the entire period of study, but in the eight years singled out here, it increased in four and fell in four others.

This crude method of analysis ignores important elements, such as differences in the relative size of the expansionary effect in the various years and the impact of other factors in these years. Possible lags in the adjustment patterns are also ignored. However, the intention here is only to establish that it is unlikely that domestic excess demand would have a strong feedback effect on domestic savings. This is argued on analytical grounds using the results of Chapter 3, and it is at least not disproven by the superficial test above.

The implication is that an increase in autonomous expenditure in the Thai economy has a stronger effect on the balance of payments than the simulations, which are based on existing models and reported previously, suggest. This conclusion further confirms the need for short-term macroeconomic models that include saving behaviour in a more realistic way.

5.4 Stabilization policies

The short-term stabilization policies of the Thai government have been subject to a number of different interpretations. Trescott (1971) described the monetary policies of the 1950s and the 1960s as 'passive'. The credit needs of the government were small as a result of a conservative fiscal policy, and the commercial banks required little central bank credit as they generally had excess reserves and could borrow from abroad. These facts, together with the rapid growth of financial savings, allowed banks to follow the domestic demand for credit without this having any negative impact on the balance of payments (see also Rozenthal 1970).

Ingram (1971) called the monetary policy 'conservative' because it maintained a high level of foreign reserves and strictly defended the value of the Baht.

Siamwalla (1975) labelled the entire package of short-term policies of the government over the period 1950–72 'passive'; various instruments of short-term policy were seldom or never used (for example, the exchange rate, tax rates, import controls, interest rates), so that only government expenditure remained as a (rather inflexible) instrument of stabilization policy. He explained the stability of the economy over this period by the great stability in the world economy (see also Trescott 1971), and by the automatic stabilization brought about by the government budget. If export prices rose, for example, the potential excess demand was curtailed by growing revenues, while government expenditure adjusted much more slowly or even fell in real terms (Siamwalla 1975).

The overall impression in this period is of an absence of any discretionary short-term policy. Given the pattern, observed above, of adjustment of internal imbalances through the balance of payments this policy seems realistic. Why would one try a stabilization policy when financial intermediation accommodates short-term saving-investment gaps? The role of monetary policy may then be interpreted as creating the conditions under which such adjustment can take place, that is creating confidence and creditworthiness, for example, by defending the exchange rate and maintaining high levels of foreign reserves.

The 1970s, with their increasing international and domestic instabilities, put this system of adjustment to the test. In that light, the excessively contractionary fiscal policy of 1974 may be seen as a shock reaction to a totally new international economic environment. In subsequent years, macroeconomic policies were less successful in maintaining stability. The macroeconomic problems of Thailand in the early 1980s may be summarized as follows:

(a) The oil price increase of 1979 hit Thailand at a moment when the economy was already slightly overheated. The level of investment was quite high over the period 1977–81 and the budget deficit had moved to a structurally higher level since the mid-1970s. These factors resulted in rapid inflation and high current account deficits.

(b) The response to the external shocks came late. Fiscal and monetary policies were accommodating and passive up to 1979–80. Gaps were filled with external borrowing. In 1981 there was a devaluation of the Baht and a slight change in the fiscal policy stance. The restrictive fiscal policies were ineffective though: the growth of expenditure was contained but the poor economic conditions led to a shortfall of revenue far below expectations so that the fiscal deficit remained high and the effectiveness of fiscal policies over the period was undermined (Wibulswasdi 1987).

(c) The fall in world market commodity prices affected agricultural income. Despite continued volume growth, the nominal value of agricultural GDP declined since 1983 and in 1986 was still below its 1983 level. With the drop in agricultural incomes, household income and also household savings fell (see Table 5.1). As private investments were also low, the private sector resource gap did not in itself create a problem, but it was inadequate to finance the public sector deficit. The high current account deficit in the years 1981–1985 was the result.

(d) The export performance of Thailand was hampered by the fact that the Baht was tied to the dollar which, since 1979, appreciated relative to the currencies of some of Thailand's major trading partners. The Baht devaluation of 1981, and even that of 1984, were not sufficient to correct for that appreciation. The result was the slowdown of export growth in the 1980s.

(e) The overvalued Baht could be defended only by an extremely high domestic real interest rate. In 1984 the real effective lending rate of commercial banks was 13 per cent. The increasing lending cost discouraged investment: private investments were low since 1982.

These factors caused the considerable fall in economic growth in the 1980s, but that did not help to reduce the current account deficit, as the poor export performance was one of the main problems. Not until 1986 was there a turnaround, which, if one wanted to be unfriendly towards policy-makers, could be ascribed mainly to external circumstances.

The devaluation of 1984 did help but was hardly enough to compensate for the appreciation of the Baht along with the dollar. But when the dollar started to depreciate in 1985 the Baht moved along and Thai exports gained gradually in competitiveness. The oil price fall in 1986 significantly reduced the cost of imports. These two factors contributed to the current account surplus of 1986, but that surplus was a sign of weakness more than strength because investment activity and production growth, and therefore import demand, were very poor in that year.

The real economic recovery started in the latter part of 1986 and gained strength in 1987; the 1987 growth rate was around 7 per cent and the expectations for 1988 are for a similar rate or even higher. The recovery of growth is carried by foreign investment and manufactured exports. The Asian surplus countries, such as Japan and Taiwan, under growing criticism and threats of trade retaliation from the USA, started to move production of export goods to Thailand. Under the impact private investment recovered and export performance improved.

Looking back, in 1988, at the economic experience of recent years, one could suggest that this period has been one of fundamental change in the policy regime in Thailand. Traditionally, the overvaluation of the currency and the price interventions by the government had kept domestic food prices low and had supported industry in general and import-dependent industry in particular. But once import substitution is completed and as long as productivity growth, and therefore income growth, in agriculture and industry is modest, industrial expansion comes to depend mainly on exports. To make that possible, Thailand had to shift from a trade regime in which an overvalued currency protected a domestic-market-oriented industry to a regime where a cheap currency would boost the international competitiveness of export industries. Such a shift is politically difficult as vested interest will suffer; the 1984 devaluation led to considerable political unrest and the eventual resignation of the finance minister. The downglide along with the dollar since 1985 provided a lucky escape: the appearance of stability in the Baht-dollar exchange rate was combined with a rapid depreciation with respect to the currencies of other main trading partners. The results of this effective depreciation on the domestic price level were cushioned by the low level of world commodity prices: domestic cost of living hardly increased.

It is clear that the traditional view that characterized Thai macroeconomic policies as cautious or passive does not hold in the late 1970s and 1980s as much as it did in earlier periods. In particular, control over fiscal policy was lost so that the fiscal balance became a problem rather than a policy instrument. This meant that monetary policies had to bear more of the stabilization task.

5.4.1 Monetary policy instruments

The execution of monetary policy has become difficult though, as might become clear from a brief review of the instruments available.

The exchange rate There have been only a few changes in the value of the exchange rate. This rate is quite sensitive politically in Thailand, as it is considered a symbol of stability. A devaluation is generally seen as an act of political suicide on the part of the Minister of Finance. This position was understandable at the time of stable international exchange rates, when the stability of the Baht was necessary to create domestic and international confidence, but it is totally inappropriate and dangerous in times of floating exchange rates.

216

The required reserve ratio for commercial banks The ratio is only infrequently changed. As banks often have excess reserves and can supplement reserves by borrowing abroad, this instrument is not very effective. Banks resent this instrument, as it increases the share of their resources on which they cannot make profits, and they use their political influence to stop rises in the reserve ratio.

The ceilings for rates of interest on deposits and for loans These are also infrequently changed. The optimal level of the domestic interest rate is determined by three factors: the need to mobilize savings, the need to stimulate investment and the need to prevent too wide a gap between domestic and foreign interest rates. Only by coincidence can the three factors be simultaneously satisfied (Wibulswasdi 1983).

In recent years the Bank of Thailand has been less active in adjusting interest rate ceilings and generally has kept the ceilings above levels that would be indicated by the three factors listed before. The intention of this policy shift is to force commercial banks to come to a more flexible interest rate management. But this has created some difficulties for the banks. Competition among them for deposits is fierce and an individual bank would fear that, if it lowered its deposit rate, others would not follow. This has created a situation in which the actual deposit rate remains close to the (high) ceiling so that substantial deposits are made, whereas the effective lending rate is further below the ceiling. Certainly for prime customers, that can also borrow abroad, banks have to adjust the lending rate according to the movements in the international interest rates. The banks can only charge a higher loan rate to smaller domestic customers. The result of the high deposit rate has been for deposits to grow rapidly and, with the poor economic conditions and high loan rate, for credit demand to increase slowly. Banks, therefore, have been relatively liquid in recent years (see data on credit/deposit ratio in Table 5.1) and have seen the spread between deposit rate and effective loan rate narrow. Profitability of the banking business has decreased since 1983 (see Nidhipabha and Arya 1987) and it is not surprising that banks continue to pressure the central bank for a more active interest ceiling policy.

The bank rate This is the interest rate at which commercial banks can borrow from the central bank. In 1980 it was significantly increased, together with an increase in the deposit and loan rate ceilings, and since then the bank rate is more actively used (World Bank 1983b; Wibulswasdi 1983; Go 1984). This could be called a shift by the monetary authorities to an 'expensive credit' policy (Panitchpakdi 1981). But as banks and large corporations can also borrow abroad, a high bank rate is only effective in curtailing domestic credit demand when the international interest rates are also high, as for example in 1979–81. But in other years, for instance 1983 and 1984, when international rates were lower, a high bank rate stimulates banks and large corporations to borrow abroad. Only the firms in the unincorporated sector and small and medium-sized corporations, which are dependent on bank credit, suffer from the high cost of credit.

The very high level of the real interest rate in recent years is difficult to explain by any short-term policy objective that the authorities could have. It should probably be explained by the need to attract foreign capital to finance the more fundamental disequilibrium in the current account caused by the growing public sector deficit. The high real deposit rates have contributed to the high level of financial savings in recent years, but the high real loan rates have discouraged private investment as can be seen in Charts 5.2 and 5.3, and this suggests that there is 'crowding-out' of private sector investment through the public sector deficit. Only in 1986 was there a turnaround, when interest rates were drastically reduced to stimulate the economy.

Credit ceiling In 1984 the central bank imposed a limit on the credit expansion allowed for that year. This was followed by wide protest, particularly from small and medium-sized companies who could not escape these controls by borrowing abroad.

The conclusion of this review of monetary policy instruments is not optimistic. Some instruments are difficult to use for political reasons; others are rather ineffective. The interest rate policy is only effective in a macroeconomic sense if the level of the international interest rate allows domestic objectives to be achieved. If that is not so, a high interest rate policy – as well as ceilings on credit expansion – may have as much effect on the sectoral allocation of credit and investment as on their overall levels. Large corporations with direct access to international financial markets do not suffer from the high cost, or the restrictions on the growth, of domestic credit.

The review of stabilization models in Chapter 1 concluded that the monetary approach models suggested controls on the expansion of domestic credit as the main instrument for the short-term management of the economy. The financial repression models claimed that an interest rate policy would be superior. The Thai experience shows that in an open and free economy, credit controls are difficult to implement. The recent experience with the expensive credit policy seems to indicate a shift towards the financial repression approach. The outcome is not very positive: financial savings increased – as they must, given a real deposit rate of return of 12 per cent in 1984 – but aggregate savings did not. The fall in private investment, partly the result of the high cost of credit, shows that investments are more sensitive to the cost of credit than the financial repression models suggest. This is in line with the expectations formulated by the neo-structuralist models. The other expectation of the latter models – that high interest rates push up costs and lead to inflation – is not confirmed by the recent Thai experience, in which inflation was very low.

Because these policies have obvious negative effects, it would seem preferable to return to the system of adjustment through foreign borrowing and to reasonable levels for the real rates of interest. That can only be done, however, if the economy is fundamentally in equilibrium. There are reasons to doubt that this condition is fulfilled. The main obstacle is the public sector deficit: its growing size and the accumulating foreign debt will, in the end, undermine the creditworthiness of the Thai economy (World Bank 1984; Kharas and Shishido 1985). Financing the public sector deficit from domestic sources is not an attractive alternative, as that would only lead to a crowding out of private investment as long as domestic savings do not increase.

It would thus appear that a successful return to short-term macroeconomic stability in Thailand requires a substantial fiscal reform. In recent years attempts in that direction have been made – partly in the context of World Bank's Structural Adjustment Loans – and some progress has been made (as the public sector savings deficit in Chart 5.4 shows), but much remains to be done.

5.5 Conclusion

Macroeconomic disturbances, in Thailand and elsewhere, may originate domestically or abroad. As observed in section 5.2, external disturbances are particularly important for the explanation of inflation. In the analysis of domestic disturbances and of adjustment patterns, the attention was focused on movements in household savings and corporate investment.

In section 5.3.1 the impact of export prices on domestic inflation and on household savings was analysed. In Thailand before the Second World War, as described by Ingram (1971), fluctuations in export earnings led to corresponding changes in the importation of consumer goods and in the transfer of trading profits to abroad. There was, therefore, no effect on the domestic economy. With the subsequent political changes and financial development, the domestic impact of increases in export earnings has changed. It leads now to an increase in household savings and in financial savings. As private investment is not predominantly finance constrained, the availability of more financial savings does not necessarily invite more investment. Also, as the real wage is likely to fall with higher export and food prices, the macroeconomic effects are far less expansionary than is sometimes suggested in the literature. This is, of course, partly related to the very special nature of the Thai economy, as an exporter of a main wage crop. But the effects can apply more generally.

In terms of policy response, there is a danger that the deflationary effects are not recognized and that the inflationary (that is price-increasing) effects of the higher export prices will lead to counter-inflationary policies that are undesirable.

The analysis, in section 5.3.2, of the effects of domestic demand expansion also led to conclusions that are somewhat at odds with conventional results obtained in a variety of macroeconomic models. There is no reason to expect that a higher level of autonomous expenditure will induce a stabilizing reaction from domestic savings. This is so particularly because household savings do not react to excess demand.

These findings confirm the importance of separating, in the productive sector of the economy, the unincorporated from the corporate sector. This breakdown has not only important implications for the sectoral balances in the economy, but it also affects significantly the analysis of short-term stabilization problems.

It may also be concluded that the role of financial intermediation in the short-term adjustment processes is not as simple as is sometimes suggested. In the financial repression models, it is asserted that an increase in the real deposit rate would lead to an increase in financial savings, and that this would enable banks to extend more credit for working capital or fixed capital so that production or investment could increase. The neo-structuralist models added that the cost of credit is likely to increase when the deposit rate rises, and that these higher costs may easily discourage investment or lead to inflation.

The analysis in this and earlier chapters provides three reasons for doubt about these mechanisms.

(a) The supply of financial savings need not be sensitive to the real deposit rate of interest. Fluctuations in the real deposit rate are mainly determined by changes in the rate of (expected) inflation. The regression in Chapter 4 failed to get a significant coefficient for the real deposit rate. Regression results of other authors that were cited gave significant results, but in one case with a positive sign and in another with a negative sign. These mixed findings may be less surprising after the analysis in this Chapter. The rate of inflation, which is the main determinant of changes in the real deposit rate, changes in response to three possible factors: changes in export prices, or in import prices or domestic excess demand pressures. But such disturbances not only have an effect on domestic inflation and the real deposit rate; they also have an income effect on the household sector, the main source of financial savings. The total effect on financial savings then is the combination of this income effect and any real deposit rate effect. The latter will always be negative in the case of an acceleration of inflation. The income effect will be positive in the case of an increase in the export prices and it is quite likely that in such a case the positive income effect will prevail over the negative substitution effect. If inflation starts with a rise in import prices or with domestic excess demand, there will be no direct effect on household income. There could be a second-round negative effect if the higher prices were to push up wage costs and the cost of living for the household firms. In these cases, there is likely to be a negative effect on financial savings. But it should be concluded that there is no unique relationship between the real deposit rate and the growth of financial savings. In the rare cases where the real deposit rate changes because of policy decisions with respect to the nominal deposit rate, the effect will be less ambiguous. Such policy changes are exceptional, however, and generally constitute small changes in the deposit rate compared to the fluctuations that the rate of inflation brings about.

(b) The second assumption underlying the financial repression models, that is that corporations are finance constrained, is also not supported by the evidence presented in this study. Large corporations and financial institutions are not exclusively dependent on domestic savings: they have alternative sources of funds abroad. It was observed that gaps between private savings and investments exist and are accommodated by variations in the (i) excess reserve holdings of financial institutions, (ii) net foreign borrowing by financial institutions and (iii) direct foreign borrowing by large corporations.

(c) These links to the international financial system are a crucial element of financial intermediation in Thailand. They enable the economy to deal with short-term fluctuations in the household savings on the one hand, and those in the corporate investments on the other, without affecting the level of desired investment and without endangering the growth of the economy. Of course, this type of short-term adjustment is only possible if, in the medium and long term, the economy is in equilibrium. If there were a continuous deficit, the resulting accumulation of foreign debt would undermine creditworthiness.

Notes

1. The expression 'short-term' in this chapter refers to year-to-year movements in economic variables, rather than to their development in the medium or longer term. In some cases it might have been desirable to trace short-term adjustment patterns within the year; and for quite a number of economic variables quarterly observations are available. However, as this chapter is more concerned with identifying general processes of adjustment than in tracing the detailed adjustment of individual disturbances it will stick to the use of annual data.

2. It will be clear that in Chart 5.1, the current account deficit is introduced with a positive sign, thus the current account surpluses of 1961 and 1966 appear as negative ratios.

3. In the formulation of equation (1) and in the subsequent charts based on it, Flow-of-Funds data have been used. In the National Accounts of Thailand savings are separated into (i) household savings, (ii) corporate savings (including private corporations and state enterprises), and (iii) savings of general government, while investments are divided into (i) the private sector (households and private corporations) and (ii) the public sector (government and state enterprises). It is clear that such a breakdown does not allow a systematic analysis of saving and investment per sector. The Flow-of-Funds data, however, have the disadvantage that the available time series is shorter; hence the use of National Accounts data in the estimation of equation (3) below.

4. This conclusion is, of course, consistent with many short-term models, including, for instance, those of the monetary approach of the IMF (see, for example, Khan and Knight

221

1981). There is a difference in that, often implicitly, the monetary approach models assume that the discrepancy between savings and investments is due to a fiscal imbalance. In the analysis above, it was shown that short-term variations in the private sector can also be the cause. As mentioned earlier, most of the other short-term models pay little attention to private sector saving and investment behaviour.

5. The Thai economy has, of course, suffered from many types of shocks, for example, the increase in oil prices. But given the focus of this study and the findings earlier in this chapter, only shocks arising from household savings and corporate investment will be discussed.

6. Thailand is a large supplier of rice to the world market, but not so large that its actions have an overriding impact on world prices of rice.

7. The model of Taylor and Rosensweig is very detailed, but data problems forced the authors to introduce assumed values for some parameters so as to be able to run the model. This should be kept in mind when interpreting the results (see Taylor and Rosensweig 1984).

8. The selection of years of excess demand was based on the criteria that an excess demand year was any year, in which (i) the ratio of Government Expenditure to GDP, or of Private Investment to GDP, increased by more than one percentage point; and (ii) the growth of domestic credit extended to the government, or of domestic credit to or foreign borrowing by the private sector, were substantially above average. Of course, these criteria can only be applied *ex post*, on the assumption that intended levels of expenditure could be realized.

6 Conclusion

This concluding chapter gives a summary of the findings of this study, and an assessment of the relevance to other developing countries of the methods applied, and of the findings on the causes and effects of financial development in Thailand.

6.1 Summary of findings

The aim of this study, as set out in the Introduction and Chapter 1, is to analyse the causes and effects of financial development in Thailand over the last 25 years. In its approach, the study tries to link the fundamental questions on financing development to more recent concerns with financial policy and stabilization. These fundamental questions, raised by early writers on economic development in the 1950s and 1960s, are (i) how to increase the resources available for investment, and (ii) how to maintain sectoral balances and stability during the process of development.

The answer to the first question depends on whether it is possible to increase domestic savings. The inflow of foreign capital may, temporarily, increase available investment resources, but in the long run it creates a debt-servicing burden that can only be managed if domestic savings increase. The second question on the stability of development depends, in the view of the classical writers, mainly on whether agricultural production can grow fast enough to generate a surplus to finance industrialization, while at the same time ensuring the satisfaction of domestic demand for basic needs (in other words, food). In these early contributions on the problems of financing development, little attention was paid to the role of the financial system.

As financial development in LDCs advanced, the concern shifted to the questions of which contribution the system could make to economic progress, and which policies would further stimulate financial development. In this later financial literature, the concern for stability is not analysed in terms of sectoral balances but in terms of macroeconomic indicators such as the budget deficit, inflation and the current account deficit.

6.1.1 A structuralist approach

This study attempts to present a reintegration of the concerns of the 'classics' into the analysis of financial development and stabilization. Questions regarding the effects of financial development and regarding optimal monetary and financial policies cannot be settled at the aggregate macroeconomic level. In answering them, one has to recognize sectoral differences in the economy. This study follows a structuralist approach in which the main sectors of the economy are separately analysed. The private side of the productive sector is split up into two main sectors according to fundamental differences in their organization of production. The unincorporated sector of small, family-based, production units operates, on the input and output side, on competitive markets. The dominant activity in this sector in Thailand is agriculture, but it also includes retail trade and services. The corporate sector, on the other hand, consists of large firms that often apply capital-intensive techniques and have some degree of market control and price-setting powers.

It is to be expected that the fundamental differences in production conditions and in the way income is generated between these two sectors have an influence on their saving and investment behaviour, both in the short and long run, and on the nature of their interaction with financial institutions.

The unincorporated sector of household enterprises is comparatively large in Thailand: about three-quarters of all households are self-employed. This can be explained by the fact that new agricultural land is still available in Thailand so that agricultural growth can take place through the expansion of acreage. There has been little pressure on labour to leave agriculture.

The growth of the corporate sector, in absolute as well as in relative terms, is due not so much to changes in the organization of production of given activities (from unincorporated to corporate forms), but more to the rapid growth of activities in productive sectors in which the corporate form of organization dominates (industry). The corporate sector in Thailand is strongly concentrated in terms of size, of geographical location and of ownership and control. A relatively small number of 'groups' may be identified, each centred around one or a few families and consisting of a number of corporations in different fields of activity. The groups that include financial institutions tend to be the largest and the most dynamic.

224

6.1.2 Disaggregated analysis of saving behaviour

This study has systematically analysed the implications of these differences in production conditions between these two segments of the private sector for (a) their saving behaviour, (b) their investment behaviour, and (c) their interactions with the financial system. The public sector is also included in the analysis but has received relatively less detailed attention.

In most conventional theories saving behaviour is derived from the consumption behaviour of the household. But household surveys, in Thailand and in other LDCs, show that most household savings come from self-employed households. This suggests these savings are the surplus of unincorporated family-based economic units that are simultaneously production and consumption unit. Household savings may therefore be interpreted as entrepreneurial income or as retained profits of the unincorporated enterprises.

Chapter 3 develops two models, one for household savings and one for corporate savings, in which these savings are explained by the production conditions faced by these two types of firms. The regression results are satisfactory, showing that the household savings ratio fluctuates strongly over time and that variations may be explained by changes in output prices and in the costs of production in household firms. The output prices in this predominantly agricultural sector are largely determined by export prices set by the world market. The main element in the cost of production is wages; so, the surplus of the unincorporated sector is sensitive to wage pressure, but this latter variable may also reflect the cost of living for household labour.

The corporate savings ratio is far more stable over time, as one would expect of firms that have some control over their own output prices. The mild fluctuations in this ratio are caused by variations in the cost of external funds, either from domestic financial institutions or from international financial markets.

6.1.3 Financial development and intersectoral transfer of resources

The household sector saves more than it uses for its own investments. Its savings surplus is increasingly deposited with financial institutions. Corporations, on the other hand, invest more than they save, and for them financial institutions are an important source of additional funds. In that way the institutions have become an indirect channel for financial resources between the unincorporated and the corporate sectors.

All available indicators show that financial development has progressed rapidly over the last 25 years in Thailand. The Flow-of-Funds Accounts, which are available on an annual basis from 1967 onwards, show that the growth of financial intermediation has two aspects:

(a) The main determinant of the growth in domestic financial intermediation has been the rise in the household savings ratio and the growing share of household savings deposited in financial institutions. These institutions use these funds to increase their loans to unincorporated and corporate enterprises.

(b) The second aspect is the increasing role of international financial markets in financial intermediation in Thailand. Not only Thai banks, but also large corporations and especially state enterprises, have increased their dealings with international financial markets.

A main question, addressed in Chapter 4, is why a growing share of household savings should be placed with financial institutions. If household savings are the profits of unincorporated enterprises, one would expect them to be used for re-investment in the household firm. But the increase in household savings has not led to an increase in household investment. Why is that so? Chapter 4 suggested three main answers to that question.

(i) The returns on investments in the unincorporated sector, compared to those in the corporate sector, are low and highly uncertain. This is because they depend on the vagaries of the world market, where the main output prices of the sector are determined. On average, returns on financial assets (that is deposits) have been good, but are also subject to the uncertainties introduced by unexpected inflation. A major factor indirectly adding to the returns on financial assets is that the rapid spread of financial institutions over the country has significantly reduced the transaction costs of financial assets.

(ii) A part of the growth of financial intermediation in the unincorporated sector is due to the gradual replacement of the unregulated money market by official financial institutions. All direct estimates and indirect indicators suggest a rapid decline in the relative size of the unregulated money market in the rural areas of Thailand, and it is likely that banks have taken over its role.

(iii) It should also be recognized that the surplus of the household sector is highly concentrated, and that a significant part of it may be in the hands of a few families (for example, those owning trading firms) which may have personal links to the 'groups' in the corporate sector. As observed before, such groups are typically involved in diverse activities, including export trade. The rural representatives of these groups may use the financial institutions to channel their surpluses to their group's urban centre.

6.1.4 Financial development and macroeconomic stability

An important consequence of the growing role of indirect finance and of

226

financial intermediation is the increased separation of saving and investment. This raises the problem of the short-term coordination of saving and investment decisions. Chapter 5 has shown that the problem of short-term stability in Thailand cannot be satisfactorily analysed in the context of an aggregated macroeconomic model. A more disaggregated and detailed analysis reveals that imbalances between *ex ante* saving and investment plans can have two sources. The main component of domestic savings, household savings, fluctuates considerably in the short term, while the others, corporate and government savings, are more stable over time. And the main element of domestic investment, corporate investment, also fluctuates strongly, while household and government investments tend to be more stable. The outcome of this is that the aggregated domestic savings tend to follow the rise and fall in household savings, and aggregated investment those in corporate investment. The macroeconomic balance between savings and investments is therefore the result of the events in these two sectors.

The fluctuations in the household savings ratio are in the first place caused by external shocks: those savings are particularly sensitive to changes in export prices. The fluctuations in corporate investment are determined more by domestic factors.

The nature of the instability, and of the adjustment process it brings, cannot be adequately understood and traced using conventional stabilization models, as these have either an aggregated saving function or a simplistic analysis of saving behaviour, and generally both.

The analysis in Chapter 5 has shown that short-term discrepancies between private savings and investments are accommodated by domestic and international financial markets. When a shortage of funds (S < I) occurs, domestic financial institutions reduce their excess reserves, and domestic financial institutions and large corporations increase their borrowing abroad. This is to make the funds available that enable the corporate sector to realize its planned level of investment. The result is a widening of the current account deficit. In the opposite case (S > I), banks will hold excess reserves and foreign borrowing is reduced.

6.1.5 Monetary and financial policies

In this study, relatively little explicit attention is given to public policy. There is relatively little government intervention in the Thai economy, as is shown in the comparatively low ratio of government expenditure to GDP. The role of state enterprises is also relatively small. These enterprises concentrate on 'traditional' public sector activities (that is, public utilities, transport and communications) and are supportive to rather than competing with the private corporate sector. The financial institutions and the corporations face relatively few restrictions in their relations with the rest of the world.

The Thai government has indirectly stimulated financial development. Some elements of financial repression are present: such as interest rate ceilings, forced government bond holding for commercial banks, and forced lending, at subsidized rates, to priority sectors. On the other hand, the interest rate ceilings have never been very low; the spread between deposit and loan rates has always been wide enough to generate good profits; and since 1970 the interest rate on government bonds has always been slightly higher than the deposit rate. The main support to financial development may well have come from indirect measures which created a feeling of confidence. Through the control on entry of new banks, existing banks knew their market to be protected. When individual institutions ran into problems, the authorities organized rescue operations to prevent a loss of public confidence. By maintaining a stable exchange rate and holding substantial foreign reserves, the monetary authorities created an international standing for Thailand that enabled banks and corporations to borrow increasingly abroad.

The government is generally supportive of the corporate sector. Political power is in the hands of a coalition of political leaders and the corporate bourgeoisie, while the unincorporated sector has no influence. So it is not surprising to find there have been no active pro-agriculture policies. Public investments in agriculture have been relatively low. The rice and rubber taxation policy and the high exchange rate have depressed agricultural incomes and returns on agricultural investments.

Just as one can analyse fiscal incidence by studying the groups, sectors or regions from which the government collects its revenue and to which its expenditures render benefits, one can also study the incidence of financial intermediation. Like the government budget, the financial system is a mechanism for the allocation of resources in the economy, and its activities have distributional implications. The broad trends, observed in Chapter 4, are that financial intermediation shifts funds from the unincorporated to the corporate sector and from the provinces to Bangkok.

In recent years the government has tried, through financial policies, to reduce these flows by imposing on financial institutions mandatory shares for agricultural and rural loans, and by offering rediscount facilities for agricultural loans. It appears that these measures have been successful in increasing the access of the unincorporated sector to the financial system, but not in stopping the net outflow of funds.

It is interesting to observe that the government chose to use the financial system as an instrument for sectoral policies, rather than applying, for instance, more general measures like an increase in the rice price or a devaluation of the exchange rate. More general measures of this type would benefit the unincorporated sector generally, but would increase the urban cost of living. The more specific measures applied through the financial institutions benefit only those persons who have access to these institutions and in the provincial setting they tend to be the richer and more powerful segments of the rural population.

The World Bank report on financial reform in Thailand (see World Bank 1983b) advised the Thai government to reduce its controls on the financial system, but this recommendation is based more on the blind faith of the World Bank in the efficiency of free markets, than on a careful analysis of the costs and benefits of financial policies. It is quite likely that if banks were free to do as they pleased, they would reduce their lending to agriculture and in rural areas to the same low levels as before the regulations were introduced. They would do so partly because loans to large urban corporations have lower administrative costs, but also because they have personal links with such corporations.

Thailand has not needed a short-term stabilization policy because its imbalances have been accommodated through financial intermediation. Such a policy would also have been difficult to implement though. The policy advice coming from available stabilization models concentrates on monetary policy instruments: in the monetary approach models of the IMF, the emphasis is on domestic credit control; in the financial repression models, it is on the interest rate. However, in a country with unrestricted and intensive links with the international financial markets, these policies are not always feasible or effective. Domestic credit controls can be evaded by borrowing abroad, and the domestic interest rate cannot move too far out of line with international rates. Under these conditions the effects of monetary policy are mainly felt by firms in the unincorporated sector and by small and medium-sized corporations; they cannot borrow directly abroad and consequently suffer from the limited availability or high cost of domestic credit.

The major macroeconomic problem for Thailand in recent years has been the structural imbalance in the public sector. The large public sector borrowing requirement has not crowded out private investment, as it has mainly been satisfied by borrowing abroad. But it has led to a rise in the current account deficit and an accumulation of foreign debt. This pattern is unsustainable in the longer run, because it will lead to an external debt that will undermine the international creditworthiness of Thailand, and therefore undermine the automatic adjustment processes of the private sector.

In IMF agreements made in recent years, and also in the terms of the Structural Adjustment Loans of the World Bank, conditionality has concentrated on the reduction of the public sector deficit. This seems a correct policy, and if the Thai government can succeed in achieving this target and bring the public sector deficit down to a sustainable level, the preconditions for automatic short-term macroeconomic adjustment will be secured.

6.2   Implications of the findings of this study

At the end of this study, it is appropriate to ask whether the approach used and the findings on Thailand are relevant for other developing countries as well.

In answering that question, it should be recognized that the Thai economy has three rather special characteristics:

(a)   It is a land surplus economy;
(b)   It exports basic food crops; and
(c)   A comparatively large proportion of its population is still active in the agricultural sector.

These three characteristics are interdependent and, taken together, are an important explanation for the economic success of Thailand.

The availability of land, together with rapid population growth, made it possible for agricultural production to develop swiftly through the extension of acreage rather than the intensification of production. The supply of food and exports could therefore expand both without much financial investment and an active government policy favouring agriculture.

Almost all agricultural crops are both exported as well as consumed at home. Government policy has allowed world market prices to determine domestic prices, so all uncertainties of the world market are borne by the producer. These uncertainties removed whatever incentives there were to invest, and they further explain the stagnation of productivity in Thai agriculture.

This model of agricultural growth explains why such a large part of the population is still active in agriculture. The low productivity explains the low average income in the sector. Most of the rest of the unincorporated sector is dependent on the fortunes of the agricultural sector for its demand or supply.

The demand arising from the extensive growth of the unincorporated sector has provided an important basis for the rapid growth of the industrial sector. But the relatively low per capita incomes in the unincorporated former have also limited the expansion of industrial output and made the growth of the sector increasingly dependent on export markets.

It could be argued that the large size of the self-employed sector is one of the factors underlying the poor tax performance of Thailand. The large number of small self-employed households are difficult for tax collectors to reach, while many of the large corporations may escape heavy taxation through investment incentives and tax evasion techniques.

These specific conditions of Thailand are not present in other LDCs. Many countries have reached the limits of their agricultural extension earlier, and can only feed their growing population and produce agricultural export crops if the productivity of the sector rises, or if they have other sources of foreign exchange earnings so that they can import food. The need to increase agricultural productivity probably requires more active government commitment to the sector, for example by large public investments, by turning relative prices in favour of the sector or by discouraging an outflow of funds through the financial system.

In many LDCs that, like Thailand, are exporters of primary commodities and thereby suffer from the vagaries of the world market, the impact on the domestic economy is different for one of the following two reasons, or both.

The first is that although the countries export primary commodities including agricultural products, they may not export food crops that are also domestically consumed. The result is that the fluctuations in the export prices do not have the direct effect on the domestic cost of living that they have in Thailand.

A second reason is that in many countries, governments do not allow the movements in international prices to affect domestic prices as directly as in Thailand. Price stabilization schemes or marketing boards function as buffers which prevent the price changes on the world market from affecting the incomes of the producers.

Under these conditions the domestic cost of living and agricultural incomes, which are the two main determinants of household savings, fluctuate less with world market prices, so it is likely that in such countries, the fluctuations in the household savings ratio are also less extreme. But that does not necessarily mean that such countries experience less instability: the fluctuations that the households do not feel, are now felt by the government through its price stabilization scheme. If the marginal propensity to save of the government were less than that of the household sector, short-term instabilities might increase, but they would be reflected more in fiscal imbalances than in fluctuations in financial intermediation, as in Thailand.

There may be many other ways in which differences in economic structure or in the policy regime would make the findings of this study quite specific to Thailand. The approach followed in this study, though, might have more general applicability.

In LDCs, and even in advanced Western countries, the productive sector may be split up into a segment of small firms operating on competitive markets, and another segment consisting of large, oligopolistic corporations. In most LDCs, the unincorporated sector is still relatively large and is likely to remain quite important to the economy. Available household surveys of many LDCs show that most of that sector's savings come from self-employed households. There is therefore sufficient justification for the explanation of household savings by the production conditions faced by household firms, as proposed in Chapter 3, rather than only from a consumption perspective.

The explicit analysis of the production conditions of household firms in the unincorporated sector would also be useful in many other areas of economic analysis, for example, in the identification of determinants of investment in agricultural innovations.

Recognition of these points will also influence the analysis of financial intermediation in other countries.

The financial system in many LDCs may suffer more from 'financial repression', and be more subject to government interventions in the interest rates and in the allocation of credit, than is the case in Thailand. Such interventions make it more difficult to identify the specific role of financial institutions in the intersectoral flows of funds. Many studies on financial repression, though, claim that these government interventions only serve to reduce the investment funds available to the unincorporated and small-scale sectors of the economy.

This study of the relatively free financial system of Thailand shows that this bias is due to the inherent nature of financial institutions as much as to the 'mistaken' government interventions. A simple act of financial liberalization would not change the nature of these institutions and remove this bias. The experience of Thailand shows that some of the government's interventions in the allocation of credit were introduced to correct for the bias in the financial system itself.

The main element of the approach followed in this study is that it interprets financial intermediation as a channel for the intersectoral flows of funds. Most studies on financial development fail to recognize this function explicitly and concentrate fully on macroeconomic aggregates. It is only when the sectoral allocation function of the financial system is recognized, and the patterns of intersectoral flows of funds identified, that an optimal financial policy may be designed.

Bibliography and references

Ajanant, J.S. Chunanuntathum and S. Meenaphant 1986. *Trade and Industrialization of Thailand*, Social Science Association of Thailand, Bangkok.

Akrasanee, N. 1981. 'Trade Strategy for Employment Growth in Thailand', in A.O. Krueger, H.B. Lary and N. Akrasanee: *Trade and Employment in Developing Countries*, pp. 393–432, University of Chicago Press.

Akrasanee, N. and J. Ajanant 1982. *Export Credit Financing in Thailand*, mimeo, Bangkok.

Amranand, P. and W. Grais 1984. *Macroeconomic and Distributional Implications of Sectoral Policy Interventions : An Application to Thailand*, World Bank staff working paper, no. 627, Washington DC.

Ando, A. and F. Modigliani 1963. 'The "Life-cycle" Hypothesis of Saving : Aggregate Implications and Tests', in *American Economic Review*, March 1963, pp. 55–84.

Aphimeteetamrong, V. 1980. *The Contribution of Financial Institutions to Thai Economic Development*, unpublished PhD thesis, University of Illinois.

ARTEP 1982. *Productivity, Wages and Minimum Wage Policy in Thailand, A framework for analysis applied to selected manufacturing industries*, ARTEP, Bangkok.

Asian Strategies Company 1982. *Euromoney Country Risk Report : Thailand, the War Across the Border*, Euromoney Publications, London.

Bain, A.D. 1973. 'Surveys in Applied Economies : Flow of Funds Analysis', in *Economic Journal*, December 1973, pp. 1055–93.

Bangkok Bank 1982. *Statistical data on Commercial Banks in Thailand*, Economic Research Division, Bangkok Bank.

Bank of England 1972. *An Introduction to Flow-of-Funds Accounting 1952–1970*, London.

Bank of Thailand. *Annual Economic Report*, published annually by the Bank of Thailand, Bangkok.

Bank of Thailand. *Quarterly Bulletin*, published quarterly by the Department of Economic Research, Bank of Thailand, Bangkok.

Bank of Thailand. *Financial Institutions in Thailand*, published annually by the Department of Economic Research, Bank of Thailand, Bangkok.

Bank of Thailand. *Production, Investment and Employment in Manufacturing, Trade and Construction Sectors*, semi-annual surveys, Department of Economic Research, Bank of Thailand, Bangkok.

Bardhan, P.K. 1980. 'Interlocking Factor Markets and Agrarian Development: A Review of Issues', in *Oxford Economic Papers,* vol. 32, no. 1, pp. 82-98.

Barreiros, L. 1985. *Distribution of Living Standards in Ecuador*, ISS- Prealc working paper no. 15, The Hague.

Baumol, W.J. 1952. 'The Transaction Demand for Cash: An Inventory Theoretic Approach', in *Quarterly Journal of Economics*, vol. 60, pp. 545-56.

Bavovada, B. 1984. 'Mobilization of Rural Savings in Thailand', in: *Economic Bulletin for Asia and the Pacific*, vol. XXXV, no. 2, pp. 45–64.

Beenstock, M. 1980. *A neoclassical analysis of macro-economic policy*, Cambridge University Press.

Berle, A.A. and Means G.C. 1967. *The Modern Corporation and Private Property* (revised), Harcourt, Brace and World, New York.

Bertrand, T. 1980. *Thailand : Case Study of Agricultural Input and Output Pricing*, World Bank staff working paper no. 385, World Bank, Washington DC.

Bertrand, T. and Squire L. 1980. 'The Relevance of the Dual Economy Model: A Case Study of Thailand', in *Oxford Economic Papers,* vol. 32, no. 3, pp. 480–511.

Bhaduri, A. 1977. 'On the Formation of Usurious Interest Rates in Backward Agriculture', in *Cambridge Journal of Economics*, vol. 1, no. 4, pp. 341–52.

Bhalla, S.S. 1978. 'The Role of Sources of Income and Investment Opportunities in Rural Savings', in *Journal of Development Economics*, vol. 5, pp. 259–81.

Bhatt, V.V. 1971. 'Saving and Flow of Funds Analysis, A Tool for Financial Planning in India', in *Review of Income and Wealth*, vol. 17, pp. 61–80.

Bird, R.M. 1971. 'Wagner's "Law" of Expanding State Activity', in *Public Finance*, XXVI, 1, pp. 1–26.

Bottomley, A. 1975. 'Interest Rate Determination in Underdeveloped Rural Areas', in *American Journal of Agricultural Economics*, vol. 57, no. 2, pp. 279–91.

234

Bruno, M. 1979. 'Stabilization and Stagflation in a Semi-Industrial Economy', in R. Dornbush and J.A. Frenkel (eds), *International Economic Policy, Theory and Evidence*, pp. 270–91, Johns Hopkins University Press, Baltimore.

Buffie, E.F. 1984. 'Financial Repression, The New Structuralists and Stabilization Policy in Semi-Industrialized Economies', in: *Journal of Development Economics*, vol. 14, no. 3, pp. 305–22.

Cameron, R. et al. 1967. *Banking in the Early Stages of Industrialisation*, Oxford University Press.

Centre for World Food Studies 1980. *A Social Accounting Matrix for Thailand, with Special Reference to the Agricultural Sector*, Research Report SOW-80-3, Amsterdam.

Chaipravat, O., K. Meesook and S. Garnjarerndee 1976. *Main Sources of Inflation in Developing ESCAP Countries, A Multi-Country Quantitative Analysis*, discussion paper no. 76/19, Department of Economic Research, Bank of Thailand, Bangkok.

Chaipravat, O., K. Meesook, and S. Garnjarerndee 1979. *Bank of Thailand Model of the Thai Economy*, discussion paper no. 79/25, Department of Economic Research, Bank of Thailand, Bangkok.

Chandavarkar, A.G. 1977. 'Monetization of Developing Economies' in: *IMF Staff Papers*, vol. XXIV, no. 3, pp. 665-721.

Chenery, H.B. 1979. *Structural Change and Development Policy*, Oxford University Press, London.

Chenery, H.B. 1983. 'Interaction Between Theory and Observation in Development', in *World Development*, vol. 10, pp. 853–61.

Chenery, H.B. and Strout A.M. 1966. 'Foreign Assistance and Economic Development', in *American Economic Review*, vol. 56, no 4, pp. 670–733.

Cole, D.C., S. Chunanuntathum and C. Loohawenchit 1986. 'Modelling of Financial Markets in Thailand', in A.H.H. Tan and B. Kapur (eds), *Pacific Growth and Financial Interdependence*, pp. 144–62, Allen & Unwin, Sydney.

Cole, D.C. and H.T. Patrick 1986. 'Financial development in the Pacific Basin Market Economies', in A.H.H. Tan and B. Kapur (eds) *Pacific Growth and Financial Interdependence*, pp. 39–67, Allen and Unwin, Sydney.

Cole, D.C. and Y. C. Park 1983. *Financial Development in Korea : 1945–1978*, Harvard University Press, Cambridge, Mass.

Cornia, G. and Jerger, G. 1982. 'Rural vs Urban Saving Behaviour : Evidence from an ILO Collection of Household Surveys, in *Development and Change*, vol. 13, no. 1, pp. 123–57.

Crockett, A.D. and O.J. Evans 1980. 'Demand for Money in Middle Eastern Countries', in *IMF Staff Papers*, Sept. 1980, pp. 543–77.

Davidson, P. 1978. *Money and the Real World* (2nd ed.), The Macmillan Press, London.

Diamond, J. 1977. 'Wagner's "Law" and the Developing Countries', in *The Developing Economies*, vol. XV, no. 1, pp. 37–59.

Dornbush, R. and Fisher S. 1985. *Macroeconomics*, McGraw-Hill, New York.

Douglass, M. 1984. *Regional Integration on the Capitalist Periphery : The Central Plains of Thailand*, Institute of Social Studies, Research Report Series, no. 15, The Hague.

Drake, P.J. 1980. *Money, Finance and Development*, Martin Robertson, Oxford.

Eichner, A.S. 1973. 'A Theory of the Determination of the Mark-up under Oligopoly', in *Economic Journal*, December 1973, pp. 1184–98.

Eichner, A.S. 1985. *Toward a New Economics, Essays in Post-Keynesian and Institutionalist Theory*, The Macmillan Press, London.

Enzewe, C. 1973. 'Structure of Public Expenditure in Selected Developing Countries: a Time Series Study', in *The Manchester School of Economic and Social Studies*, vol. XLI, no. 4, pp. 430–63.

Evans, M.K. 1969. *Macroeconomic Activity; Theory, Forecasting and Control*, Harper & Row, New York.

Feder, G. 1986. 'Land Ownership Security and Farm Productivity : Evidence from Thailand', mimeo, October 1986.

Feder, G., T. Onchan and T. Raparla 1986. 'Land Ownership Security, Access to Credit and Land Policy in Rural Thailand', mimeo, April 1986.

Feeny, D. 1982. *The Political Economy of Productivity, Thai Agricultural Development, 1880–1975*, University of British Colombia Press, Vancouver.

FitzGerald, E.V.K. 1986. *Kalecki on the Financing of Development : Elements for a Macroeconomics of the Semi-Industrialised Economy*, working paper no. 17, Institute of Social Studies, The Hague.

Friedman, M. 1957. *A Theory of the Consumption Function*, Princeton University Press, NJ.

Friend, I. and I.B. Kravis 1957. 'Entrepreneurial Income, Saving and Investment', in *American Economic Review*, vol. XLVII, no. 3, pp. 264–301.

Fry, M.J. 1978. 'Money and Capital or Financial Deepening in Economic Development', in *Journal of Money, Credit and Banking*, no. 10, 464–78.

Fry, M.J. 1980. 'Saving, Investment, Growth and the Cost of Financial Repression', in *World Development*, vol. 8, pp. 317–27.

Fry, M.J. 1982. 'Models of Financially Repressed Developing Economies', in *World Development*, vol. 10, no. 9, pp. 731–50.

Galbis, V. 1977. 'Financial Intermediation and Economic Growth in Less Developed Countries : A Theoretical Approach', in *Journal of Development Studies*, January 1977, pp. 58–72.

Galbis, V. 1979. 'Money, Investment and Growth in Latin America, 1961–1973', in *Economic Development and Cultural Change*, vol. 27, no. 3, April 1979, pp. 423–43.

236

Galbraith, J.K. 1967. *The New Industrial State*, Signet Books, New York.

Galbraith, J.K. 1975. *Economics and the Public Purpose*, Penguin Books, Harmondsworth.

Garnjarerndee, S. 1981. 'Pattern of Household Financial Savings in Thailand since 1960', in Bank of Thailand, *Quarterly Bulletin* vol. 21, no. 2, June 1981, pp. 15–20.

Garnjarerndee, S. 1982. 'Flow-of-Funds Accounts of Thailand', in *Quarterly Bulletin*, Bank of Thailand, vol. 22, no. 2, pp. 25–34.

Ghatak, S. 1981. *Monetary Economics in Developing Countries*, The Macmillan Press, London.

Giovannini, A. 1983. 'The Interest Elasticity of Savings in Developing Countries : The Existing Evidence', in *World Development*, vol. 11, no. 7, pp. 601–7.

Go, E.M. 1984. *Domestic Resource Mobilization through Financial Development; Thailand*, Asian Development Bank, Manila.

Goldsmith, R.W. 1969. *Financial Structure and Development*, Yale University Press, New Haven and London.

Goldsmith, R.W. 1983. *The Financial Development of India, Japan and the United States*, Yale University Press, New Haven.

Griffin, K. 1970. 'Foreign Capital, Domestic Savings and Economic Development', in *Oxford Bulletin of Economics and Statistics*, vol. 32, no. 2, pp. 99–112.

Grinols, E. and J. Bhagwati 1976. 'Foreign Capital, Savings and Dependence', in *Review of Economics and Statistics*, vol. LVIII, no. 4, pp. 416–24.

Grootaert, C. 1986. *The Role of Employment and Earnings in Analysing Levels of Living. A General Methodology with Applications to Malaysia and Thailand*, LSMS working paper, no. 27, World Bank, Washington DC.

Gupta, K.L. 1971. 'Dependency Rates and Savings Rates: Comment', in *American Economic Review*, vol. LXI, no. 3, pp. 469–71.

Gupta, K.L. 1984. *Finance and Economic Growth in Developing Countries*, Croom Helm, London.

Gurley, J.G. and E.S. Shaw 1960. *Money in a Theory of Finance*, Brookings Institute, Washington DC.

Gurley, J.G. and E.S. Shaw 1967. 'Financial Structure and Economic Development', in *Economic Development and Cultural Change*, vol. 15, no. 3, pp. 257–68.

Hammer, J.S. 1986a. 'Population Growth and Savings in LDCs: A Survey Article', in *World Development*, vol. 14, no. 5, pp. 579–91.

Hammer, J.S. 1986b. 'Children and Savings in Less Developed Countries', in *Journal of Development Economics*, vol. 23, pp. 107–18.

Harrod, R.F. 1939. 'An Essay in Dynamic Theory', in *Economic Journal*, vol. 49, pp. 14–33.

Hewison, K.J. 1981. 'The Financial Bourgeoisie in Thailand', in *Journal of Contemporary Asia*, vol. 11, no. 4, pp. 395–412.

Hewison, K. 1986. 'Capital in the Thai Countryside: The Sugar Industry', in *Journal of Contemporary Asia*, vol. 16, no. 1, pp. 3–17.

Hicks, J. 1967. *Critical Essays in Monetary Theory*, Clarendon Press, Oxford.

Hilferding, R. 1981. *Finance Capital : A Study of the Latest Phase of Capitalist Development*, (translation and Introduction by T. Bottomore) Routledge & Kegan Paul, London.

Hongladarom, C. 1982. 'Structure of the Thai Economy and its Implications for Industrial Relations in Thailand', in Hongladarom, Chira (ed.), *Comparative Labour and Management: Japan and Thailand*, pp. 64–111, Thammasat University Press, Bangkok.

Holtsberg, C. 1980. *Income Distribution Implications of the Thai Rice Price Policy*, ILO WEP working paper, January 1980, Geneva.

Houthakker, H.S. 1965. 'On Some Determinants of Saving in Developed and Underdeveloped Countries', in E.A.G. Robinson (ed.), *Problems in Economic Development*, pp. 212–27, Macmillan, New York.

Howard, D.H. 1978. 'Personal Saving Behaviour and The Rate of Inflation', in *The Review of Economics and Statistics*, vol. LX, no. 4, pp. 547–54.

Ingram, J.C. 1971. *Economic Change in Thailand 1850–1970*, Stanford University Press, California.

IMF 1977. *The Monetary Approach to the Balance of Payments*, IMF, Washington DC.

Islam, R. 1983. 'Poverty, Income Distribution and Growth in Rural Thailand', in Azizur Rahman Khan and Eddy Lee (eds): *Poverty in Rural Asia*, pp. 205–30, ILO (ARTEP), Bangkok.

Jansen, K. 1982. *State, Policy and the Economy*, Institute of Social Studies, research report no. 12, The Hague.

Jansen, K. (ed.) 1983. *Monetarism, Economic Crisis and the Third World*, Frank Cass, London.

Jung, W.S. 1986. 'Financial Development and Economic Growth: International Evidence', in *Economic Development and Cultural Change*, vol. 34, no. 2, pp. 333–46.

Kaldor, N. 1955. 'Alternative Theories of Distribution', in *Review of Economic Studies*, vol. 23, pp. 94–100.

Kalecki, M. 1976. *Essays on Developing Economies*, The Harvester Press, Sussex, England.

Kapur, B.K. 1976. 'Alternative Stabilization Policies for Less-developed Economies', in *Journal of Political Economy*, vol. 84, no. 4, part I, August 1976, pp. 777–95.

Keller, P.M. 1980. 'Implications of Credit Policies for Output and the Balance of Payments', in *IMF Staff Papers*, September 1980, pp. 451–77.

Kelley, A.C. and J.G. Williamson 1968. 'Household Saving Behaviour in the Developing Economies: The Indonesian Case', in *Economic Development and Cultural Change*, April 1968, pp. 385–403.

Keuning, S.J. 1985. 'Segmented Developments and the Way Profits Go: the

238

Case of Indonesia', in *Review of Income and Wealth*, series 31, no. 4, pp. 375–95.

Keynes, J.M. 1936. *The General Theory of Employment, Interest and Money*, The Macmillan Press, London.

Khan, M.S. and M.D. Knight 1981. 'Stabilization Programs in Developing Countries: A Formal Framework', in *IMF Staff Papers*, March 1981, pp. 1–53.

Kharas, H.J. and H. Shishido 1985. *Thailand: An Assessment of Alternative Foreign Borrowing Strategies*, World Bank staff working paper no. 781, World Bank, Washington, DC.

Kirakul, S. 1986. *Mobilisation of Informal Sector Savings in Thailand*, Department of Economic Research, Bank of Thailand, Bangkok.

Kirakul, S., A. Sriphayak and P. Ploydanai 1984. 'Household Savings', in *Quarterly Bulletin*, Bank of Thailand, Dec. 1984, pp. 21–49.

Knudsen, O. and A. Parnes 1975. *Trade Instability and Economic Development*, Lexington Books, Massachusetts.

Krongkaew, M. 1980. *The Distributive Impact of Government's Policies : An Assessment of the Situations in Thailand*, discussion paper no. 83, Faculty of Economics, Thammasat University, Bangkok.

Krongkaew, M. 1985. 'Agricultural Development, Rural Poverty, and Income Distribution in Thailand', in *The Developing Economies*, vol. XXIII, no. 4, pp. 325–46.

Kuramochi, T. 1987. *The Impact of Monetary Policy on Financial Development: a Case Study of Thailand*, MA thesis, Faculty of Economics, Thammasat University, Bangkok.

Laidler, D.E.W. 1977. *The Demand for Money, Theories and Evidence* (2nd ed.), Dunn-Donnelley, Harper & Row, New York.

Lee, J.-K. 1971. 'Exports and the Propensity to Save in LDCs', in *Economic Journal*, vol. 81, no. 322, pp. 341–51.

Lee, S.Y. and Jao, Y.C. 1982. *Financial Structures and Monetary Policies in Southeast Asia*, The Macmillan Press, London.

Leeahtam, P. 1985. 'Some Aspects of the Recent Adjustment Efforts in Thailand: the Twin Deficits', in *Quarterly Bulletin*, Bank of Thailand, Bangkok, September 1985, pp. 57–65.

Leff, N.H. 1969. 'Dependency Rates and Savings Rates', in *American Economic Review*, vol. LIX, no. 5, pp. 886–96.

Leff, N.H. 1976. 'Capital Markets in the Less Developed Countries : The Group Principle', in R.I. McKinnon (ed.): *Money and Finance in Economic Growth and Development*, pp. 97–126, Marcel Dekker Inc., New York.

Leff, N.H. 1979. 'Monopoly Capitalism and Public Policy in Developing Countries', in *Kyklos*, vol. 32, pp. 718–37.

Leff, N.H. and K. Sato 1980. 'Macroeconomic Adjustment in Developing Countries: Instability, Short-run Growth and External Dependency', in *The Review of Economics and Statistics*, May 1980, pp. 170–9.

Lewis, W.A. 1954. 'Economic Development with Unlimited Supplies of Labour', in *The Manchester School*, May 1954, pp. 400–47.

Likitkijsomboon, P. 1985. *Taxation and Income Distribution in Thailand: A Case Study for 1981*, MA thesis, Faculty of Economics, Thammasat University, Bangkok.

Lipton, M. 1977. *Why Poor People Stay Poor; Urban Bias in the World Development*, Temple & Smith, London.

Lluch, C., A.A. Power and R.A. Williams 1977. *Patterns in Household Demand and Saving*, published for the World Bank by Oxford University Press, New York.

Long, M. 1968. 'Interest Rates and the Structure of Agricultural Credit Markets', in *Oxford Economic Papers*, July 1968, pp. 278–88.

McKinnon, R.I. 1973. *Money and Capital in Economic Development*, Brookings Institution, Washington DC.

McKinnon, R.I. 1980. 'Financial Policies', in J. Cody, H. Hughes, D. Hall (eds): *Policies for Industrial Progress in Developing Countries*, pp. 93-120, Oxford University Press, London.

Maizels, A. 1968. *Exports and Economic Growth of Developing Countries*, Cambridge University Press, London.

Marglin, S.A. 1984. *Growth, Distribution and Prices*, Harvard University Press, Cambridge, Mass.

Marzouk, G.A. 1972. *Economic Development and Policies, Case Study of Thailand*, Rotterdam University Press.

Mathieson, D.J. 1980. 'Financial Reform and Stabilization Policy in a Developing Economy', in *Journal of Development Economics*, no. 7, 359–95.

Meer, C.L.J. van der 1981. *Rural Development in Northern Thailand, an Interpretation and Analysis*, Krips Repro, Meppel.

Meesook, K. 1978. *Regional Distribution of Commercial Bank Services in Thailand*, discussion paper 78/24, Department of Economic Research, Bank of Thailand, Bangkok.

Meesook, K. 1979. *Industrial Distribution of Labour Force and Income in Thailand, Change in the Process of Economic Growth*, discussion paper 79/26, Department of Economic Research, Bank of Thailand, Bangkok.

Meesook, K.M. and C. Jivasakdiapimas 1981. *The Relationship Between Money and Credit and Economic Activity: Thailand*, discussion paper 81/36, Department of Economic Research, Bank of Thailand, Bangkok.

Meesook, O.A. 1979. *Income, Consumption and Poverty in Thailand, 1962/63 to 1975/76*, World Bank staff working paper, No. 364, World Bank, Washington DC.

Mellor. J.W. 1973. 'Accelerated Growth in Agricultural Production and the Intersectoral Transfer of Resources', in *Economic Development* and Cultural Change, vol. 22, no. 1, pp. 1–16.

Mikesell, R.F. and J.E. Zinser 1973. 'The Nature of the Savings Function in

Developing Countries: A Survey of the Theoretical and Empirical Literature', in *Journal of Economic Literature*, vol. XI, March 1973, pp. 1–26.

Mitra, A. 1977. *Terms of Trade and Class Relations, An Essay in Political Economy*, Frank Cass, London.

Modigliani, F. 1986. 'Life Cycle, Individual Thrift, and Wealth of Nations', in *American Economic Review*, vol. 76, no. 3, pp. 297-313.

Modigliani, F. and R. Hemming (eds) 1983. *The Determinants of National Saving and Wealth*, The Macmillan Press, London.

Modigliani, F. and E. Tarantelli 1975. 'The Consumption Function in a Developing Economy and The Italian Experience', in *American Economic Review*, December 1975, pp. 825–42.

Moore, M. 1984. 'Political Economy and the Rural–Urban Divide, 1967–1981', in *Journal of Development Studies*, vol. 20, no. 3, pp. 5–27.

Morell, D. and C.-A. Samudavanija 1981. *Political Conflict in Thailand: Reform, Reaction, Revolution*, Oelgeschlager, Gunn and Hain, Cambridge, USA.

Mundle, S. 1985. 'The Agrarian Barrier to Industrial Growth', in *Journal of Development Studies*, vol. 22, no. 1, pp. 49–80.

Mundle, S. and K. Ohkawa 1979. 'Agricultural Surplus Flow in Japan, 1888-1937', in *The Developing Economies*, vol. XVII, no. 3, pp. 247–65.

Musgrove, P. 1978. 'Determinants of Urban Household Consumption in Latin America: A Summary of Evidence from the ECIEL Surveys', in *Economic Development and Cultural Change*, vol. 26, no. 3, pp. 441–65.

National Economic and Social Development Board (NESDB). *National Income of Thailand*, published annually by NESDB, Bangkok.

National Economic and Social Development Board (NESDB) 1983. *Fact Book on Labour, Employment, Salaries and Wages*, NESDB, Population and Manpower Planning Division, Bangkok.

National Economic and Social Development Board (NESDB) 1985. *Summary Direction of the Sixth National Economic and Social Development Plan*, NESDB, Bangkok, October 1985.

National Economic and Social Development Board (NESDB) and Bank of Thailand 1982. *Flow-of-Funds Accounts of Thailand, 1982* edition, published by the National Account Division, Office of the National Economic and Social Development and the Research Department of the Bank of Thailand, Bangkok.

National Economic and Social Development Board (NESDB) and Bank of Thailand 1983. *Flow-of-Funds Accounts of Thailand, 1983 edition*, published by the National Account Division, Office of the National Economic and Social Development and the Research Department of the Bank of Thailand, Bangkok.

National Economic and Social Development Board (NESDB) 1986. *Flow-of-Funds Accounts of Thailand, 1986 edition*, published by National Accounts Division, NESDB, Bangkok.

National Economic and Social Development Board (NESDB) and World Bank (IBRD) 1982. *A Social Accounting Matrix for Thailand 1975*, NESDB, Bangkok.

Newlyn, W.T. 1977. *The Financing of Economic Development*, Clarendon Press, Oxford.

Nidhiprabha, B. and G. Arya 1987. *Efficiency in the Thai Financial Sector*, Thai Development Research Institute, Bangkok.

Nontapunthawat, N. 1973. *Financial Capital Flows in the Balance of Payments of Thailand*, unpublished PhD thesis, Purdue University.

Nontapunthawat, N. 1978. *Financial Capital Flows and Portfolio Behaviour of Thai Commercial Banks*, Research Report Series no. 5, Faculty of Economics, Thammasat University, Bangkok.

Nurkse, R. 1953. *Problems of Capital Formation in Underdeveloped Countries*, Basil Blackwell, Oxford.

O'Connor, J. 1973. *The Fiscal Crisis of the State*, St. Martin's Press, New York.

Onchan, T. 1985. *Informal Credit and the Development of Non-farm Enterprises in Thailand*, research paper, USAID Thailand.

Onchan, T., Y. Chalamwong and S. Aungsumalin 1974. *Agricultural Credit in Chainat Province in Thailand*, research report no. 9, Department of Agricultural Economies, Faculty of Economies and Business Administration, Kasetsart University.

Osotsapa, S. 1987. *Impact of Low Agricultural Prices on Asian Agriculture*, paper no. 3004, Faculty of Economics, Chulalongkorn University, Bangkok.

Panayotou, T. (ed.) 1985. *Food Policy Analysis in Thailand*, Agricultural Development Council, Bangkok.

Panitchpakdi, S. 1981. *Issues in Banking and Finance in Thailand 1975– 1980*, printed by Marketing Media LP, Bangkok.

Papanek, G.A. 1972. 'The Effect of Aid and Other Resource Transfers on Savings and Growth in Less Developed Countries', in *Economic Journal*, September 1972, pp. 934–50.

Papanek, G.F. 1973. 'Aid, Foreign Private Investment Savings, and Growth in Less Developed Countries', in *Journal of Political Economy*, vol. 81, no. 1, pp. 120–30.

Pasinetti, L. 1961. 'Rate of Profit and Income Distribution in Relation to the Rate of Economic Growth', in *Review of Economic Studies*, vol. 29, pp. 267–79.

Patrick, H.T. 1966. 'Financial Development and Economic Growth in Underdeveloped Countries', in *Economic Development and Cultural Change*, vol. 14, pp. 174–89.

Phipatseritham, K. and K. Yoshihara 1983. *Business Groups in Thailand*, research notes and discussion paper no. 41, Institute of Southeast Asian Studies, Singapore.

Phongpaichit, P. 1982. *Employment, Income and the Mobilisation of Local Resources in Three Thai Villages*, ILO/ARTEP, Bangkok.

Polak, J.J. 1957. 'Monetary Analysis of Income Formation and Payments Problems', in *IMF Staff Papers*, vol. 6, pp. 1–50.

Polak, J.J. and V. Argy 1971. 'Credit Policy and the Balance of Payments', in *IMF Staff Papers*, March 1971, vol. XVII, no. 1, pp. 1–24.

Pongtanakorn, C., C. Sussangkarn, K. Khatikarn and Y. Chalamwong 1987. *The Impact of Agricultural Product Prices Changes on Labor Absorption in Thai Agriculture: A non-linear Programming Approach*, Thai Development Research Institute, Bangkok.

Potter, J.M. 1976. *Thai Peasant Social Structure*, University of Chicago Press.

Prasartset, S. 1980. *Thai Business Leaders, Men and Careers in a Developing Economy*, published by Institute of Developing Economies, Tokyo.

Prasartset, S. 1981. 'The Impact of Transnational Corporations in the Economic Structure of Thailand', in *Alternatives, A Journal of World Policy*, vol. VII, no. 4, pp. 431–50, December 1981.

Prasartset, S. 1982. *Some Aspects of Government–Business Relations in Thailand and Japan*, mimeo, Faculty of Economics, Chulalongkorn University, Bangkok.

Prasartset, S. 1985. 'Crisis of the Transnationalization Model of Accumulation: the Thai Case', in *Transnationalization, the State and the People: the Case of Thailand*, South-east Asian Perspective Project, UN University.

Ram, R. 1982. 'Dependency Rates and Aggregate Savings: A New International Cross-Section Study', in *American Economic Review*, vol. 72, no. 3, pp. 537–44.

Ramangkura, V. and P. Amranand and Associates 1981. *Thailand: Long-term Prospects for Economic Development 1980–1990*, mimeo.

Rojpibulstit, S. 1976. *Bank Competition in Thailand*, unpublished MA Thesis, Thammasat University, Bangkok.

Rozental, A.A. 1970. *Finance and Development in Thailand*, Praeger, New York.

Saith, A. 1985. ' "Primitive Accumulation", Agrarian Reform and Socialist Transitions: An Argument', in *Journal of Development Studies*, vol. 22, no. 1, pp. 1–48.

Schimmler, H. 1979. *'Towards Distinguishing between Traditional and Modern Activities in the National Accounts of Developing Countries'*, Development Centre Papers, OECD, Paris.

Securities Exchange of Thailand (SET) 1982. *Fact Book '82*, SET, Bangkok.

Seers, D. 1983. 'Structuralism vs Monetarism in Latin America: A Reappraisal of a Great Debate, with lessons for Europe in the 1980s', pp. 110–26, in K. Jansen (1983).

Sen, A. (ed.) 1970. *Growth Economics, Selected Readings*, Penguin Books, Harmondsworth, England.

Sen, A. K. 1970. 'Introduction', in A.K. Sen (ed.), *Growth Economics*, pp. 9–40, Penguin Books, Harmondsworth, England.

Shaw, E.S. 1973. *Financial Deepening in Economic Development*, Oxford University Press, New York.

Siamwalla, A. 1975. 'Stability, Growth and Distribution in the Thai Economy', in Puey Ungphakorn and others: *Finance, Trade and Economic Development in Thailand, Essays in Honour of Khunying Suparb Yossundara*, pp. 25–48, Sompong Press, Bangkok.

Siamwalla, A. 1978. *Inflation in Thailand in the 1970s: Its Causes and Consequences*, discussion paper no. 61, Faculty of Economics, Thammasat University, Bangkok.

Siamwalla, A. and S. Setboonsarng 1987. *Pricing Policies of Four Major Agricultural Commodities in Thailand, 1960–1984*, Thai Development Research Institute, Bangkok.

Silcock, T.H. 1967. 'Money and Banking', in T.H. Silcock (ed.), *Thailand, Social and Economic Studies in Development*, Duke University Press, Durham, NC.

Sinsup, P. 1976. *A Summary Research Report on Private Capital Formation in Agricultural Sector of Thailand for Crop Year 1974–75*, paper no. 1903, Faculty of Economics, Chulalongkorn University, Bangkok.

Siricharoengseng, S. 1987. *Thai Household Saving Behaviour under an Alternative Saving Concept: an Analysis of Cross-Section Data 1981*, MA thesis, Faculty of Economics, Thammasat University, Bangkok.

Skinner, G.W. 1958. *Leadership and Power in the Chinese Community of Thailand*, Cornell University Press, Ithaca.

Skully, M.T. 1985. *Asean Financial Co-operation Developments in Banking, Finance and Insurance*, The Macmillan Press, London.

Song, B.-N. 1981. 'Empirical Research on Consumption Behavior: Evidence from Rich and Poor LDCs', in *Economic Development and Cultural Change*, vol. 29, no. 3, pp. 597–611.

Sundararajan, V. 1985. 'Debt-Equity Ratios of Firms and Interest Rate Policy', in *IMF Staff Papers*, vol. 32, no. 3, pp. 430–74.

Taylor, L. 1981. 'IS/LM in the Tropics: Diagrammatics of the New Structuralist Macro Critique', in W.R. Cline and S. Weintraub (eds): *Economic Stabilisation in Developing Countries*, The Bookings Institution, Washington, DC.

Taylor, L. 1983. *Structuralist Macroeconomics*, Basic Books, New York.

Taylor, L. and Rosensweig, J.A. 1984. *Devaluation, Capital Flows and Crowding-Out: A Computable General Equilibrium Model with Portfolio Choice for Thailand*, mimeo, MIT.

Thai Development Research Institute (TDRI) 1986. *Financial Resources Management*, prepared for TDRI 1986 Year-end Conference, TDRI, Bangkok.

Thai Development Research Institute (TDRI) 1987. *Prospects for Thai Economic Development*, TDRI, Bangkok.

Thirlwall, A.P. 1974a. 'Inflation and the Savings Ratio Across Countries', in *Journal of Development Studies*, vol. 10, no. 2, pp. 154–74.

Thirlwall, A.P. 1974b. *Inflation, Saving and Growth in Developing Economies*, The Macmillan Press, London.

Thisyamondol, P., V. Arromdee and M.F. Long 1965. *Agricultural Credit in Thailand, Theory, Data, Policy*, Kasetsart University.

Tobin, J. 1958. 'Liquidity Preference as Behaviour Towards Risk', in *Review of Economic Studies*, vol. 25, pp. 65-86.

Tobin, J. 1965. 'The Theory of Portfolio Selection', in F.H. Hahn and F.P.R. Brechling (eds): *The Theory of Interest Rates*, The Macmillan Press, London.

Trairatvorakul, P. 1984. *The Effects on Income Distribution and Nutrition of Alternative Rice Price Policies in Thailand*, research report no. 46, International Food Policy Research Institute, Washington, DC.

Trescott, P.B. 1971. *Thailand's Monetary Experience, The Economics of Stability*, Praeger, New York.

Tritasavit, P. 1978. *Labor Policy and Practices in Thailand: A Study on Government Policy on Labor Relations: 1932–1976*, unpublished PhD dissertation, New York University.

Tsiang, S.C. 1969. 'The Precautionary Demand for Money: An Inventory-Theoretical Analysis', in *Journal of Political Economy*, Jan./Feb. 1969, pp. 99–117.

United Nations/ESCAP. 1985. *Economic and Social Survey of Asia and the Pacific 1984*, UN/ESCAP, Bangkok.

Usher, D. 1967. 'Thai Interest Rates', in *Journal of Development Studies*, vol. 3, no. 3, pp. 267–79.

Usher, D. 1978. *The Economics of the Rice Premium*, discussion paper no. 60, Faculty of Economics, Thammasat University, Bangkok.

Viksnins, G.J. 1980. *Financial Deepening in ASEAN Countries*, Pacific Forum, Honolulu, Hawaii.

Visser, A.P.R. 1978. *Een Dorp in de Centrale Vlakte van Thailand*, doctoral dissertation, Utrecht.

Vongpradhip, D. 1986. 'Urban Unorganized Money Markets in Thailand' in *Quarterly Bulletin*, Bank of Thailand, Bangkok, vol. 26, no. 2, pp. 27-45.

Vongvipanond, P. 1980. *Finance in Thailand's Industrial Development Context*, a report prepared for the NESDB, Thai University Research Association, research report no. 1A, Bangkok, mimeo.

Vongvipanond, P. 1981. *Local Operations of Transnational Banks, Foreign Financial Institutions in Thailand : A Study of Regulatory Framework and their Role in the Development Process*, research report prepared for UN Centre on Transnational Corporation, New York.

Wai, U.T. 1972. *Financial Intermediaries and National Savings in Developing Countries*, Praeger, New York.

Wai, U.T. 1977. 'A Revisit to Interest Rates Outside the Organized Money Market of Underdeveloped Countries', in *Banca Nationale del Lavoro Quarterly Review*, vol. 2, no. 122, pp. 291–312.

Warren, B. 1977. *Inflation and Wages in Underdeveloped Countries: India, Peru and Turkey 1939–1960*, Frank Cass, London.

Wasow, B. 1979. 'Saving and Dependence with Externally Financed Growth', in *Review of Economics and Statistics*, vol. LXI, no. 1, pp. 150-4.

Weber, W.E. 1975. 'Interest Rates, Inflation and Consumer Expenditures', in *American Economic Review*, vol. 65, no. 5, pp. 843-58.

Weisskopf, T.E. 1972. 'The Impact of Foreign Capital Inflow on Domestic Savings in Underdeveloped Countries', in *Journal of International Economics*, 2 (1972), pp. 25–38.

Wibulswasdi, C. 1983. 'Strategies and Measures to Maintain Thailand's Economic Stability in the 1980s' in *Quarterly Bulletin*, Bank of Thailand, vol. 23, no. 4, pp. 27–47.

Wibulswasdi, C. 1987. *Recent Thai Experiences in Economic Management*, paper presented at Malaysian Economic Association Convention, Kuala Lumpur, November 1987.

Wijnbergen, S. van 1982. 'Stagflationary Effects of Monetary Stabilization Policies: A Quantitative Analysis of South Korea', in *Journal of Development Economics*, 10, pp. 133–69.

Wijnbergen, S. van 1983. 'Credit Policy, Inflation and Growth in a Financially Repressed Economy', in *Journal of Development Economics*, 13 (1983), pp. 45–65.

Wijnbergen, S. van 1985. 'Macro-economic Effects of Changes in Bank Interest Rates; Simulation Results for South Korea', in *Journal of Development Economics*, 18 (1985), pp. 541–54.

Wong, J. 1979. *ASEAN Economics in Perspective. A Comparative Study of Indonesia, Malaysia, The Philippines, Singapore and Thailand*, The Macmillan Press, London.

Wood, A. 1975. *A Theory of Profits*, Cambridge University Press.

World Bank 1978. *Thailand: Toward a Development Strategy of Full Participation. A Basic Economic Report*, World Bank, Washington, DC.

World Bank 1982. *Thailand, Program and Policy Priorities for an Agricultural Economy in Transition*, World Bank, Washington, DC.

World Bank 1983a. *Thailand, Rural Growth and Employment*, A World Bank Country Study, World Bank, Washington, DC.

World Bank 1983b. *Thailand, Pespectives for Financial Reform*, World Bank, Washington, DC.

World Bank 1984. *Thailand, Managing Public Resources for Structural Adjustment*, World Bank, Washington, DC.

World Bank 1986. *Thailand: Growth with Stability, A Challenge for the Sixth Plan Period: A Country Economic Report*, World Bank, Washington, DC.

World Bank 1987. *World Development Report*, Oxford University Press, New York.

Index